SHAKESPEARE'S DRAMATIC MEDITATIONS

AN EXPERIMENT IN CRITICISM

SHAKESPEARE'S DRAMATIC MEDITATIONS

An Experiment in Criticism

by

GIORGIO MELCHIORI

CLARENDON PRESS · OXFORD
1976

Oxford University Press, Ely House, London W.1

GLASGOW   NEW YORK   TORONTO   MELBOURNE   WELLINGTON
CAPE TOWN   IBADAN   NAIROBI   DAR ES SALAAM   LUSAKA   ADDIS ABABA
DELHI   BOMBAY   CALCUTTA   MADRAS   KARACHI   LAHORE   DACCA
KUALA LUMPUR   SINGAPORE   HONG KONG   TOKYO

0 19 812073 7 ✓

*Printed in Great Britain
by William Clowes & Sons, Limited
London, Beccles and Colchester*

PREFACE

I SKETCHED out a first version of this book directly in English in the autumn of 1971; in the following academic year I put those hastily written pages to the test of viva voce delivery as a course to my students in the University of Rome. The result was an Italian text which was published in July 1973 under the title *L'uomo e il potere—Indagine sulle strutture profonde dei Sonetti di Shakespeare* (Torino, Einaudi). A Fellowship, generously granted by the Leverhulme Foundation at Wolfson College, Cambridge, for the Michaelmas and Lent terms of 1973–4, gave me the time and means to take full advantage of the lively discussion the book had aroused upon publication in Italy, and to reappraise the whole subject in the light of new experiences and of material which had not been available to me before.

The present version is, I hope, better informed, and eliminates some of the uncertainties of its Italian predecessor, but does not claim to be in any way final. I must state at the outset that this is not a study of the Sonnets as a whole, or of their achievement, their main themes, etc.; I chose deliberately to isolate some trees out of the wood. The book is about which trees to look at, and what the chosen ones can show us. I am still of the opinion expressed in the introduction to the Italian edition:

This book originated out of a deep mistrust in the validity of literary criticism and its practice, both on the page and in the lecture room. It was actually written in a couple of months, though Shakespeare's Sonnets had 'lived' with me for at least twenty years, since I had translated some and edited all of them for use in class. This practical application has produced a dissatisfaction with, and roused questions and doubts about the function of criticism at a time when, in trying to keep up with what is supposed to be technological progress, literary criticism is reaching unprecedented levels both of specialization and massification. The competition in the critical market has encouraged the production of useless and superfluous objects, and the consumer is hardly in a position to judge how functional are the offerings pressed on him. What follows is by no means market research in order to ascertain what is most suited to a certain more or less academic public (this is the great temptation of the cultural operator nowadays), but rather an experiment in trying out, perhaps amateurishly, some old and new tools of critical production, in order to test not only their efficiency but their actual usefulness and functionality within the context of today's existential predicament.

Chapter I tries to account for the choice of subject, placing it in its socio-historical as well as its linguistic context, while the analyses of single sonnets in the rest of the book should suggest how far that context is relevant to us today. In chapters II, IV, and V the sections with code no. 0 are meant to provide the philological and historical-critical premises, those with code no. 1 examine formal structures, while those with code no. 2 attempt the indispensable transition from form to content. In chapter III the examination of semantic values (code no. 1) precedes that of logical and metrical structures (code no. 2), while the sections with code no. 3 check meanings against formal structures. The Interchapter between III and IV should act as a cautionary interlude against dogmatic assumptions of critical methods and the critics' proneness to identify structural elaboration with aesthetic achievement. Indeed, the whole book should sound a warning both against conferring the status of art on any work that conforms to a certain critical model or responds to a certain critical method, and against considering universally valid any critical theory or approach simply because it can be successfully applied to certain works of art.

My debts to scholars and friends are numberless. Apart from those listed in the bibliographical references, I wish to repeat my acknowledgement to those whom I had already mentioned in the Italian version. What I learned from William Empson, I. A. Richards, L. C. Knights, as well as, with some friendly disagreement, from Marcello Pagnini, goes well beyond the few mentions in the notes. The same is true of my old friend Walter Lever, while Winifred Nowottny took time off her edition of the Sonnets to read and comment on an earlier typescript of this book, Marvin Spevack provided useful computerized data of the Sonnets, Agostino Lombardo promoted my edition of the text some years ago, and Christine Brooke-Rose stimulated my curiosity to explore certain critical problems. What I owe to a number of Continental critics will be apparent to all those familiar with the present debate on formalism, structuralism, and semiotics in France, Italy, the U.S.S.R., and the rest of Europe, but I wish to mention in particular Umberto Eco who is the author of the most exciting writings I have been exposed to in the last few years.

In the Italian edition I expressed my gratitude to Terence Spencer, George Hunter, Clifford Leech, Dame Helen Gardner, Muriel Bradbrook, and a number of Shakespearian scholars for their constant help and friendship. This debt has since increased, especially towards the Mistress of Girton, who was material in securing for me the Fellowship at Wolfson, where I enjoyed the generous hospitality of President Morrison and the Fellows. The reshaping of the book owes much to my stay in Cambridge, through the friendly contacts with Raymond Williams, John Holloway, George Steiner; if I do not mention a score of other names it is only because our shared interests were not strictly Shakespearian, but I learnt no less from them. I cannot omit Philip Edwards's and Nicholas Brooke's contributions both in specific learning and in amicable hospitality, and Raymond Brett gave me the opportunity of trying out the substance of the book in a series of lectures at the University of Hull. I. R. Willison of the British Library (British Museum), Peter Sheldon of the Brynmor Jones Library (University of Hull), and the staff of the Cambridge University Library have been of great help.

The Italian version bore a dedication to my old Italian friends Dario Puccini and Stefania Piccinato, who, together with Renato Oliva and Vanna Gentili, through a constant exchange of opinions by no means confined to Shakespeare or problems of criticism, provided the living context of the following pages. But my wife Barbara, who strongly contested each word of this book, is the one really responsible for its existence.

CONTENTS

CHAPTER I

THE USE OF STATISTICS

0. With this key: a foreword on method. The number of
editions of Shakespeare's Sonnets, the commentaries, volumes,
and exegetic essays which are concerned with them runs into
thousands; some justification for adding another book to this
pile seems to be called for—the more so in that the suspicion that
literary criticism and exegesis have been reduced to a mere
exercise of ingenuity, a gratuitous game, is not without foundation. This suspicion is likely to be strengthened by a glance
through the following pages, in that the method followed in
approaching the Sonnets, the use of tables, schemes, and diagrams gives the whole work a pseudo-experimental air of trying
to catch up with the latest fashion, instead of honestly looking
for the poetic value or even the message which this work can
have for us today.

The chief obstacle to this honest approach, in the case in
question, lies in the fact that the Sonnets are the major *non-
dramatic* work of the greatest dramatic poet of all time. Anyone
who is looking for the poetry or for a message in Shakespeare's
work has had full opportunity to find both of these in his plays.
The Sonnets—pure lyric or private poetry in contrast with the
public poetry of the stage, in which the author objectifies himself in his characters—have for this reason been approached
above all either as formal exercises on a very high level, as
extremely useful documents to demonstrate Shakespeare's
mastery within the context of the poetic culture of his age, or as
allusive confessions of a private and even secret predicament,
cris du cœur, expressions of what Eliot, using a dangerously empiric classification, called the first voice of poetry, that of the
poet who is talking to himself—or to nobody.[1]

Sonnet criticism has for a long time followed this second path,
at least since the moment when, in a monstrosity of introverted
literary formalism, 'the Sonnet to the Sonnet', Wordsworth

[1] T. S. Eliot, *The Three Voices of Poetry* (London, 1953), p. 4.

declared: 'with this key Shakespeare unlocked his heart'. Even today there are those who read the Sonnets in terms of the poet's 'heart', and who speak of the mystery of the sexual ambiguity which surrounds them. But, in contrast with this trend, there has been a shift in recent times, from Empson's exploration of their poetic ambiguity in 1930, down to the symbolic and contextual interpretations of the 1950s and '60s in which the poetic experience has been faced as a whole, and with greater rigour. Parallel with these, the last ten years have shown a substantially new approach in the analysis of the Sonnets which have become a happy hunting-ground for all schools of structural and semiological criticism. It is true that in the past, although they were using a different terminology, such critics as Empson, Mizener, Winifred Nowottny, and Schaar[2] provided analyses of sonnets or sonnet groups which took into consideration their formal structures, though without renouncing the complex play of other elements, ranging from the author's psychology to the objective conditions in which the sonnets were composed. More recently, however, through the close analysis of specific sonnets by Samuel Levin,[3] Marcello Pagnini,[4] and finally Jakobson and Jones, whose exploration of Shakespeare's verbal art in Sonnet 129 set out to be normative,[5] we have reached such a rigorous application of semiotic and structural instruments as to exclude all spurious matter;

[2] W. Empson, *Seven Types of Ambiguity* (London, 1930), *Some Versions of Pastoral* (London, 1935); A. Mizener, 'The Structure of Figurative Language in Shakespeare's Sonnets', *Southern Review*, v, 1940; W. Nowottny, 'Formal Elements in Shakespeare's Sonnets I–VI', *Essays in Criticism*, ii. 1, January 1952; C. Schaar, *An Elizabethan Sonnet Problem: Shakespeare's Sonnets, Daniel's Delia and Their Literary Background* (Lund, 1960). The books by M. Krieger, *A Window to Criticism: Shakespeare's Sonnets and Modern Poetics* (Princeton, 1964), with its postscript 'The Innocent Insinuations of Wit: The Strategy of Language in Shakespeare's Sonnets', in the same author's *The Play and Place of Criticism* (Baltimore, 1967), pp. 19–36, and S. Booth, *An Essay on Shakespeare's Sonnets* (New Haven, 1969), are more conscious of a structural background.

[3] S. Levin, *Linguistic Structures in Poetry* (The Hague, 1962), pp. 51–8 (on Sonnet 30).

[4] M. Pagnini, 'Lettura critica (e metacritica) del Sonetto 20 di Shakespeare', *Strumenti Critici*, iii. 1 (February 1969), pp. 1–18, included in the same author's *Critica della funzionalità* (Torino, 1970), pp. 121–41. Other recent Italian contributions to the structural analysis of the Sonnets: A. Serpieri, *I sonetti dell'immortalità* (Milano, 1975), and R. Rutelli Quintavalle, *Saggi sulla connotazione: tre sonetti di Shakespeare* (Torino, 1975), on Sonnets 86, 87, and 104.

[5] R. Jakobson and L. G. Jones, *Shakespeare's Verbal Art in Th'Expense of Spirit* (The Hague, 1970).

but the validity of such metacritical analyses is in practice limited to the identification of possible interpretative parameters, which in fact they refrain from applying. They have not, that is to say, avoided the pitfall against which Romano Luperini warns us: 'The viewpoint of the structural critic is not in the least, as he would have it, objective, neither is it an empiric viewpoint. It is, instead, abstract, a transcendental *apriori* which formalizes the empiric datum in its own image.' [6]

There is the risk that the inquiry, instead of being the clinical examination of a living organism to discover the mode of its existence, might turn into an autopsy carried out on a corpse; it can even be suspected that, in order to facilitate their analyses, the analysts themselves cause the death of the object of their examination. For this reason, I. A. Richards, in a review which in effect is the reworking of the whole essay by Jakobson and Jones on Sonnet 129,[7] suggests, taking a hint from another essay of Jakobson, 'Subliminal Verbal Patterning in Poetry' (1970), a further road to be followed which reaches beyond the analysis of the formal structures, extending it into the field of depth-psychology and into a wider historical and cultural context. The impression nevertheless remains that the strictly organized and historically limited form of the sonnet tempts one to circumscribe an inquiry to the formal aspects alone, isolating and imprisoning it in pre-established categories which precede the very act of creation, so as to suppress all truly critical considerations. Even this most recent approach to the Sonnets, which should have provided an effective antidote to the still flourishing tendency to read them as confessional and autobiographical poems, contains the seeds of an involutionary tendency leading us back in the direction of the first alternative: considering them as little more than very skilful formal exercises.

In order to get beyond this critical impasse it will be necessary in the first place to reassess the importance of the instruments used, recognizing their usefulness but considering them no more than instruments with certain limited functions; and remembering that none of them, taken alone, is *the* key to an interpretation of the Sonnets, in the same way that the Sonnets

---

[6] *Marxismo e letteratura* (Bari, 1971), p. 76.
[7] I. A. Richards, 'Jakobson's Shakespeare: the subliminal structures of a Sonnet', *TLS*, 28 May 1970, pp. 589–90.

themselves, taken as a whole, are not *the* key to Shakespeare's 'heart'. In other words, the approach must be such as to permit the converging use of a variety of hermeneutic methods to arrive at an overall interpretation, and, at least implicitly, an evaluation. At this point another observation of Luperini's seems relevant:

> once the absolute and universal value of the structure has been excluded, and once the object has been put back in its real socio-economic dimension, and is seen from a real point of view, the internal rules which govern its functioning must be ascertained. The research techniques of Russian formalism and even of structuralism can, in so far as they are techniques, be utilized not only to provide the correct historical view of literary forms and genres, but also to ascertain the historical meaning of the literary work, which is to be found not so much in its exterior theses and its explicit ideology as in its way of capturing reality and formally organizing it in terms of a meaning which it would be arbitrary to overlook as being conditioned by that very organization.[8]

We must guard, on the other hand, against the danger of over-emphasizing content and context (whether historical or socio-economic) at the expense of the forms of expression. Shakespeare's Sonnets present a further complication: in their case the formal organization, at least at the level of a prosodic system, is 'given', it exists before the act of composition (this is not true in the case of his dramatic works which constantly invent new forms of organization, which only at a later period become normative for him and for other authors). The sense, then, in the Sonnets is not determined by that organization, but rather by the way in which reality is captured within a preconstituted formal framework. In this case, therefore, two distinct operations are required: in the first place it is necessary to establish the norm of the formal organization of the English sonnet, taking into consideration the historical and cultural context in which it was born and developed; in the second place the distinctive characteristics (internal as well as purely external) of the 154 Sonnets of Shakespeare must be identified, both as a whole and in the single poems, ascertaining the variations in that context both on the diachronic level (the general historical evolution of the context) and on the synchronic level

[8] Op. cit., pp. 80-1.

(the individual position of Shakespeare as a thinking mind in a precise context).

The books of Lever,[9] Cruttwell,[10] and Muriel Bradbrook[11] have successfully attempted something of this kind—but in spite of the sound historical and aesthetic foundations of their interpretations, they do not altogether escape the suspicion of relying too much on personal impressions however brilliant and stimulating. It seems to me therefore worthwhile to proceed to a more factual selection of the samples, basing this in the first place on a statistical analysis. The purely empirical and technical character of this approach is deliberately adopted to avoid all temptation to sentimentalize or aestheticize the relation between author and reader, pinning it down instead to a precise working hypothesis.

A comparative analysis of the word-frequencies in five of the most representative collections of sonnets of the last ten years of the sixteenth century (Shakespeare's collection was not published till 1609, but the composition of most of the sonnets must date back to the period in question) provides us with the normative basis of a literary genre in a precise moment in history, and an indication of the more obvious individual deviations; once the more significant among the outstanding elements in Shakespeare's collection have been identified—those elements, that is to say, which mark it off from the other four under consideration as constituting his particular norm or convention—I shall proceed to isolate the single poems or groups of poems which stand out as different, which react from the inside against this newly instituted convention. These doubly atypical sonnets, if it proves possible to establish their aesthetic validity and their peculiar manner of organizing reality, are the richest in suggestions with regard to the underlying thought: thought which on account of its very originality has been unable to find expression in any other formal organization except one which, though keeping the prosodic rules, overturns all other structural conventions.

The data and tables discussed in this first chapter are only a starting-point, without any value in themselves; they do not

[9] J. W. Lever, *The Elizabethan Love Sonnet* (London, 1956); cf. *Sonnets of the English Renaissance*, selected and edited by J. W. Lever (London, 1974).

[10] P. Cruttwell, *The Shakespearean Moment and its Place in the Poetry of the Seventeenth Century* (London, 1954).

[11] M. C. Bradbrook, *Shakespeare and Elizabethan Poetry* (London, 1951).

represent a method of inquiry, but are the factual presuppositions for a study which proposes to utilize a number of converging critical instruments to justify the analysis in depth of the four sonnets in which Shakespeare's thought and feeling are best articulated. Formally atypical, they are a momentary reconciliation of the tensions, contradictions, and internal ambiguities of that thought and feeling, rejecting the self-imposed norm of the other sonnets.

1. The five samples: grammatical functions.   The five sonnet sequences of the 1590s used for the lexical tests have been chosen because, in their case, computerized data were readily available. A wider selection from the sonneteers of the time— the only time in which, for a brief and unexpected season, the sonnet sequence flourished in England—would have been more satisfactory. But for the purposes of a summary inquiry, which makes no claim to strict scientific analysis, I thought that the data provided by Herbert Donow in his *Concordance to the Sonnet Sequences of Daniel, Drayton, Shakespeare, Sidney and Spenser* [12] were sufficient. These five sequences, by critical consensus, achieve authentic poetic dignity as against the plethora of minor versifiers who mechanically repeat themes and patterns used by their contemporaries or predecessors (the Italian Petrarchists, the French poets of the Pléiade and Desportes, and, in England, the occasional sonnets of Sir Thomas Wyatt and the Earl of Surrey). The sequences under consideration, besides Shakespeare's sonnets, are:

Sir Philip Sidney, *Astrophil and Stella*, 1591 (only the 108 sonnets).
Samuel Daniel, *Delia*, 1592 (50 sonnets).
Michael Drayton, *Ideas Mirrour*, 1594 (51 sonnets).[13]
Edmund Spenser, *Amoretti*, 1595 (89 sonnets).

[12] Carbondale and Edwardsville, 1969.
[13] Drayton kept on for a quarter of a century modifying, rearranging, adding to, and subtracting from his sonnet sequence, so that the last of its many editions ('Idea', in *Poems*, 1619) includes 63 poems, only 18 of which were in the 1594 collection. Donow tabulated both the first and the last editions, but in this book I have not taken into account the later *Idea*, as being outside the period under consideration; but I have sampled it while preparing my statistical tables, with interesting results. Both in general pronominal frequencies and in the proportional distribution of pronouns, as well as in word-frequencies, Drayton's tendency seems to be away from the early tradition and to follow (at a distance) Shakespeare's lead.

These sequences are, moreover, the ones to which students of Shakespeare's Sonnets most often refer for the identification of sources or of parallels.

They can therefore be considered a sufficiently representative context within which to study the characteristics of a literary genre as strictly limited in time and space as the Elizabethan love-sonnet. It would be more accurate to speak in terms not of a genre but of the model for a system of signs subject to a strict formal organization, clearly distinguished in respect of the infinite variety of other possible organizations of signs. As Donow writes in the introduction to his *Concordance*, speaking of its possible uses, it is 'an invitation . . . to observe poets working in a tight convention, manifesting their poetic personalities in a controlled environment. By examining poems in a situation where the effects of semantic difference are minimized, we can study style as an abstraction, apart from meaning.'[14] I would like to add that an over-all survey of the five sequences can provide, on an empirical plane, the general norms of the English sonnet of the late sixteenth century, while a comparison of the distinctive features of the single collections enables us to point out some of the individualizing traits of each particular poet.

One of the first uses of the *Concordance* is to indicate the words which occur most frequently (see Appendix, Table I).

It appears that the words with the highest frequencies (occurring on an average at least 1·5 times per sonnet) comprise the definite article *the*, the conjunction *and*, the prepositions *to*, *of*, *in*, and *with*, *that* (both as pronoun and conjunction) and, significantly, both the first person singular pronoun and possessive adjective, *I* and *my*. In the group of frequencies between 1·0 and 1·2 are, beside the indefinite article *a* and the conjunction *but*, three pronominal forms: *her*, *thy*, and *me*. The high incidence of deictic forms and especially pronominal expressions, above all in the first person (5 out of the 15 most frequent words, with *my* topping the list in absolute in both Sidney's and Drayton's collections), is a fact which is worth taking into consideration. In a middle position between the two frequency groups listed above there is the only word with a connotative function, *Love*: but it must be borne in mind that it serves both as noun and verb and

---

[14] Donow, op cit., pp. vi–vii.

that the inflected forms (*love's, loves, lovest, loved,* and *loving*) have been included in the count.

As is to be expected, with this one exception the most frequent words are those with a merely grammatical or demonstrative function.[15] But even within these obvious limits, the specific anomalies in the figures of the single sequences have a certain interest, serving, if for nothing else, to confirm the conclusions generally reached on the language of the single authors by aesthetic criticism. The high-incidence indices (as high as 5) in Daniel's and Drayton's collections confirm their relative linguistic and lexical poverty, their greater monotony; their faithful following of convention is demonstrated also by the fact that they show no outstanding variations from the norm: though in different arrangements, the words most used in their sonnets coincide on the whole with the over-all maximum frequencies in the five collections. In Sidney, on the other hand, there is a more uniform distribution of the commonest words (he never reaches the proportion of three such words in any one sonnet), bearing witness to a greater attention to lexical variety; easier to explain, even if symptomatic, is the low incidence of *thy* and *her*: in the first case it is the poet's rank which leads him to prefer the more impersonal *your* (which occurs 67 times with an incidence of 0·75); the explanation of the relative scarcity of *her* lies in the fact that Sidney's mistress (unlike the recipients of Spenser's and Shakespeare's sonnets) has a name, Stella, and the poet usually addresses her in this way instead of using a pronoun: Stella is mentioned no less than 74 times, while Daniel invokes Delia 18 times, and Drayton his Idea (who is more of an abstraction than a woman) only three times.

All Spenser's deviations from the norm tend to stress the abstract literary character of his compositions. I will deal later with his disinclination to mention *Love*; but his limited use of the indefinite article *a* as compared with his use of the definite article *the* is significant, the use of *the* being notably higher than the average: Spenser prefers the absolute, the idea of the thing to the thing itself. Still more significant is the lower incidence of all pronominal expressions, including the first person; *thy* is

---

[15] The only inflected verbal form, *is*, appearing more than once per sonnet in Spenser and Shakespeare, is an auxiliary with strictly grammatical functions.

practically absent, and is scarcely compensated for by the 67 *yours* to be found in the collection: the *Amoretti* are addressed to an anonymous figure not as if she were alive and present but as if she existed on a purely intellectual plane, and should therefore be celebrated in the third person. She is spoken *about* rather than *to*.

This is the exact opposite of what happens in Shakespeare, in whose Sonnets not only the possessive but also *thou* and *thee* are present in a very high proportion. The other anomaly in the Shakespearean frequency tables, the rare occurrence of the feminine *her*, requires no explanation: obviously a feminine pronoun plays little part in compositions addressed, for the most part, to a man.

This shows that the reasons for the variations from the norm of the grammatical and deictic functions depend rather on content than style; nevertheless it seems clear that most of these variations concern the pronominal forms, terms which frequently carry, beside their grammatical function, a denotative or even a connotative function. It seems therefore worth while to pursue this line of inquiry a step further.

2. Pronouns and public relations. In a language like English in which the verbal conjugations are restricted to a paradigm almost without desinential variations, the pronouns and other pronominal expressions play a very important part. The pronouns are the main semiotic pointers, they indicate and determine the communications of the sentence, setting up a network of relations which, in the last analysis, can be extended to the more strictly social field, telling us to whom the forms of expression are addressed, and what they wish to express. They are, in other words, the vehicles of communication. In the five sonnet sequences the percentage incidence of the pronominal forms with respect to all the words used is extremely high, and varies within narrow limits from a minimum in Spenser of 12·25 per cent to a maximum of 14·17 per cent in Shakespeare. A much wider variation, on the other hand, is to be found in the single authors in the distribution of pronouns according to person, number, and gender (see Appendix, Table II).

Taking the five collections as a whole, the pronominal forms for the *first* person account for 43·8 per cent of the total, those of

the *third* person for 30·6 per cent, and those of the *second* for only
25·6 per cent. This distribution is indicative of the way in which
the specific function of the sonnet was understood within the
more general field of lyric poetry. The sonnet, in the first place,
is the expression of the *I*, of the poet who voices his own feelings:
this accounts for the confessional interpretation of Shakespeare's
Sonnets mentioned above.

The *I* is followed not by *thou/you* but by the third person,
which is often used in an impersonal sense. In other words, the
poet either speaks of himself, or places himself in relation to the
external world observed objectively or with a certain detachment, without establishing a dialogue with others. The second
person is the least used: the *I* has no need of a direct interlocutor, and only occasionally apostrophizes the reader or addresses
directly the loved object or his patron with prayers, supplications
or even invectives. The norm of the use of personal pronouns is
in any case revealing: the closed form of the sonnet lends itself
above all to the expression of the speaker's own feelings, and
therefore to the contemplation and detached meditation on the
surrounding world. Only rarely is there any direct relationship
established with one or more interlocutors.

This attitude qualifies the English sonnet at the outset as élite
poetry, made possible by a society with a definite class structure,
in which the court poet celebrates his own *I*, and places it at the
centre of a clearly defined world, in a position from which it can
contemplate from above and with detachment the rest of mankind which does not share the same culture. His poems circulate
in manuscript in the closed circle of his friends, like private letters
speaking essentially about himself. This is the case of Sir Philip
Sidney, the model of the English courtier, poet and soldier,
ready to give his life in defence of a foreign country. His sonnets,
composed between 1580 and 1584, were published in a pirated
edition five years after his death in 1586, to confirm the myth of
the perfect man of 'virtù'. Samuel Daniel, in the dedication to
Delia, the first collection of sonnets composed in the wake of
Sidney, and dedicated to Sidney's sister Mary, Countess of Pembroke (the mother of that William Herbert held by some critics
to be the youth to whom Shakespeare's Sonnets were dedicated),
upholds the convention of the private character of the sonnets,
justifying their publication in the following terms:

Right honorable, although I rather desired to keep in the private passions of my youth, from the multitude, as things utterd to my selfe, and consecrated to silence: yet seeing I was betraide by the indiscretion of a greedie Printer, and had some of my secrets bewraide to the world, uncorrected: doubting the like of the rest, I am forced to publish that which I never ment. But this wrong was not onely doone to mee, but to him [Sidney] whose unmatchable lines have indured the like misfortune; Ignorance sparing not to commit sacriledge upon so holy Reliques.[16]

Drayton, meanwhile, was composing his sonnets to *Idea* and all kinds of fashionable poetry to draw attention to his merits, and in the hope of entering the circle of aristocracy by marrying the daughter of his noble patron (the fact that he failed in this attempt, and that he was condemned to the role of diligent, pedantic, and frustrated poet is irrelevant). It should be noticed that in all three cases, the affirmation of the *I*, although for different reasons, is revealed by the absolute predominance of first person pronominal forms in their poetry, which reaches (and in Drayton exceeds) about 50 per cent of the total number of pronouns employed.

This gives rise to a consideration of the introduction of the sonnet form into England. Obviously such a short and compact form can only be the vehicle for individual messages, in contrast with the narrative function which poetry assumes in the epic. On the other hand, the Petrarchan sonnet was in its turn the culmination of a process which attempted to impose a logical order on lyrical expression, which otherwise ran the risk of being reduced to the level of pure exclamation; that is to say, it attempted to structure the expression of feeling according to the scheme of the syllogism, the skeleton key of logics. But just as the logical syllogism tends to become sophistry, so the sonnet in the sixteenth century loses more and more the sense of its original rational rigour and is reduced to a mere prosodic scheme, and as such it was introduced into England. The startling paradox replaces the precise reasoning and organization of feelings which was at the basis of the sonnet which does not, however, lose its characteristic of self-expression, the concentration on the speaking *I*. The cultural élite in England adopted the sonnet as a useful container rather than as an organic form of

16 *Delia, Contayning certayne Sonnets*, etc. (London, 1592), sig. A2.

expression imposed by the content. It is sufficiently compact and brief to allow for the development of a conceit, which does not involve the three-cornered logical play of the syllogism, but is rather a sequence of oxymora culminating in a final paradox; this is the reason why the prosodic and rhythmic scheme has been changed from the Petrarchan model of octave and sestet to the three independently rhyming quatrains plus a rhymed couplet.

The English sonnet is the typical expression of the poet who is either already at the top of fortune's hill[17] or who hopes to reach it. Not for nothing was it first introduced by two noblemen, Sir Thomas Wyatt and the Earl of Surrey, while the first sonnet sequence was the work of Sir Philip Sidney. This gives rise to a foreseeable instrumentalization of the sonnet: from a form of expression proper to an élite it becomes a kind of passport to a privileged social and cultural position. Daniel's dedication quoted above is symptomatic, with its transparent fiction of his being forced to publish compositions which he pretends are the fruit of leisured ease. The spate of sonnet sequences which flood the printers and booksellers between 1592 and 1598 are not the symptom of a poetic explosion, but the exploitation of the relatively recent technical development of printing to affirm and bear witness to the social advancement of their authors, just at a time when the traditional class hierarchy was changing. Celebrating their ideal mistresses on the printed page—Diana and Parthenope, Phillis and Licia, Zepheria and Coelia, Cynthia and Alcilia and Chloris and Fidella and Diella and Laura(!) and Alba[18]—Henry Constable and Barnabe Barnes, Thomas Lodge and Giles Fletcher, William Percy and Richard Barnfield, William Smith and Bartholomew Griffin and Richard Linche and Robert Tofte and Nicholas Breton (so many worthy gentlemen who have been justly forgotten) laid their claim on behalf of the culturally up-

[17] I am thinking of the title of John Danby's illuminating book, *Poets on Fortune's Hill* (London, 1952), rather than of the passage in *Timon*, I. i, from which it is taken.

[18] The virgin-queen was identified with Artemis, the virgin-goddess; such names as Diana, Parthenope, Cynthia, and Delia are implicit tributes to her, even if the 'real' (or pretended) mistresses are merely court ladies. Most of these sequences are reprinted in *Elizabethan Sonnets newly arranged and indexed*, with an introduction by Sidney Lee, 2 vols. (London, 1904).

to-date for a right of entrance into the magic circle of the
aristocracy or the court: social climbers, it is true, and sometimes shabby enough, but the involuntary promoters and at the
same time the fruit of a more general movement tending to re-
place the primacy of blood with that of merit: meritocracy
rather than aristocracy.[19]

In point of fact, however, merit was only one of the two keys
by which the new middle class was trying to open the doors to
power. The right key turned out to be the other one, that of
conquest in the field of trade and economics; and while the
dreams of the intellectual were limited to a selfish aspiration to
rise into the higher class, closing the door at once behind him as
soon as he had crossed the threshold of the palace of power,
those of the enterprising merchant and industrious artisan con-
tributed to form a wider awareness of the crisis of that hierarchic
system which culminated in the king's 'body politic'.[20] The so-
called Puritan or middle-class revolution of the mid-seventeenth
century sprang from this source, certainly not from the mistaken
ambitions of a horde of sonneteers whose sole aim was to turn
the existing system to their own personal advantage. They considered that it was their duty to conform faithfully to the current
aristocratic conception of the function of lyric poetry as the
patrimony of the privileged few.

A greater poet, like Edmund Spenser, on the other hand, is
so acutely conscious of this practical utilization of poetry as a
means of social climbing within the framework of a clientèle
system, that he refuses to copy the forms used by his protectors
and patrons in order to place himself on a level with them; in
Poets on Fortune's Hill John Danby stresses the emblematic

[19] They would aim at creating a new leisured class, whose composition is clearly
suggested, e.g., by 'R. S. of the Inner Temple, Gentleman', in the sub-title of the
book of poems he collected in 1593 in memory of Sir Philip Sidney, *The Phoenix
Nest. Built up with the most rare and refined workes of Noble men, woorthy Knights, gallant
Gentlemen, Masters of Arts, and brave Schollers*.

[20] See L. Stone, *The Crisis of the Aristocracy, 1558–1641* (Oxford, 1965), and, for a
clear statement of the current controversy on the reasons for the social changes in
those years, see Stone's introduction to his *Social Change and Revolution in England
1540–1640* (London, 1965). Cf. Chr. Hill, *Society and Puritanism in Pre-Revolutionary
England* (London, 1964), and, by the same, *Intellectual Origins of the English Revolution*
(London, 1965). An essential treatment of the literary repercussions of the social
changes is to be found in P. N. Siegel, *Shakespearean Tragedy and the Elizabethan
Compromise* (New York, 1957), pp. 3–78; finally, for the conception of the 'body
politic' see E. H. Kantorowicz, *The King's Two Bodies* (Princeton, 1957).

character of the anecdote (almost certainly apocryphal) narrated by Aubrey: Spenser walking off in a huff after being kept waiting for hours in the ante-chamber of Sir Philip Sidney to whom he had sent the first cantos of his poem, and Sidney, once he had read the manuscript, sending out in search of its author and loading him with gifts. Danby goes on:

Spenser's is the poetry of accretion and accumulation, the poetry of display . . . the difference between Spenser and Sidney has to do, I think, in part, in addition to the difference in their endowments, with the difference in their poetic situation as members of their community. Sidney is on the top of Fortune's hill, whereas Spenser is not. Spenser's poetry must win him preferment, and then maintain him in place in the body of the world. For Sidney poetry is the private devotion to truth. For Spenser it must also be the public vindication of his claim to recognition as a poet.[21]

The whole of Spenser's poetic output follows two main lines, the one to assert his cultural superiority over that very world which he is so anxious to enter, the other to modify from within the poetic models which that world offers, thereby asserting his own individuality. His sonnets are only one aspect, and certainly not the most important, of his personal tactics in aristocratic integration, but they are well worth taking into consideration, returning once more to the table of pronominal frequencies which, as I have said, can furnish significant data if we bear in mind the variations from the norm. It is, too, a way of verifying Danby's conclusion when he writes: 'For Sidney, we have said, poetry was truth, whereas for Spenser poetry was prestige.'[22]

The first and most obvious comment is that in Spenser's *Amoretti*, alone of the five sequences, the dominant pronoun is not *I* but the third person, which accounts for almost 50 per cent of the pronominal forms; the first person accounts for only 36 per cent, and the second for just over 16 per cent. Such a wide deviation from the norm can only mean that Spenser wishes to stand as far off as possible, that his celebration (in this case not of his patron but of his mistress) may have all the dignity which an impersonal tone can confer. The object of his celebration, his mistress (the feminine third person singular in his collection reaches the very high incidence of 25 per cent) is contemplated with insistence but also with a respectful detach-

[21] Op. cit., p. 35.   [22] Op. cit., p. 36.

ment, not as an interlocutor but as the focal point of contemplation and meditation, so as to stress the poet's intellectual gifts. Poetry as prestige: but prestige not only of the poetizing subject but also of the poetized object. It is the characteristic attitude of the court poet—while Sidney, who is writing above all about himself, and who mentions his Stella 74 times, is a courtier by natural right, a nobleman first, and then also a poet.

In Shakespeare's Sonnets too there is a marked deviation from the norm in the use of pronominal forms, but in the opposite direction to Spenser. Once again it is the first person which predominates, but not to the same extent as in Sidney, Daniel, and Drayton. The ambiguous circumstances of publication, the dedication signed by the bookseller Thorpe instead of by the author, go to show that, like Sidney's collection and unlike the collections of his other predecessors, Shakespeare's Sonnets were not in fact intended for publication, but should have circulated separately in manuscript within a narrow circle of friends, men of letters, and possible patrons; a circle only tangentially touching the one for which *Astrophil and Stella* was destined. I spoke of separate sonnets in that Shakespeare's collection has not the same unity of thematic development which characterizes the sequences deliberately prepared for publication. The most notable variation in respect of the other collections remains, however, Shakespeare's use of the second person, which is almost as frequent as that of the first: 37·2 per cent as against 40·3 per cent, while in the other poets under consideration the highest percentage reached is 20 per cent. What is the meaning of the disruption of the normal pronominal order: I → her/him → thou/you? In the first place, Shakespeare is breaking with the tradition of the sonneteer as a court poet or an aristocrat. He opens a dialogue: rather than contemplating his interlocutors from on high or paying them respectful and detached homage, he involves them in debate. He behaves, that is, as *par inter pares*, or as man to man. On the other side, this balance between *I* and *thou*, this direct exchange, this dialogue, is also an obvious demonstration of the dramatic and theatrical character of his poetic genius, even when using the lyrical form. There is no need to labour this point, except to note that it is simply his profession as a playwright, as a man of the theatre, which places him on a totally different plane from that of the other sonneteers of his time, in respect of the social hierarchy in which they were trying to find a place.[23]

The other outstanding deviation in the frequency tables regarding Shakespeare's use of pronominal forms is that he scarcely uses the feminine third person singular pronoun as compared to the masculine. But the reason for this has already been given, and there is no need to go over the same ground. What should be recognized instead as the characteristic feature of Shakespeare's Sonnets as compared with those of his contemporaries is the balanced predominance of *I* and *thou* rather than the distance between *I* and *she*.

3. The connotations of love and the importance of the atypical. Passing to a consideration of the frequencies of words with connotative value (naturally, occurring on the whole much less than words with grammatical and deictic functions), Shakespeare seems at first sight to fit more easily into the norm, even to the point of conventionality (see Appendix, Table III).

As we have already seen, *Love*, both as verb and noun, leads in the work of all five poets; only in Spenser is it used to a lesser extent and is approached by the adjective (occasionally used as a noun) *fair*, meaning both 'beautiful' and 'just': the most ambitious of court poets celebrates love in terms of the chivalrous aesthetic ideal. The privileged position of *eyes*, strengthened by the wide use of the verb *to see* by all the sonneteers, bears witness not so much to the visual element (although this carries a certain weight) as to the continuance of the courtly convention which holds sight to be the purest and most refined of the five senses, and the best vehicle of the world of feeling. The eyes give sense to the heart, and the celebration of the war and the alliance between *eye* and *heart* is a commonplace in all these authors, finding its most effective expression in the diptych of Shake-

---

[23] On the theatrical profession and its social status, see M. C. Bradbrook, *The Rise of the Common Player* (London, 1962), and G. E. Bentley, *The Profession of Dramatist in Shakespeare's Time* (Princeton, 1971); on social aspects of Elizabethan and Jacobean drama see L. G. Salingar, G. Harrison, and B. Cochrane, 'Les Comédiens et leur public en Angleterre de 1520 à 1640' and other important essays by different hands in *Dramaturgie et société*, ed. Jean Jacquot (Paris, 1968), vol. ii; and two remarkable full-length studies in Italian: V. Poggi, *L'uomo e le corti nel teatro elisabettiano* (Bologna, 1968), and V. Gentili, *Le figure della pazzia nel teatro elisabettiano* (Lecce, 1969).

spearian sonnets (nos. 46 and 47) in which the initial contrast resolves itself in the joint sublimation of both.[24]

More significant than the substantial agreement in the frequency of the main connotative terms within the five sequences are the anomalies which are to be found in one or another of them. The frequency of *self* (usually high, but almost non-existent in Drayton) is not significant in so far as this word, which many times, and particularly in Shakespeare, stands for the individuality of the speaker or his interlocutor, is often used as a mere suffix in reflexive pronouns. Rather we should note the high incidence in Drayton of words less commonly used by other authors: *world* (0·6), *tears* (0·53), *sighs* (0·47); this is merely further evidence of the stereotyped character of his poetry: his microcosm is constantly threatened by storms of tears and tempests of sighs.[25]

The anomalies of some of Shakespeare's word-frequencies give rise to a different argument. In his Sonnets, immediately after *Beauty* (0·54—physical beauty as a reflection of inner beauty), comes *Time* (0·51), often personified, and *true/Truth* (0·44—the quality of being genuine and sincere, faithfulness as well as truth), words which in no other author exceed 0·32 (time) and 0·29 (truth) respectively—while *heart*, which in other poets shows a high frequency level, in Shakespeare only just reaches 0·4. Here we are dealing with fundamental and typical motives of Shakespeare's poetry: his preoccupation with the pressure of time, his recognition of the temporal and transitory dimension of human existence, and his determination to defy time and death without trying to escape into another dimension; the exaltation of *Truth* is an affirmation of the necessity to remain faithful to oneself and to one's condition as a man, to be frank; and this authenticity—an essentially moral quality

[24] On the debate between the eye and the heart, going back to the medieval allegory of the Court of Love, see L. C. John, *The Elizabethan Sonnet Sequences, Studies in Conventional Conceits* (New York, 1938), pp. 93–102. W. H. Auden, in his introduction to the Signet edition of the *Sonnets* (New York, 1964), p. xxxiii, remarks: 'The Petrarchan distinction, employed by Shakespeare in a number of his sonnets, between the love of the eye and the love of the heart, is an attempt, I think, to express the difference between these two kinds of beauty [public and personal] and our response to them.'

[25] The incidence is drastically reduced in the 1619 edition of Drayton's *Idea: world*=0·25, *tears*=0·15, *sighs*=0·19. Shakespeare hardly used the last two words at all in the Sonnets: *tears* six times (=0·04), and *sighs* only twice (=0·01).

—can constitute, together with beauty, a passport to immortality (see Sonnets 14, 54, 79, 101, and 105, besides Interchapter, § 1 of the present book). The theme, as most commentators have repeated, is of Horatian and Ovidian origin, but in Shakespeare it takes on a new ethical quality, over and beyond its Renaissance usage which is essentially aesthetic. Shakespeare, while using the themes of court poetry as his starting-point, breaks free of the convention in this way: while Love remains in his Sonnets, as for all other poets, the privileged theme, it is no longer for him either the idealization of a conventional sentiment (as shown by the reduced incidence of *heart*) or a courtly game, but is rather an inescapable component of the human condition, a conflict between the life of the senses and an innate ethical need. This brief comment on one feature of Shakespearian word-frequencies is sufficient to show the individuality of his collection of sonnets as compared with the other contemporary sequences.

To summarize: the norm of Shakespeare's Sonnets is characterized on the connotative level by the prevalence of the word *Love* (they are explorations and expressions of the infinite variety of love) in relation to Beauty, Time, and Truth; on the level of communication Shakespeare's work stands out from that of the other sonneteers on account of the high frequency of the second person, setting up a dialogue, a vital and dramatic I–thou relationship.

This is the norm. Nevertheless, in some of his Sonnets, and notably in the more memorable ones, this norm is no longer observed—on the contrary, it is radically reversed. *Love* disappears entirely, and the balance between the first and second person pronouns is overthrown by the absence of either one or the other, or even of both. Now, while respect of a norm, however individual that norm may be, can enable us to read the constants of recurring themes, it is indeed the deviations from that norm which become very relevant for the discovery of the underlying meaning. I wish therefore, at this point, having established the individual norm of Shakespeare as a sonnet writer, to discover the deviations from it, and examine more closely those sonnets in which they occur, on the assumption that such deviations may reveal more directly the thought of the author beyond the self-imposed personal conventions and tricks of style which are merely the stock-in-trade of his poetic craft. The starting-point will be once again deviations in his use of pronouns, the absence of *I* and *Thou*.

4. The I-less sonnets and the economy of Venus.

Although the first person singular dominates the pronominal forms in the Sonnets (*I* occurs 351 times, *me* 168, *my* and *mine* 455, making a total of 974, with an average incidence of 6·35 per sonnet), it is completely absent in twenty of them, that is to say in nos. 1, 3, 4, 5, 6, 7, 8, 9, 11, 53, 56, 67, 68, 69, 70, 77, 84, 94, 95, and 129. Sonnet 2 can also be added to the list in so far as the one *my* in it does not refer to the speaker but is part of what the 'Thou' says in reported direct speech, so that its logical value is that of the second rather than of the first person. It is also remarkable that in all these sonnets (with the exception of 3, 8, 9, 56, and 70) the key connotative word *Love* is likewise absent. Obviously there is no dialogue in these sonnets: the speaking *I* does not attempt to open a dramatic debate with his interlocutor—at the most, as in Sonnets 1 and 53, he uses the impersonal plural *we*; in five cases the interlocutor himself disappears: in Sonnets 5, 67, 68, 94, and 129 not even the second person is to be found. The 67–68 sonnet-diptych performs an abstract eulogistic function: the beauty of the poet's friend is the epitome of all past beauties; but elsewhere, in Sonnets 94 and 129, the dialogue is replaced by a dialectic within the one character, Man himself; I shall return more fully to this point later. More often, however, in the I-less sonnets, the tone adopted is that of apostrophe: reproof (69), apology (70), homage (53 and 77), warning (84 and 95), but above all exhortation (56 and 1–11). This hortatory character is particularly marked in the first sonnets, which are worth considering at this point in greater detail.

The sonnets from 1 to 9 plus 11, atypical on account of the absence of the first person, are part of the only group of Shakesperian sonnets which can be clearly identified and isolated, in that they all deal with a common subject: they are an invitation to the poet's young friend and/or patron to marry and to generate children. The definition 'marriage' or 'generation sonnets' has therefore been given to this group of poems which in the 1609 edition were numbered 1–17; from the formal point of view they can effectively be isolated in that they totally invert Shakespeare's norm in the use of pronominal forms: while in the whole collection the relation between the first person singular and the second is 51·1 to 48·9, in the seventeen marriage sonnets it is 16·3 of the first as against 83·7 of the second (see Appendix, Table IV).[26]

Moreover, in this group of sonnets dialogue disappears: it is a case of the poet's self-effacement in relation to the addressee. The author wishes to be simply an exhorting voice, an anonymous counsellor or the conscientious steward who promotes his master's interests. It is hardly surprising that, confronted at the beginning of the collection by this group of sonnets, we get the impression that the young man to whom they are addressed must be a nobleman of high rank, which accounts for the identification of the Earl of Pembroke or the Earl of Southampton with the mysterious 'Mr. W. H.'. Even though it is true that in love-poems (but can poems in which *love* is never mentioned be classified in this way?) the loved object is always considered as lord and sovereign, whatever his actual rank may be, yet the tone of these sonnets is so strictly linked to a hierarchical conception as to give the impression of an almost masochistic humility, as of a work which is in a certain sense commissioned. This does not imply a negative aesthetic judgement—much of Renaissance art was born because it was commissioned by either ecclesiastic or lay patrons; none the less it is significant

---

[26] Taking into consideration only the first eleven sonnets, the difference between first and second person is even more marked: only 5·2 per cent for the first person (incidence =0·54), against 94·8 per cent for the second (incidence =9·9); the increased use of 'I' in the later marriage sonnets (nos. 12–17) seems to testify to that 'growth of intimacy' that John Dover Wilson sees in them, in the notes to his edition of the *Sonnets* (Cambridge, 1966), pp. 91–2. The change from *thou* in sonnets nos. 1–12 and 14, to *you* in nos. 13 and 15–17, on the other hand, does not seem to be particularly significant, and contradicts the conclusions reached by recent linguistic studies on the use of the singular and plural second person pronouns in Shakespeare's plays. See, as an example of the method, Angus McIntosh's analysis of the relation Celia–Rosalind, "'As You Like It": a grammatical clue to character', in *A Review of English Literature*, iv. 2 (April 1963), pp. 68–81, reprinted with additional notes in *Patterns of Language*, by A. McIntosh and M. A. K. Halliday (London, 1966), pp. 70–82; the paper in its final form is particularly valuable for the bibliographical references it provides. Obviously the usage in the plays is unconnected with that in the Sonnets, since it appears that, dramatically, the passage from *thou* to *you* marks the reverse process from that 'growth of intimacy' postulated in the Sonnets. I feel that a linguistic study of the different *persons* in pronominal usage is far more rewarding in the field of non-dramatic poetry.

that the only one of these first sonnets in which not only the first but also the second person (repeated obsessively in the others) is absent, that is to say Sonnet 5, stands out in an extraordinary way. Although the theme is the same, and the sonnet in effect is a prelude to no. 6, while the eulogistic attitude is just as marked, yet the absence of 'thou' gives it a peculiar quality of lyrical reflection, and seems to allow it a greater freedom in the use of imagery.

The group of marriage sonnets as a whole gives the impression of being an elegant series of variations on a single theme, a poetic experiment on a high level, composed for a practical purpose, but which finds its most genuine notes when the poet, going outside the limits of the specific argument, contemplates the 'wastes of Time' and makes war upon this 'bloody tyrant' using the weapon of poetry. Sonnet 15, though only the prelude to no. 16 which fits completely into the main theme of the whole group, ignores the central theme of the invitation to wed and to procreate, concentrating instead on the function of poetry as an antidote to death. This latter theme is repeated more fully in nos. 18 and 19, sonnets which are probably outside the group of marriage sonnets though linked to them by lexical and iconic affinities.

I have deliberately spoken of group rather than sequence when referring to the marriage sonnets, in that the order in which they appeared in the 1609 edition is not necessarily the one intended by the author, and 17 is in any case a very odd number for a complete sequence; critics who are anxious to observe poetic decorum try to add no. 18 to the hypothetical sequence, and some even add 19 and 20 (see Interchapter, below). E. K. Chambers sees the sequence as completed by no. 126, which is not a sonnet but a series of six rhymed couplets.[27] In any case, the first seventeen sonnets form a sufficiently homogeneous complex, with a strict connecting theme; the impression that we are dealing with a series of experimental variations on a set theme is reinforced by the great variety of logical and syntactical schemes and of semantic organizations which they reveal, while strictly respecting the prosodic pattern of the English sonnet. The poet tries to explore, within these narrow and possibly self-imposed confines of form and content, the vari-

[27] *William Shakespeare, A Study of Facts and Problems* (Oxford, 1930), i, p. 562.

ous possibilities offered by his means of expression. So Sonnets 2, 12, and 15 are applications, with inner variations, of the syllogistic scheme, balanced on the correlative adverbs so dear to Petrarch *When* and *Then*: all three open with *When*, but while in no. 2 *Then* is to be found already at the beginning of the second quatrain, in nos. 12 and 15 *When* is repeated again in the octave (at lines 3 and 5 of Sonnet 12, and only at 5 of Sonnet 15), and *Then* instead opens the third quatrain, suggesting the logical division of the Italian sonnet into octave and sestet. Sonnets 4, 8, 9, 16, and 17 explore the various possibilities of the interrogative opening gambit, nos. 7, 10, and 13 the exclamatory opening gambit, and no. 3 its imperative variant. Sonnets 1 and 11, which respect the English structure more faithfully, are tripartite meditations on the proposed theme, with a more rigorous continuity of development which is worked out in the final couplet; no. 14 is the elegant elaboration of a typical sixteenth century conceit, and lastly no. 5, perhaps the best of all, is also the most complex on account of the wealth of inner movement based on a serried play of antitheses supported by the arrangement of the sounds; it is not for nothing that this sonnet, as noted earlier, is the most atypical in the group also on account of the total absence of *Thou*.

The ordering of the marriage sonnets, on the other hand, reflects in microcosm the ordering of the whole collection. There are two undisputed poetic diptychs, Sonnets 5–6, and 15–16, but it is impossible to tell how far the arrangement of the others is deliberate or whether it is purely casual. Winifred Nowottny, in an exemplary essay,[28] has convincingly demonstrated the structural unity of the first six, basing her argument above all on the alternating images through which the constant theme takes shape. She defines the first sonnet as a 'litany of images', one for each line, which will then be taken up again in the others; in the second she traces two dominant currents: images taken from nature (or agriculture), and others from the world of business and economics. Those from agriculture are dominant in the third and fifth sonnets, those from economics in the fourth and sixth, the latter concluding the series with a

---

[28] 'Formal Elements in Shakespeare's Sonnets I–VI', pp. 76–84; for a more recent reconsideration of the marriage sonnets see Philip Martin, *Shakespeare's Sonnets: Self, Love and Art* (Cambridge, 1972), pp. 15–30.

not altogether successful attempt to also reabsorb the images
from nature. But the search for iconic repetitions cannot easily
be taken further. Sonnets 7, 8, and 14, while maintaining the
invitations to procreate, each develop a single metaphor, producing an effect not unlike that of the euphuistic conceit. They
are respectively applications of topoi relating to the Sun, to
Music, and to Astrology. On the other hand, the last three sonnets of the group (nos. 15, 16, and 17) are not so much linked by
the repetition of the by now familiar images, as by internal
variations on the theme, which here is that of time's wastes as
opposed to the desire for immortality: in no. 15 the immortality
is conferred by poetry, in no. 16, which is both the formal and
syntactic continuation of the argument, immortality is conferred
by children; lastly Sonnet 17 tries to blend the two themes in a
synthesis which remains purely external. But the most frequent
and variously interlocked arguments used in the remaining sonnets, from no. 9 to 13, are still and mainly based on natural
and/or economic imagery.

This play of pervasive and recurring metaphors is worth
examining. It has already been noted that the two main streams
are images from nature and conceits based on economic operations. It is not surprising that an invitation to procreate should
find its most effective iconic organization in a network of
references to what Shakespeare himself calls 'great creating
nature'. The poet logically associates with it the scriptural doctrine of *increase*, that is to say the Creator's commandment to
nature and man 'to bring forth fruit and multiply'.[29] But, as
Lever has pointed out,[30] the derivation is filtered through a
series of Renaissance texts, in which the invitation in Genesis is
placed in open contrast with the traditional Christian (and
more specifically Roman) celebration of virginity as a supreme
virtue. One of the most important of these, Erasmus's epistle
De Conscribendis, was included in Thomas Wilson's widely circulated treatise, *Arte of Rhetorique* (reprinted nine times between
1553 and 1585), under a title which could hardly fail to attract
the attention of anyone who, like Shakespeare, intended to deal

---

[29] Genesis 1:22 and 28. All scriptural quotations are from the 'Bishop's Bible'
based on the 'Geneva' version in the 1592 edition checked against those of 1579
and 1583. The gloss on 'God blessed them' in 1:22 in all editions says: 'That is, by
the vertue of his word hee gave power to his creatures to ingender.'
[30] J. W. Lever, *Eliz. Love Sonnet*, pp. 190–3.

with the subject he handles in the marriage sonnets: 'An epistle
to perswade a yong Gentleman to mariage'. The arguments
were repeated by Sidney in his *Arcadia*, both in verse, in the
Eclogue of Geron and Hister (book I), and in prose, in the
speech of the evil Cecropia to induce the pure Philoclea to break
her vow of chastity (book III, ch. 5, sec. 2); and they are used
again by Leander in Marlowe's *Hero and Leander* (1593). But in
the case of both Cecropia and Leander, the invitation to bear
children is directed toward women; Shakespeare instead in his
Venus and Adonis (1593) uses it as one of Venus's arguments in
the seduction of Adonis (lines 169–74):

> Upon the earths increase why shouldst thou feed,
> Unlesse the earth with thy increase be fed?
> By law of nature thou art bound to breed,
> That thine may live, when thou thy selfe art dead:
>   And so in spite of death thou doest survive,
>   In that thy likenesse still is left alive.

It is interesting to note how Adonis (the masculine ideal of
'virtù', in this courtly debate between Virtue and Lust in the
spirit of Castiglione's *Courtier*, but echoing also the tradition of
the late medieval moralities) replies to Venus's enticing logic
(lines 791–2):

> You do it for increase, ô straunge excuse!
> When reason is the bawd to lusts abuse.

The arguments used by Venus were not restricted to a repetition
of the doctrine of *increase*,[31] but extended also to most of the

[31] It has hardly been noticed that the doctrine of increase as an argument against
virginity, with all its economic and even political implications, is found in another
Shakespearian context: it is enunciated by a despicable but not unsympathetic
character, the *miles gloriosus* Parolles in *All's Well*, I. i: 'It is not politicke, in the
Common-wealth of Nature, to preserve virginity. Losse of Virginitie, is rationall
encrease, and there was never Virgin got, till virginitie was first lost . . . Keepe it
not, you cannot choose but loose by't. Out with't; within ten yeare it will make
it selfe two, which is a goodly increase, and the principall it selfe not much the
worse.' The economic terminology is precise, and there is the same fusion with elements derived from the literal interpretation of the parable of the talents which we
find, e.g., in Sonnet 6 ('That use is not forbidden usery, / Which happies those that
pay the willing lone; / That's for thy selfe to breed an other thee, / Or ten times
happier be it ten to one'). That is why I would favour Dover Wilson's (following
Hanmer) emendation of *two* into *ten*, rather than Hunter's (New Arden Shakespeare, following Harrison) *ten yeare* into *the year*. See on this my essay 'Shakespeare
and the New Economics of his Time', *Review of National Literatures*, iii. 2 (Fall
1972), pp. 123–37.

other persuasions employed in the marriage sonnets to convince the young recipient to generate children. Above all in lines 157–68 and 755–68 of *Venus and Adonis* we find the theme of narcissism (cf. Sonnets 1, 9, 10), of the necessary use of beauty (cf. Sonnets 2, 4, 9), the idea that children are the posthumous life of the father (Sonnets 4, 6, 7, 9, 10, 13, etc.), that a refusal to procreate is the equivalent of suicide (Sonnets 9 and 10), and that the body of a man who does not produce children becomes his tomb (Sonnet 3); lastly the invitation to be prodigal, which, however, is meant as an encouragement not to accumulate unproductive capital, but to invest it wisely (Sonnet 1, 2, and especially 9)—from which follows the corollary on the necessity of practising legal usury, making interest on the capital which in this case is beauty—a motive to which Shakespeare returns extremely frequently in this group of Sonnets (cf. nos. 1, 2, 4, 6, 9, 11, 13).

So Venus, in Shakespeare's version, transfers a biblical doctrine from the natural to the economic field. This explains how it comes about that the various economic operations—from money-lending to the principles of inheritance, from trading to capital investment—furnish the second main stream of imagery in the marriage sonnets. In fact there is a very high proportion of economic and financial terminology, hardly present in the rest of the collection, in these seventeen sonnets.[32] It has been noted that other sonneteers have made use of the same vocabulary; but the examples usually quoted—Sonnet 18 of *Astrophil and Stella* and Sonnet 10 of *Ideas Mirrour*—show no signs of Shakespeare's consistency and competence in handling these images: they are isolated exercises of wit, practical conceits serving to divert the reader, or rather, as Raymond Southall has effectively demonstrated,[33] the imagery characteristic of a society in which wealth and its accumulation is a supreme value.

[32] Among words used nearly exclusively in the marriage group, the most noticeable—apart from the obvious *increase, breed, sap, lusty*—are the inflected forms of *thrift, heir, husbandry, repair,* and *use,* the last in the specific acceptations of rate of interest and capital investment. See the penetrating comments of M. M. Mahood, *Shakespeare's Wordplay* (London, 1957), pp. 52 and 100–2, on the puns on *use* and *husbandry* in the marriage sonnets, and again M. Krieger's exploration of the poet's linguistic strategy in Sonnets 12 and 15, and of his play on *use* in the marriage sonnets ('The Innocent Insinuations of Wit').

[33] R. Southall, *Literature and the Rise of Capitalism* (London, 1973), especially chapter II, 'Love Poetry in the Sixteenth Century', pp. 21–85. The book, published

In Shakespeare, on the other hand, we find a clear awareness of the new economic mechanisms created by the birth of modern capitalism, superimposed upon the traditional moral tirades of the court poets against Avarice. The unorthodox application of economic metaphors in the marriage sonnets contrasts with the continuation in the seventeenth century of the moralistic trend according to which Usury—justified by Shakespeare in Sonnet 6—is associated by Thomas Dekker with Lust in his 1606 pamphlet with the significant title *The Seven Deadly Sins of London*: 'The Usurer lives by the lechery of money, and is bawd to his own bags, taking a fee, that they may engender,' a conceit which is taken up again in the 'Portrait of an usurer' in Sir Thomas Overbury's *Characters* (printed as late as 1614): 'he puts his money to the unnatural act of generation'.[34]

In the marriage sonnets Shakespeare goes back to another scriptural text, this time from the New Testament, the parable of the talents (Matthew 25:14–30) where the servant who puts his master's money to use is praised for his diligence: but Shakespeare does not use the story in the biblical sense as moral allegory, offering it rather as a pattern for behaviour in the field of economics.[35] These sonnets then reflect Shakespeare's awareness of the transition which was taking place at the time, a transition from an agricultural economy in the hands of the landed aristocracy to the progressive assertion of a merchant class accumulating wealth through commercial and banking

at the same time as the original Italian version of the present study, corroborates my argument with a wealth of documentation extending to such plays as *The Merchant of Venice* and *Troilus and Cressida*, and the section 'The Commerce of Affection' (pp. 50–60), touching also on the marriage sonnets, runs parallel with the present paragraph on 'the economy of Venus'.

[34] The quotations are from L. C. Knights, *Drama and Society in the Age of Jonson* (1937), new edn. (Harmondsworth, 1962), pp. 138–41; but cf. R. H. Tawney, *Religion and the Rise of Capitalism* (1926), 1938 edn., esp. pp. 48–67 and 155–96.

[35] The most relevant verses, echoed in Sonnets nos. 4, 6, 9, 11, and 13, are 27–30: 'Thou oughtest therefore to have put my money to the Exchangers, and then at my comming should I have received mine owne with vantage. Take therefore the talent from him, and give it unto him which hath ten talents. For unto every man that hath, it shall be given, and he shall have abundance, and from him that hath not, even that he hath, shall be taken away. Cast therefore that unprofitable servant into utter darkness: there shall be weeping and gnashing of teeth.' Though only the Authorized Version was so bold as to restore the word *usury* (Vulgate: *usura*) instead of *vantage* in verse 27, the 1592 Bishops' version pointedly annotated 'Exchangers': 'Table mates which have their shop bulkes or tables set abroad, where they let out money by usurie.'

operations, threatening the privileges of blood. The poet, composing these sonnets with a practical purpose—as an invitation to put an end to celibacy—adopts the arguments of Venus as opposed to those of the ideal Adonis (Sir Philip Sidney, the 'virtuous' youth no longer in step with the times), and gives the traditional metaphorical references (the doctrine of *increase*, the parable of the talents, the images based on the procreative powers of nature) a new and immediate relevance which is founded on the objective socio-economic context of his time.

This explains why in this group of sonnets, notwithstanding their prothalamic function, the incidence of the word *Love* should be extremely low: in this new context marriage is not a question of love but is an economic transaction—the upkeep and transmission of property, useful alliances of financial interests, a last defence against the encroaching middle class and lower gentry which advance the values of industry, of productive work, against those of hereditary nobility.[36] Paradoxically the defence is possible through those very means (the economy of Venus) which orthodox morality, linked to chivalric and Christian ideals (Adonis!), refuses; Shakespeare's position, and the position taken up in his Sonnets, cannot be other than ambiguous in the face of a choice between the new capitalist ethic with its Puritan overtones (another paradox: Venus and Calvin find themselves in the same camp), and the traditional ethic which guarded the privileges of the landowning aristocracy. But it is from precisely this ambiguity that the marriage sonnets draw their vitality, leaving the 'occasion' and the hortatory tone far behind. The transposition of the doctrine of increase from the field of nature to that of finance, where it meant capital investment for a solid interest, finds its justification; and so does the interpretation of the parable of the talents in concrete rather than spiritual terms: the good steward must be an efficient stock-exchange operator.

Lastly, even the images drawn from nature lose in these sonnets their traditional character of abstract celebration in terms of aesthetic beauty and providential bounty, to be replaced by concern with concrete principles of good husbandry: ploughing (Sonnet 3), the distillation of perfume from flowers (Sonnets 5 and 6), cattle-rearing (Sonnet 6), harvesting (Sonnet 12), graft-

---

[36] See L. Stone, *The Crisis of the Aristocracy, passim.*

ing (Sonnet 15), the cultivation of flowers and plants (Sonnet 16). Nature is made fertile by means of technical competence and the good management of the property (husbandry, Sonnets 3 and 13), as taught in so many handbooks, from John Fitzherbert's *The Boke of Husbandry* (1535) to Gervaise Markham's *The English Husbandman* (1613) and *Cheape and Good Husbandry* (1614);[37] in other words, it is nature instrumentalized in the interests of the land-owners, not a garden of Eden: the middle-class man from the prosperous agricultural town of Stratford-on-Avon, though perhaps as yet not personally involved, could certainly not be ignorant of the current polemic concerning enclosures, a polemic which was the distant prelude of the Civil War.[38]

5. The non-You sonnets: dramatic meditations. The absence of the first person in the Sonnets, even if it makes possible in a few cases a historical vision of Shakespeare's awareness of the human condition in his time, is an impediment to the dialogue, to the theatrical quality, which I postulated as the distinctive characteristic of Shakespeare's Sonnets compared with the collections of his contemporaries. If this is true in the cases where the 'I' is either non-existent or self-effacing, in homage to his lord, then it is even truer in the cases when the missing party is the interlocutor, the 'Thou' he is addressing— the second person singular of the personal pronoun. Yet the number of sonnets in which the second person is absent is higher than that where there is no first person. The sonnets in question are: 5, 21, 23, 25, 33, 63, 64, 65, 66, 67, 68, 94, 105, 116, 119, 121, 124, 127, 129, 130, 138, 144, 145, 153, 154.[39] To these

---

[37] Dr. Ambrosoli, an expert in sixteenth-century European agronomical theory, tells me that English treatises on husbandry are mainly derived from continental models, but while their Italian and French sources are large, beautifully produced books obviously intended for the libraries of a small group of aristocratic land-owners, their English counterparts are mostly badly printed hasty compilations limited to the practical and technical aspects of agriculture, addressed to the yeoman farmers and the literate tenants, free-holders, and copy-holders.

[38] When writing this I was of course unaware of Edward Bond's imaginative exploitation of Shakespeare's involvement in the Welcombe enclosure: see E. Bond, *Bingo* (London, 1974), and cf. S. Schoenbaum, 'Shakespeare played out, or much ado about *nada*', *TLS*, 30 August 1974.

[39] C. Schaar (*Sonnet Problem*, pp. 127–9) isolates a very similar group of sonnets when he remarks that 'Out of Shakespeare's 154 sonnets, 134 contain the figure of *apostrophe*', and lists the twenty sonnets without it: they are obviously all 'non-You'

should be added those sonnets where the pronominal forms do not refer to human beings, but to personifications: Love (Sonnets 56, 137, 148), the Muse (Sonnets 100, 101), Time (Sonnets 19 and 123), and lastly the Soul ('Poor Soul', Sonnet 146). Thirty-three all told, more than one-fifth of the total. Must we therefore conclude that, when we have added to these the I-less sonnets, over 30 per cent of Shakespeare's Sonnets lack the dramatic quality, the clash between I and Thou, which is so generally recognized as their distinguishing feature?

It is interesting that G. K. Hunter, in a perceptive essay 'The dramatic Technique of Shakespeare's Sonnets' mentions precisely Sonnet 129—the only one in which neither the first, the second nor the third person appear[40]—among the examples of this technique. In fact in some of these non-You sonnets the dramatic effect is obtained by a different method; or rather the adjective 'dramatic' can also be applied to them, but with a different connotation from its use when applied to the rest of the collection. Normally in Shakespeare's Sonnets we find a truly dramatic dialogue between two characters: the *persona* of the poet himself (the speaking I, not the man William Shakespeare) and a 'you', the actor playing the role of a lovely boy, a worthy or unworthy mistress, possibly a rival poet. The poems are dramatic in so much as the speaker and his interlocutors act out a drama. As G. K. Hunter observes, the overwhelming emphasis put by critics on the biographical and psychological elements in Shakespeare's Sonnets, is due to the fact that he is not 'a passionate autobiographical poet whose confessions are cut short by his conceits, so much as ... a *dramatist*'. And more specifically:

The subject-matter and the rhetoric may be that of the Petrarchan tradition, the effect may sometimes seem Metaphysical, but the uniquely Shakespearean quality of the sequence is not to be explained by either of these labels. We have here what we might expect: a dramatist describes a series of emotional situations between persons (real or fictitious) in a series of separate short poems; the Petrarchan instruments turn in his hands into means of expressing and concentrating the great human emotions, desire, jealousy,

sonnets, but the two lists are not co-extensive—in Sonnets 21, 23, 25, 105, 116, though not using *thou* or *you*, the poet apostrophizes (using the imperative with the auxiliary *let*) either the reader, or himself, or people at large.

[40] The point is stressed by Jakobson and Jones, op. cit., p. 16.

fear, hope and despair, and of raising in the reader the dramatic
reactions of pity and terror by his implication in the lives of the
persons depicted.[41]

All this is correct, as applied to the generality of the 1609
collection. But I submit that some of the sonnets without a *you*
or when the *you* is the poet's own 'soul', are exceptions: they are
dramatic in a different way, or rather in the same way as
Donne's poems are dramatic. They represent a conflict not between characters, their actions and feelings, but *within* one
character. It is on this level that the definition holds, and we
can agree with Richard Levin in considering also 'Sonnet
CXXIX as a "Dramatic" Poem'.[42] The question is: are not
most lyrical poems in the whole history of poetry dramatic in
this sense? If one has to reply in the negative, it is because in
most cases the inner debate is indeed 'emotion recollected in
tranquillity', not so much with detachment as with assurance:
the poet knows the replies to the questions posed by his conflicting feelings. In Shakespeare on the other hand, as in much
of Donne, the tension remains, the feelings and thoughts are
actors in a performance played on the stage of the author's
mind: the poet-actor does not define his passions, he lets them
speak out in their own persons. So the sonnets without obvious
dialogue are not descriptive of the poet's meditations, but they
are meditations *in action*, and since his sense of the theatre made
him constantly suit the action to the word and the word to the
action, they share the language and the technique of the great
tragic soliloquies with the same concentration of semantic
values, the same unresolved tensions and contradictions.
Granted, then, the dramatic quality of nearly all of Shakespeare's Sonnets (apart from the feeble conceits of 145, 153, and
154, and the mere descriptions of some of the others, e.g. 67 and
68 on the boy's beauty, 127 and 130 on the mistress), I would,
for the sake of clarity, maintain a distinction between the 'you'
and the 'non-You' sonnets, between those instituting a kind
of fully dramatic dialogue with two or three characters (I–you–
he/she), and those where the drama is acted within a single

[41] G. K. Hunter, 'The Dramatic Technique of Shakespeare's Sonnets', *Essays in
Criticism*, iii. 2 (April 1953), pp. 152–64.
[42] R. Levin, 'Sonnet CXXIX as a "Dramatic" Poem', *Shakespeare Quarterly*,
xvi (1965), pp. 175–81.

character, the speaker's (I am not saying Shakespeare's) mind; the latter I would call meditative sonnets, though without the static implications of the reflective sonnets of a Sidney or a Spenser.

In the 1609 Quarto there are no less than 25 non-You sonnets; but, apart from the merely descriptive or conceited ones mentioned above, most of the rest are meditations—dramatic or not—on the canonical subject of traditional sonneteering: Love. So, at least in appearance, they conform with the current convention of such collections as *Delia*[43] or *Ideas Mirrour*, largely made up of non-dramatic (non-You) variations on love-themes, in sharp contrast with the dramatic directness of the rest of Shakespeare's *canzoniere*. It is significant that Sonnet 145, that A. Gurr, on very convincing evidence (l. 13 *hate away—Hathaway*) believes to be the first written by Shakespeare among those preserved,[44] should be of this type; and in fact it has the air of a youthful imitation of a fashionable literary genre. Of the same type are the two sonnets that the unknown compiler of the *Passionate Pilgrim* included in his collection of 1599 together with miscellaneous spurious material, and which in the 1609 Quarto edition were published as Sonnets 138 and 144. These must have been the sonnets which circulated most widely in manuscript, and which led Francis Meres to speak, as early as 1598, of 'his [Shakespeare's] sugred sonnets among his private friends.'[45] It is hardly necessary to point out that these two sonnets do not use the second person and are presented as definitions of love, conforming to models which have already been used; only after a careful reading can we observe how far they are heretical in respect of that religion of Love proclaimed by contemporary sonneteers (see later, Interchapter, §§ 0 and 1).

Now, the special claim I am making for nos. 94, 121, 129, and subordinately 146, is that they—though non-You (except for the last, where *you* is, against all convention, not the loved

[43] The linguistic, structural, and conceptual affinities—within an obvious convention—between many Shakespearian sonnets and Daniel's work, have been studied by Claes Schaar (*Sonnet Problem*); he extended the search to other contemporary sonneteers in his *Elizabethan Sonnet Themes and the Dating of Shakespeare's Sonnets* (Lund, 1962).

[44] A. Gurr, 'Shakespeare's First Poem: Sonnet 145', *Essays in Criticism*, xxi. 3 (July 1971), pp. 221–6.

[45] No derogatory intention attaches to the fulsome adjectivation (mellifluous, hony-tongued, sugred) in Francis Meres' *Palladis Tamia*.

one or Love itself, but the subject's Soul)—are not true to type
in that they ignore the ruling theme, Love, which is the main
feature of the whole genre, a genre which is indeed defined as
the Elizabethan *love*-sonnet.[46] These four sonnets are dramatic
meditations on less conventional subjects, and it is surprising
that so few readers have noted the peculiar features which dis-
tinguish them from the rest of the collection. Instead of Love,
the subjects are those I referred to in connection with the ambiguity of Shakespeare's attitude towards the upheaval in traditional ethical values in the moment of history in which he was
living. These sonnets are explorations of the contradictions—in
themselves dramatic—existing in the various views on the
exercise of power, social behaviour, sex, and religion. These
inner contradictions are presented by Shakespeare in their
agonic phase, without proposing any solution, but with an intense awareness of all the forces at play. This gives these four
sonnets a rich texture of meanings and a formal complexity
which can only be even partially brought out by means of a
minute and unrelenting inquiry both on the levels of form and
content, involving the utilization of a number of critical instruments. There is no single key to the sense—even if Sonnets 94,
121, 129, and 146 can themselves be used as keys to open not
the heart but the mind and craft of Shakespeare. In the following chapters, each of which is concerned with one of the four
'problem' sonnets, I intend to carry out this analysis with the
aid of all available critical instruments. A value-judgement on
their poetic quality is implicit in their very choice.

Excursus: A note on numerology. The abundance of
figures and statistics in the present chapter may have led the
reader to expect some reference to a subject which has become
somewhat fashionable in recent times, namely numerology.
There is no doubt that from the Middle Ages till at least the

---

[46] See J. W. Lever's book already quoted, and for an extremely perceptive history
of the evolution of the sonnet-form in England and its implications, see John Fuller,
The Sonnet in 'The Critical Idiom' series (London, 1972). Surveying the later
English uses of the form, it should perhaps be noticed that in the nineteenth century
the sonnet came to be considered the proper vehicle not of love but of meditative
and philosophical poetry; as William T. Going remarks ('Matthew Arnold's Sonnets', *Papers in Language and Literature*, vi. 4 (Fall 1970), pp. 387–406), in Arnold's
twenty-nine sonnets the theme of love, appearing in his other verse, is never
touched upon, while all his other major themes are present.

eighteenth century a good deal of attention was devoted to
numerical correspondences and symmetries, and this is particularly true of poetry, which is indeed an art of magic 'num-
bers'. But while it is unquestionable that a poet like Spenser,
with his erudite and deliberately archaic and esoteric cultural
background, would feel all the attraction of numerical correspondences—as the recent volumes of A. Kent Hieatt and
Alastair Fowler have demonstrated—with Shakespeare we are
on much less safe ground. The most sustained attempt at
finding a numerological rationale in the Sonnets as they are
arranged in the 1609 Quarto was made once again by Alastair
Fowler (in chapter 9 of *Triumphal Forms: Structural Patterns in
Elizabethan Poetry* (Cambridge, 1970), pp. 183–97); but even
renouncing, for the sake of the symbolic total, Sonnet 136,
accepting the implications of a belief that the sequence of the
poems in the Quarto was devised by Shakespeare himself, and
admiring the ingenuity of Fowler's argument, there remains the
impression of an inordinate amount of juggling with hardly
demonstrable surmises. It is therefore the more surprising that,
in postulating that Shakespeare arranged his Sonnets in the
figure of a 'pyramid of 153' (a biblical figure, corresponding to
that of the total catch of fish in John 21:11), Fowler should not
have advanced the one argument in its favour that could carry
conviction: viz., seventeen being the basis of such a pyramid,
this would account for the fact that the first seventeen sonnets
are a separate self-sufficient group (the marriage sonnets, see
§ 4 above). They form the solid base of a sonnet pyramid higher
than any other in his time: a peculiar justification for the fact
that his generation sonnets stop at so ominous a number.
Seventeen, numerologists tell us, is particularly *infaustus* because associated with castration.

   Who is going to explore the subconscious implications of an
invitation to a 'fair boy' to marry and procreate children
repeated exactly *seventeen* times?

From 1609 Quarto, sig. F4ᵛ:

94

They that haue powre to hurt, and will doe none,
That doe not do the thing, they most do showe,
Who mouing others, are themselues as stone,
Vnmooued, could, and to temptation slow:
They rightly do inherrit heauens graces,
And husband natures ritches from expence,
They are the Lords and owners of their faces,
Others, but stewards of their excellence:
The sommers flowre is to the sommer sweet,
Though to it selfe, it onely liue and die,
But if that flowre with base infection meete,
The basest weed out-braues his dignity:
    For sweetest things turne sowrest by their deedes,
    Lillies that fester, smell far worse then weeds.

CHAPTER II

LILIES THAT FESTER:
THE STRATEGY OF SONNET 94
AND THE ETHICS OF POWER

0.1. The world of It. In the introductory remarks to the second of his Clark Lectures for 1970–1, Professor L. C. Knights says:

The things that really concern us are of course things with which our connexion is personal and direct [. . .]—all these belong to the world that Martin Buber defined as the world of *I* and *Thou*, the world of relationship. But man cannot live exclusively in the world of *Thou*: there is also the world of *It*, the world that can be, has to be, manipulated and arranged, and that necessarily affects the quality of the personal world—[. . .] Conflicting needs and desires have to be adjusted; and although in a small social group there is always the possibility of arrangement in the spirit of relationship, in larger social structures arrangement is inevitably a matter of the play of conflicting interests within the world of *It*. One name for large-scale arrangements of this kind is politics.[1]

This long quotation seems in order when facing a sonnet— no. 94—in which there are no first or second person pronouns or possessives, but a number of third person expressions: not the world of *I* and *Thou*, but the world of *It*, *They*, and the *Others*. And, as it happens, Sonnet 94 seems to be the one *political* sonnet of Shakespeare. Professor Knights does not mention the sonnet on this occasion, but its opening words are explicit: *They that have power* . . . The fact that it is political, and therefore not in line with the subject-matter of the rest of the Sonnets, is the reason why no. 94 is considered a difficult poem. In its turn, the difficulty accounts perhaps for what Mr. Booth calls 'its current vogue'.[2] A number of critics[3] have variously pointed out the

---

[1] L. C. Knights, *Public Voices* (London, 1971), p. 30; this lecture is on Shakespeare.

[2] S. Booth, *An Essay on Shakespeare's Sonnets*, p. 152.

[3] The discussion on Sonnet 94 was opened by William Empson who in 1933 devoted to it a whole chapter of *Some Versions of Pastoral* (pp. 89–115); he was

relevance to its interpretation of *Measure for Measure* (Angelo, the corrupt moralist), *Henry IV* (Prince Hal's morality), Matthew 25:14–30 (the parable of the talents, which looms large in the marriage sonnets), and Matthew 4 and 5 (the Sermon on the Mount). Perhaps I find myself once again most attracted by the essential and pithy remarks of L. C. Knights in an early essay of his, which underline the moral ambiguity of the argument by placing it not only side by side with *Measure for Measure*, but as a kind of half-way house between the economic doctrine expounded in Sonnets 1–17 and the sexual morality of Sonnet 129, to which 94 'forms an interesting complement'.[4] I would, however, take issue with Knights's parenthetic remark that Sonnet 94 is 'not altogether successful'.[5]

The success of a poem is largely assessed, at least on a technical level, by an analysis of its structures, and I feel that even detailed line-by-line commentaries such as those provided by Hilton Landry and Philip Martin, though extremely illuminating, fail in precisely this. And the failure is due to the fact that

---

followed by L. C. Knights, 'Shakespeare's Sonnets', *Scrutiny*, iii (September 1934), pp. 146–7, included in his *Explorations* (London, 1946), pp. 40–65; then John Crowe Ransom, 'Shakespeare at Sonnets', *The World's Body* (New York, 1938), and the same author's weak rejoinder to Empson's analysis, 'Mr. Empson's Muddles', *The Southern Review*, iv (Winter 1938), pp. 322–39, esp. 328–31; Hallet Smith, *Elizabethan Poetry. A Study in Conventions, Meaning and Expression* (Cambridge, Mass., 1952), pp. 188–91; E. Hubler, *The Sense of Shakespeare's Sonnets* (Princeton, 1952, repr. New York), pp. 102–6; J. W. Lever, *Eliz. Love Sonnet*, pp. 216–21; M. M. Mahood, *Shakespeare's Wordplay*, pp. 98–100; A. S. Gérard, 'The Stone as Lily: A Discussion of Shakespeare's Sonnet XCIV', *Shakespeare Jahrbuch*, xcvi (1960), pp. 155–60; H. Landry, *Interpretations in Shakespeare's Sonnets* (Berkeley, 1963), pp. 7–27; J. Winny, *The Master-Mistress: A Study of Shakespeare's Sonnets* (London, 1968), pp. 163–9; S. Booth, op. cit., pp. 152–67; and Philip Martin in *The Critical Survey* (Summer 1969), included in his already mentioned *Shakespeare's Sonnets*, pp. 30–44.

[4] L. C. Knights, 'Shakespeare's Sonnets', p. 147.

[5] This feeling, already voiced by Empson, is echoed by Hubler and others; a typical attitude is that taken by Miss Mahood (op. cit., p. 99): '*Measure for Measure* seems to me a great but unsatisfactory play for the same reason that Sonnet 94 is, on its own scale, a great but unsatisfactory poem: in each case Shakespeare is emotionally too involved in the situation to achieve a dramatic clarification of the issues.' Harriett Hawkins, in *Likenesses of Truth in Elizabethan and Restoration Drama* (Oxford, 1972), pp. 51–2, develops this hint in respect of *Measure for Measure*: 'The intense personal involvement aroused by the first half [of the play] is not sustained or even permitted in the second half. In short, the first half of the play has the power to hurt; the second half will do none. The play refuses to do the thing it most did show. The first half moves others (us) to desire tragedy, and then the second half asks them (us) to be unmoved, cold, and to temptation slow.'

they cannot help seeing this sonnet within the context of the surrounding ones, from 92 to 96, addressed to the 'lovely boy'.[6] True, Landry states at one point that Sonnet 94, 'like Sonnets 66, 121, 125, and 129, is timeless, general and unique";[7] but apart from the fact that he refrains from pursuing this line of argument any further, it should be noted that Sonnets 66 and 125 are far from being 'general': they address the poet's *love* (66, line 14), or the usual *thee* (125), while 94, 121, and 129 have the truly extraordinary distinction of *not* mentioning love *and* not using any second person pronominal forms. Sonnet 94, having no *I* or *Thou*, but insisting on *They* and *Other*, is an even more special case; this is why I propose to consider it in the first place completely out of context, as a poem not included in a sequence, and to see what we can make of it when lacking an immediate frame of reference.

1.0. Metrical and logical pattern.   Sonnet 94 is, first and foremost, an artefact. Our first task is to see *how* it is made, and if and how it works. From the formal point of view—metrics, rhymes, line-divisions—it is a typically 'regular' Shakespearian sonnet. There are no enjambments and each quatrain ends with a heavier punctuation (:) and is therefore self-contained. A closer examination shows, though, that the first two quatrains are closely linked together: (a) They open with the same word *They* which is the main grammatical subject of both; (b) Syntactically they form a single paragraph, and the first quatrain, constituted by three relative clauses, is dependent on the second for its subject and main sentence; (c) All subjects and verbs, in the first two quatrains, are in the plural.

[6] Philip Martin (op. cit., pp. 39–41) is more guarded: 'in 94 these materials [from Sonnets 92–3 and 95–6] have not only been transmuted, they have been compounded with others ... Without becoming abstract the poetry is more generalized, more lofty, more compressed. Much more is happening: we recognize that, even if we know that some of it eludes us. And if it does so, it is not so much because the *events* referred to are not stated, as because the poet's concerns have become so much deeper and more complex.' The 'private' contextual angle is quite tenable in the terms suggested by such critics as Lever, Landry, Winny, and Martin, but it can be taken to extremes of fatuity, as in Ransom's remarks that Sonnet 94 'has proved obscure to commentators, but I think it is clear if taken in context, as an imaginary argument against the friend's relation with the woman, or with any woman, exactly opposite to the argument of the sonnets which open the sequence'. (*The World's Body*, p. 297.)

[7] H. Landry, op. cit., p. 10. In another part of the book Landry describes as 'virtually unique' Sonnets 66, 129, 146; see below, ch. IV, § 0.2.

Quatrains I and II (lines 1–8), then, form a single unit, in spite of the marked pause at the end of the fourth line, a unit corresponding to the octave in the Petrarchan sonnet.

Quatrain III (lines 9–12) starts a wholly new sentence, with a separate subject, a different structure, and a different number (all nouns and verbs are in the singular).

There is, then, a definite break after line 8, and in fact most modern editors rightly substitute a full stop for the colon at the end of the line.

The final couplet (lines 13–14) reverts from the singular to the plural, but is syntactically and logically linked with the previous quatrain, opening with the consecutive adverb *For*, and following up its nature imagery.

We are confronted, as so frequently in Shakespeare, with a double structure: metrically the sonnet is of the English type, but from the point of view of the logical structure it is Petrarchan, with a clear division into octave and sestet.

1.1. Octave versus sestet.   More than divided, octave and sestet seem unrelated to each other: they use different codes. In the octave the subjects are persons, men (*They, others*), in the sestet the subjects are flowers, weeds, 'things': Animate versus Inanimate, or, the world of Men versus the world of Nature. There is therefore a relation between the two parts, but it is a relation by contrast. And it is enough to remember the dominating doctrine of correspondences in the sixteenth century, to recognize a further relation: the world of Nature reproduces exactly the microcosm of Man, and vice versa. In other words, the one (the world of Nature) is a metaphor for the other (the world of Man)—*the sestet is a metaphor for the octave.* It will be useful to keep this in mind when exploring the meaning of the sonnet.

The technique employed by Shakespeare in Sonnet 94 is juxtaposition. In the octave we are presented with actual subjects (or objects). The sestet superimposes on them a set of metaphors:[8] flower → They; weed[s] → Others. Axiomatically, what is true of the metaphor is true of its referent. So we are

---

[8] Cf. A. S. Gérard, 'The Stone as Lily', p. 159: 'l. 9 echoes in metaphorical terms the moral statement of l. 1'; I am not sure though that I agree with the inference that Gérard draws from this statement; see also Ph. Martin's remarks on the subject, op. cit., p. 33.

implicitly invited, in the closing couplet, to apply the conclusions—the 'moral'—reached in respect of flowers and weeds
to the *They* and *Others* of the octave.

1.2. The lexical level. The final couplet deserves most
attention since it holds the whole sonnet together. And it does
this through an extremely skilful choice and placing of words. I
remarked before on its being closely linked with the third
quatrain through grammar and imagery. The link is even
clearer on the lexical level, where $_{13}$*sweetest* picks up *sweet*, the
rhyme-word of line 9 (the opening line of the sestet); and
$_{14}$*weeds*, the very last rhyme-word of the sonnet, and therefore
in a very strong position, echoes *weed* in line 12, which is the
last of quatrain III. The relevance of these repetitions becomes
clearer if we take the whole of the sestet and look at the only
word-roots that appear twice in different lines (Fig. 1).

nouns		adjectives
flower	9	sweet
	10	
flower	11	base
weed	12	base*st*
	13	sweet*est*
weeds	14	

Fig. 1. Iterative words in the sestet of Sonnet 94

Two antithetical nouns (flower versus weed) and two antithetical adjectives (sweet versus base), the latter with the
further refinement of each being once in the positive and once
in the superlative form.

The couplet, then, is indispensable to complete the antithetical lexical symmetry suggested by the third quatrain;
significantly it contains one noun and one adjective semantically antithetical: *sweetest* versus *weeds*.

In only one point does the couplet not agree with quatrain
III: the number used ($_{12}$*weed* → $_{14}$*weeds*). But this provides the
link with the octave (all plural), and is a means of holding
together the entire sonnet. Remaining on the lexical level,
another link is provided by the fact that the *only* two word-

roots common to both octave and sestet are to be found in the
second line of the octave and the first (second from the end) of
the couplet.

> 2. That *doe not do* the *thing*, they most do showe,
> 13. For sweetest *things* turne sowrest by their *deedes*,

The correspondence is once again through antithesis: *deeds*
(affirmative) versus *do not do* (negative); *things* in line 13 is
concrete, being the equivalent of 'Lilies' and 'flower', and
carries a positive meaning (sweetest), while *thing* in line 2 is
abstract, and acquires a negative connotation through its
correspondence to *hurt* in the first line.

The couplet fulfils a double function: it completes the unity
of the sestet and, by reflecting back on the octave, reveals the
structural relation between the two apparently independent
parts of the poem.

The whole sonnet, then, presents a perfect mirror-structure,
and develops all the possibilities of the binary principle. It is
now time to look at the application of this principle to its two
units (octave and sestet), which are in turn each formed by two
sub-units.

1.3. The octave.   The basic logical and syntactical structure
of the octave has already been summarily described (§ 1.0).
The word recurring most frequently in the eight lines is the
pronoun *They* (lines 1, 2, 3 [themselves], 5, 7), with the logical
function of subject of the main clauses in 1, 5, and 7 (in 6 it
does not appear but it is understood); in 2 it is the subject of a
sub-relative clause, while in 3 (themselves) it is in a predicative
position. Next comes *Others*, also a pronoun, appearing first in
quatrain I (line 3) in the accusative case and then in quatrain
II (line 8) as a subject, parallel with *They* which occupies the
same position in the previous line. So we get the typical binary
opposition *They* versus *Others* in both sub-units of the octave.

We have already seen that, syntactically, the first sub-unit is
dependent on the second. In fact sub-unit I, beginning with the
main subject *They*, proceeds through a series of relative pronouns: ₁*that*, ₂*That*, ₃*Who*, which establish three relative clauses,
the first two covering one line each and the third covering two
lines (the whole of line 4 is in apposition to *themselves* in line 3).

The logical progression of the lines in quatrain I is therefore
1.1.2.

Quatrain II follows an identical pattern, 1.1.2, establishing
a perfect correspondence between the two sub-units of the
octave. But in this case, instead of relative clauses, we have a
series of parallel, co-ordinated main sentences. The quatrain
begins once again with the subject *They*, like quatrain I, which
is not repeated but clearly understood in the next line; in fact
line 6 repeats with the utmost fidelity the sequence of logical
functions in line 5: subject → verb → genitive → object, with
the conjunction *And* supplying the function of subject. Lines 7
and 8 show in their turn an identical sequence of grammatical
functions with each other, but are soldered into a single sentence, in spite of the change of subject (*They/Others*) by sharing
a single verb-function:

> 7. pron. → aux. verb (copula) → noun[s] → prep. →
>   poss. adj. → noun.
> 8. pron. → noun → prep. → poss. adj. → noun.

Many secondary features would be worth noticing, but I
propose to do that later, when dealing with the semantic and
semiotic aspects of the sonnet. For the present it will be sufficient
to stress the absolute structural balance between the two sub-
units of the octave and within each separate sub-unit.

1.4. The sestet. The sestet need not detain us long. I have
already pointed out (§ 1.2) the lexical links between its two
sub-units (quatrain III and couplet), and their antithetical
correspondence (singular versus plural). What remains to be
said is that, syntactically, the quatrain provides a reversed
alternation of binary patterns: line 9 is a statement, line 10 is a
limiting clause to the same (*though*); in their turn, lines 11–12,
beginning with *But*, act as a conditional sentence in respect of
the sentence formed by lines 9–10, establishing the same relation
existing between the minor and the major premises in a syllogism. Again, if we consider lines 11–12 in themselves, we find
that the first is a limiting clause (*if*) to the statement contained
in the second, the reverse or mirror-pattern of the sentence in
lines 9–10.

Finally the couplet is formed of two parallel statements, in two complete co-ordinated sentences filling a line each, and fulfils the same function in respect of the previous quatrain as does the conclusion in respect of the two premises in the syllogistic pattern. The logical progression of the lines in the whole sestet is therefore 2.2.2.

1.5. The structural schema. From what has been said up to this point, the structural schema shown in Fig. 2 can be produced.[9] This is, of course, a merely formal pattern. But it goes a long way to show the success of the poem as a living linguistic and syntactical organism, a living structure resulting from the careful balancing and interweaving of a double series of meaningful binary oppositions.

In order to see whether or not this structure is also valid on the level of meaning, a fresh approach is required—the analysis must move from the form of the sonnet's meaning to the meaning of its form.

2.0. The relevance of *Edward III*. Distracted by situational analogies with *Measure for Measure* and *Henry IV*, commentators of Sonnet 94 have generally overlooked the obvious context to which reference should be made. They are all careful to point out that line 14, 'Lillies that fester, smell far worse than weeds', is identical with the apocryphal *Edward III*, II. i. 451, but they hardly bother to look at that play, generally assuming that its unknown author (possibly young Shakespeare himself) has simply borrowed that line from the sonnet written earlier, since the line, in Swinburne's words, appears more like 'a theft from Shakespeare's private store of undramatic poetry than a mis-application by its own author to dramatic purposes of a line too apt and exquisite to endure without injury the transference from its original setting'.[10] The assumption is not wholly warranted. To begin with, the line in *Edward III* occurs in the course of a lengthy speech which is nothing else but a repertory of 'sententiae' on the corruption of power, and it fits perfectly

---

[9] All quotations from the sonnets are from the 1609 Quarto; I have also made ample use, of course, of the New Variorum Edition, *The Sonnets*, ed. H. E. Rollins, 2 vols. (Philadelphia, 1944). In all quotations from XVI and XVII century texts I have modified only the Elizabethan printers' usage which made no distinction between *u* and *v*, using a typographical *v* for both when in initial position, and a typographical *u* when medial.

[10] Quoted by K. Muir, *Shakespeare as Collaborator* (London, 1960), p. 12.

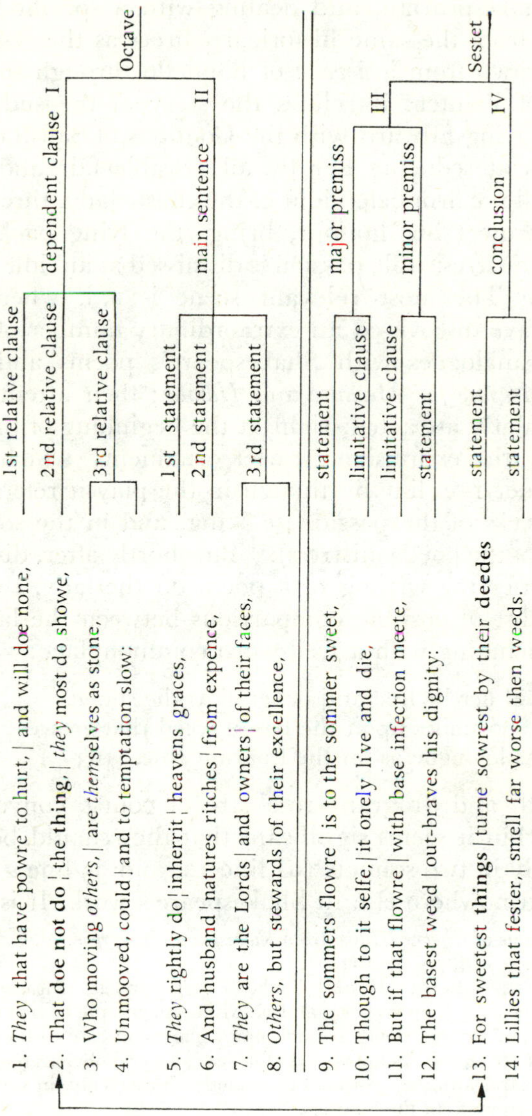
1. *They* that have powre to hurt, | and will doe none,
2. That **doe not do** ¦ the **thing**, | *they* most do showe,
3. Who moving *others*, | are *them*selves as stone,
4. Unmooved, could | and to temptation slow;
5. *They* rightly do ¦ inherrit ¦ heavens graces,
6. And husband ¦ natures ritches ¦ from expence,
7. *They* are the Lords | and owners ¦ of their faces,
8. *Others*, but stewards | of their excellence,
9. The sommers flowre | is to the sommer sweet,
10. Though to it selfe, | it onely live and die,
11. But if that flowre | with base infection meete,
12. The basest weed | out-braves his dignity:
13. For sweetest **things** | turne sowrest by their **deedes**
14. Lillies that fester, | smell far worse then weeds.
1st relative clause
2nd relative clause
3rd relative clause
dependent clause I
Octave
1st statement
2nd statement
3rd statement
main sentence II
statement
limitative clause
limitative clause
statement
major premiss
minor premiss
III
Sestet
statement
statement
conclusion
IV

Fig. 2. Structural schema of Sonnet 94

into its context. Besides, it is a part of a 'detachable' section of the play (I. ii. 90–166 and the whole of Act II) considered as the most Shakespearian, and dealing with a specific episode not derived from the same historical sources as the rest of the play, but drawn from a *novella* of Bandello through the usual mediation of Painter: it relates the story of the sudden infatuation of King Edward with the Countess of Salisbury, and his attempts at seducing her by all possible fair and unfair means—until the firm behaviour of the chaste lady, threatening suicide to protect her honour, brings the King back to his senses, and the irresistible passion is dismissed as an 'idle dream' (II. ii. 200).[11] The most relevant scene is II. i, where commentators have discovered an extraordinary number of verbal and iconic analogues with Shakespeare's poems and plays, especially *Measure for Measure* and *Hamlet*; their attention has been particularly attracted, right at the beginning of the scene (line 10) by the expression 'scarlet ornaments' which occurs also in Sonnet 142, line 6 (though in the play it refers to the blushing cheeks of the passionate King, and in the sonnet to the red lips of the poet's mistress).[12] But shortly after, discussing with a courtier the writing of a poem on the lady, the King gives a full list of possible comparisons between the lady and the sun, concluding with a well-worn commonplace:

> Bid her be free and generall as the sunne,
> Who smiles upon the basest weed that growes
> As lovinglie as on the fragrant rose. (163–5)

'Basest weed' and 'fragrant rose' are of course conventional expressions, but it seems significant that they should be found identical only in two sonnets (94 line 12, and 95 line 2 respectively)[13] and nowhere else in Shakespeare's work. It is hardly

---

[11] All quotations of *Edward III* are from *Shakespeare's Apocrypha*, ed. C. F. Tucker Brooke (London, 1908), pp. 67–102.

[12] See A. Platt, 'Edward III and Shakespeare's Sonnets', *Modern Language Review*, vi (October 1911), pp. 511–13, and K. Muir, op. cit., pp. 10–11; C. Schaar (*Sonnet Themes*, pp. 117–35) devotes much more space and care to the analogies between *Edward III* and the Sonnets, but still misses several obvious ones and the parallelism in moral attitude, so that he concludes (mistakenly, in my opinion) that the play borrows from the Sonnets.

[13] Sonnet 95, a bitter reproach and warning to the friend who hides sin in beauty, 'like a canker in the fragrant Rose', can be considered as a personal and private application of the 'political' climate of thought evoked in Sonnet 94. The two sonnets are by no means complementary: at most, they testify to Shakespeare's

likely that the author of *Edward III* should have borrowed freely expressions from different Shakespearian sonnets, putting them together in the current conceit on the indiscriminate generosity of the sun. It is much more probable that Shakespeare, writing different sonnets, remembered passages of a play which he knew, and more particularly the scenes that he either wrote himself or revised, especially since one of them dealt specifically with the writing of a lyric and the language of love-poetry. What I am suggesting, then, is that Sonnet 94—and a good number of the others—were written *after* and not before *Edward III*.[14]

The play of reminiscence is even more marked in the second part of II. i, and it extends to situational as well as verbal echoes. It is here we find also quite obvious parallels with *Measure for Measure*, and this is not surprising, since the leading character is placed in an extremely ambiguous moral position, reminiscent of that of Angelo, the corrupt moralist in the later play. In *Edward III* the King, blinded by his passion for the Countess of Salisbury, turns to her father, the Earl of Warwick, who is not aware of this sudden infatuation of his master, and obtains from him an oath of absolute allegiance. Having got it, Edward proceeds (340–5):

> And therefore, Warwike, if thou art thyselfe,
> The Lord and master of thy word and othe,
> Go to thy daughter; and in my behalfe
> Comaund her, woo her, win her anie waies,
> To be my mistress and my secret love.

Now, the second of the lines quoted is undoubtedly echoed in Sonnet 94 line 7 with a typical ironical deformation—the same kind of deformation we find elsewhere in the sonnet. In the play Warwick is in honour bound to commit a most dishonourable

ability to extend and reduce at will his range within the same formal frame. All the same, it is significant to find the lines in *Edward III* echoed in two consecutive sonnets linked by a conceptual affinity though on a very different scale.

[14] Among the many parallels between *Edward III* and other sonnets, unnoticed by Schaar, I may mention *Edward III*, I. ii. 95–7, 'Whose beauty tyrant[s] feare, / As a May blossome with pernitious winds, / Hath sullied, withered, overcast and donne', and Sonnet 18, line 3, 'Rough windes do shake the darling buds of Maie'. K. Muir (op. cit., pp. 10–30) has pointed out a number of echoes of *Edward III* in *later* and not in possibly earlier plays of Shakespeare, particularly *Measure for Measure*.

action (inducing his daughter to break her marriage vow). He must do it to prove that he is Lord and master of his social status, represented by his word and oath to *his* Lord and master, the King. In Sonnet 94 the righteous people in authority are in their turn Lords and owners, not of their inner integrity but of their outer appearances:

> They are the Lords and owners of their *faces*,
> Others, but stewards of their excellence: (lines 7–8).

They, in the sonnet, are in the position of the King, not Warwick, who, though Lord and master of his word, is in fact but a steward of the King's excellence. What they rule and own is not (like Warwick, the faithful steward) their word and honour, but merely their *'faces'*.[15] The usual Shakespearian contrast between reality (truth) and appearance is subsumed here in its political connotation. The mighty, only apparently just, have absolute control over outer forms; the others, their stewards, may be honest like Warwick, and masters of their honour, but are in honour bound to serve the 'excellence', that is to say the superior state, of their Lords and masters,[16] whatever form this superiority may take.

2.1. Sidney versus *Edward III* (lines 1–4). We are sharply reminded of the basic subject of the Sonnet: the implications of the exercise of power. And the context of *Edward III*, II. i, helps us again in this. Warwick, oath-bound, is aware of the desperate ambiguity of his position: he knows that the King's will is wrong and evil, but he must convey to his daughter the 'message' from the King. He tells her (384–6):

> The mighty king of England dotes on thee.
> He that hath power to take away thy life,
> Hath power to take thy honor;

[15] See the use of *face* in Sonnet 93, lines 2–3: 'so loves face, / May still seeme love to me, though alter'd new', and cf. Ph. Martin, op. cit., pp. 31, 37, and 40–1; for *face* in *Richard II* see § 2.11 below.

[16] The question whether *their* refers to *stewards* (so that 'stewards of their [own] excellence' would be a parallel construction with 'owners of their [own] faces' in the previous line), or to *owners*, is idle; the sense does not change whether we paraphrase 'they are the stewards to the superior rank of the Lords and owners', or 'they are stewards to those who rank higher than themselves'. But Martin (op. cit., pp. 37–8) suggests another interesting interpretation: 'Others are humble enough to make themselves stewards of the talents given them—excellent to begin with, but improved by industry'.

The obvious reminiscence of the second of these lines in the opening of Sonnet 94,

> They that have powre to hurt, and will doe none,

is extremely instructive and reveals Shakespeare's strategy in the poem—I would call it a political strategy. The question whether or not, in setting out to write it, he meant to generalize the problem raised by his relation to the young man, is irrelevant: whether an aristocrat or a commoner, the lover as such is always, and traditionally, a king, a prince, a ruler, a sun, the wielder of love-power. The true subject, direct or metaphorical, is the behaviour of those who have power. And Shakespeare starts off with Sidney's traditional and still chivalrous view of the paternalistic benevolent tyrant. Commentators have referred to *Arcadia*, II. 15. 6: 'but the more power he hath to hurt, the more admirable is his praise that he will not hurt'[17] (*posse et nolle, nobile*, according to the ancient wisdom of the Latin proverb). But the poet's position is not one of unquestioning acceptance of the old saw; it is rather an exploration of its truth and wisdom. They that have power to hurt others but refrain from it, are they really praiseworthy? Their virtue in abstaining is merely passive, not active, consists in not doing, rather than doing. What if they cause others (their stewards or subjects) to do the 'thing' (deed or misdeed) that they 'do not do'? The relevant context and predicament of Warwick in *Edward III* must have presented itself to the poet's mind not as the answer to the question, but as a convincing way of putting it. So on to the three-member syntactical and logical structure suggested by Sidney:

(1) He that has power to hurt (2) and will not hurt (3) is admirable,

is superimposed the model provided by *Edward III*:

---

[17] Lever (*Eliz. Love Sonnet*, pp. 217–18) explores the context in which the sentence occurs in the story of Prince Plangus in *Arcadia*. The starting-point is a situation surprisingly similar to that of Edward III and Lady Salisbury: the Prince woos 'a private mans wife of the Principal Citie of that Kingdome'. But the outcome is quite different from that of the episode in the play: Prince Plangus enjoys the lady, and when he later finds that his own father is in love with her, surrenders his claims to her love. Lever sees in this a reflection of the supposed triangular affair poet–friend–mistress.

(1) He that has power to hurt (2) and will not hurt (3) has power to force others (his stewards) to (ill) doing.

In order to prepare the alternative, Shakespeare, in the first place, has extended members (1) and (2) of this structure to the whole of the first quatrain. The extension is obtained, as we have seen (§§ 1.0 and 1.3 above), through the addition of parallel relative clauses, and it produces a progressive dislocation of meaning:

> They that have powre to hurt, and will doe none,
> That doe not do the thing, they most do showe,
> Who moving others, are themselves as stone,
> Unmooved, could, and to temptation slow:

We move from potential action (the exercise of power), through refusal of action ('will do none') and negative action ('do not do'), to action by proxy ('moving others'), implying a loss of personal humanity ('as stone, unmoved, cold'); indeed what is lost is that animation that distinguishes man from lifeless matter. But the last hemistich is significant: 'and to temptation slow'— the negation is qualified. *They* are not *immune* from temptation, but *slow* to it; we have already been told that *They* are personally unmoved, but can and do move *Others*: now, after denying and refusing to act, the stimulus to action given by temptation can be delayed by the only type of action *They* are ready to do—action by proxy. Their temptation will be satisfied by means of the *others*, 'the stewards of their excellence' mentioned in the next quatrain.[18]

---

[18] Landry (op. cit., pp. 7 and 23) quotes most appropriately a passage from Th. Roger's *A Philosophical Discourse Entitled, The Anatomy of the Mind* (1576): 'that man which is never moved in mind, can never be either good to himself or profitable to others'. This attitude, as Eleanor Prosser points out in *Hamlet and Revenge* (Stanford, Calif., 2nd ed., 1971), pp. 164–5, was characteristic of sixteenth-century humanistic idealism, and she quotes an even more pertinent passage from Sir Richard Barcklay's *A Discourse of the Felicitie of Man: or his Summum Bonum* (London, 1598), pp. 599–600: 'For hee deserveth not the name of a good man, that forbeareth to do evill, as though good were a privation, & a defect from evill . . . For good is not a defect, but an effect: not placed in idleness but in doing.' In his turn, Philip Martin (op. cit., p. 39) reads the poem as 'a piece of grave irony', and, in considering the 'stone' image, makes an extremely perceptive observation (p. 35): 'Looking more closely still for a moment at "[they] are themselves as stone", one notices how the phrase, when dwelt upon, acquires a shape similar to that of a sentence like "He was himself as Hamlet". They are themselves as stone, stone expresses their nature: the more they are like stone, the more fully they are themselves.'

2.2. Hamlet's 'rightly' and Malcolm's 'graces' (line 5).

At this point the third member of the statement mentioned above, so long postponed, can spread out over the whole of the second quatrain. The opening line is in fact a masterpiece of ambiguity:

> They rightly do inherrit heavens graces,

a statement which at first seems perfectly in line with Sidney's conclusion: They are admirable. But there is a false ring to it. No reader who is in the least familiar with his Bible can miss the echo from the Sermon on the Mount (Matthew 5:5): 'Blessed are the meek: for they shall inherit the earth.'[19] Shakespeare has had recourse once again to the technique of ironical substitution, or inverted quotation, that we saw before: if the meek inherit the earth, the mighty[20] must inherit 'heaven's graces'; viz. meek: earth:: mighty: heaven. The equation can only be sardonic, being in flat contradiction with biblical doctrine (e.g., Isaiah 5:15: 'And man shall be brought downe, and man shall be humbled, even the eyes of the proude shall be humbled.'); and we are given warning of the sardonic tone by the opening adverb, 'rightly': correctly, according to rules. Ingram and Redpath[21] remind us that this is 'the only use of the word "rightly" in the poems. Of the twenty-three uses of the word in the plays, not one bears the moral or legal sense of "rightfully", "justly", "legitimately", or "of right". Here the meaning must be "truly" or "really" or "indeed".' As a matter of fact, the predominant meaning in the plays is 'correctly', 'in the right form', or even 'according to the accepted norm'. And

---

[19] See S. Booth, op. cit., p. 156.

[20] Cf. the lines of *Edward III*, II. i. 384–5, already quoted: 'The mighty king of England . . . He that hath power'. I strongly disagree with Elias Schwartz's denial of the existence of irony in the sonnet: cf. 'Shakespeare's Sonnet XCIV', *Shakespeare Quarterly*, xxii. 4 (Autumn 1971), pp. 797–8. On the contrary, James Winny (*The Master–Mistress*, p. 165) is surely right in considering the first quatrain 'a dispassionate, unhurried dissection of character which reveals step by step the meanness of spirit lying behind a mask of rectitude and abstinence'. After pointing out Shakespeare's delaying tactics in 'holding back the main clause of his sentence until the fifth line', Winny remarks on the latter: 'If his ironic tone were not evident, the inconsistency of this conclusion with the picture of arid, ungenerous nature which it follows, and the bitter energy of the line, should reveal Shakespeare's purpose'.

[21] *Shakespeare's Sonnets*, ed. W. G. Ingram and T. Redpath (London, 1964), p. 214.

let us look at the best-known occurrence of the word, in Hamlet's famous monologue 'How all occasions do inform against me', IV. iv. 53–6:

> Rightly to be great
> Is not to stirre without great argument,
> But greatly to find quarrell in a straw
> When honour's at the stake.

Hamlet's situation at this turning-point of the play, when he realizes the moral necessity of action and revenge, is curiously akin to the ethical predicament of the mighty in the sonnet. The proper criterion of greatness is in remaining unmoved, unless by very weighty matters; this corresponds to the code of behaviour indicated in the first quatrain of the sonnet. 'But'— the cold rule of unmoved greatness, underlined by the initial 'rightly', *must* be broken when a superior ethical principle— honour—is at stake.[22]

Warwick's dilemma in *Edward III* is of the same kind, but complicated by his being a steward rather than a master. In *Hamlet* it is a case of (morally) right versus rightly (logically correct), made clear by the placing of another adverb, 'greatly' in antithetical parallelism with 'rightly'. By contrast with 'greatly', 'rightly' acquires a negative connotation, through an obvious mental process of substitution. We expect *rightly* versus *wrongly*, but find instead *greatly*; now, the opposite of *greatly* in the present acceptation, would be *meanly*; this last adverb reflects therefore its negative associations on the first member of the *rightly* versus *greatly* antithesis. So 'rightly' comes to mean 'merely according to the correct rules of logical behaviour', but

---

[22] Derek A. Traversi's extended discussion of these lines in *Hamlet* seems to me very relevant (*An Approach to Shakespeare*, 3rd ed. revised and expanded (Garden City, N.Y., 1969), ii, p. 41); he takes the passage in connection with Falstaff's speech on honour in *1 Henry IV*, v. i, and comments: 'Reason, it is suggested, does not allow a man to act except upon a sufficient cause, upon the foundation of "great argument"; but "honour", based on natural feeling, insists that it is right and noble to act "greatly", with magnanimity, even when "reason" has concluded that the ground for action is an inadequate "straw". Falstaff's realistic skepticism has, in short, been taken up into a mood at once deeper and less conclusive, based no longer on the detached observation of reality but upon an intimate sense of conflict. "Honour", satirically conceived in the earlier comic spirit, has now become a necessary good, an incentive to action of a kind with which Falstaff had never been concerned; but, in the mood in which Hamlet considers it, it is also less than acceptable to reason.'

in contrast with the higher ethical code.[23] In the same way in Sonnet 94 *rightly* means 'correctly, according to the rules of formal logic': according to such rules, if the earth is inherited by the meek, the mighty would expect to inherit the earth's opposite—heaven's graces.

The question now is: what are these *graces* conferred by heaven upon those 'that have power'? It has been remarked that the choice of the word *graces* (not Grace, so important and ambiguous a word in Shakespeare's last plays, especially *Winter's Tale*) is ironical, with its implication of 'pleasing qualities', superficial charm.[24] But since the subject here is 'They that have power', the natural inference is that the poet is referring to the heavenly gifts of the rulers, listed by Malcolm to a bewildered Macduff (*Macbeth*, IV. iii. 91 ff.):[25]

> The King-becoming Graces,
> As Iustice, Verity, Temp'rance, Stablenesse,
> Bounty, Perseverance, Mercy, Lowlinesse,
> Devotion, Patience, Courage, Fortitude,
> I have no rellish of them [. . .].

The context is familiar enough, as well as its close source in Holinshed: Macduff has suggested that Malcolm, as the rightful heir of the slaughtered Duncan, should rescue Scotland from Macbeth's tyranny;[26] Malcolm, in order to test Macduff's trustworthiness, represents himself as tainted with all vices, and therefore unfit as future ruler of the country. The scene is worth considering, as perhaps Shakespeare's most extensive 'political' statement in any of the plays, where—in Tillyard's well-known words[27]—he 'finally settled his account with his idea of the

---

[23] Philip Martin (op. cit., p. 35–6), though following a different line of reasoning, points out very convincingly the ambiguity of 'rightly' in the context of the sonnet.

[24] Landry, op. cit., p. 23 and note 28, p. 147.

[25] Sonnet 94 and this passage in *Macbeth* are brought together in passing by W. R. Elton, *King Lear and the Gods* (San Marino, Calif., 1966), p. 213.

[26] Macbeth is never called 'king' in the play except by the witches and by Lady Macbeth, while, from III. vi onwards, he is referred to fifteen times as 'tyrant'; the latter term descends directly from the Morality tradition, with Herod as prototype, and the only other characters so defined in Shakespeare's plays are Richard III (twice), Caesar as seen by Brutus's party (three times), Leontes (so called by Paulina in *Wint.*, III. ii), and Prospero as seen by Caliban (three times); in *3 Henry VI*, III. iii, Edward IV is called 'tyrant' by Warwick's party, but in IV. iv Queen Elizabeth retorts the appellation on Warwick himself.

[27] E. M. W. Tillyard, *Shakespeare's History Plays* (London, 1944), p. 317.

good ruler', opposed both to Duncan's fideistic acceptance of
his kingly role as due to him by divine right, and to Macbeth's
usurpation of power by violence and deceit. In spite of the
implicit homage to James I's view of 'a Kings duetie in his
office'[28] contained in the very list of the king-becoming graces
or princely virtues,[29] I would agree with Agostino Lombardo's
reading of the scene:

The passage from the world of Duncan to that of Malcolm is in fact
the passage from the Middle Ages to the Renaissance: the 'prince'
whom Malcolm, directly or indirectly, is portraying, as the opposite
of the tyrant, is a modern ruler: he acknowledges the basic values
of the past, embodied in Duncan, but lives and acts in the present;
he is getting ready to restore the broken order, but knows that the
restoration can be achieved only by human means; he wants to get
back his lost crown, but knows that he must, in the first place,
deserve it.[30]

Malcolm includes 'Lowlinesse', that is to say that 'Meekness'
that 'inherits the earth', among the 'King-becoming Graces'.[31]
If we revert to Sonnet 94, we find that 'They that have power'
do not put to the test their 'graces' through action; they 'rightly
inherit' them. Line 5 of the sonnet (written presumably before

---

[28] Such is the title of Book II of James's *Basilikon Doron* (wr. 1599, pub. London,
1603), containing a list of what he calls 'Princely vertues' (*The Political Works of
James I*, ed. C. H. McIlwain (Cambridge, 1918), pp. 37–8); in his edition of
Macbeth (Cambridge, 1947), Dover Wilson remarked that at this point in the
scene Shakespeare conflated Holinshed's narrative with borrowings from King
James's treatise, and this was taken up by Henry N. Paul (*The Royal Play of
Macbeth*, New York, 1950), who saw the whole play as a tribute to the new
sovereign. Lily B. Campbell, discussing 'Political Ideas in *Macbeth* IV. iii', *Shakespeare Quarterly*, ii (October 1951), pp. 281–6, saw in this scene Shakespeare's support
for all the King's 'pet political ideas', including those of the divine right and of the
obedience due even to a bad king. A more balanced view seems that of Irving
Ribner, 'Political Doctrine in *Macbeth*', *Shakespeare Quarterly*, iv (1953), pp. 202–5:
'although Shakespeare did not hesitate to flatter King James by repeating the
monarch's own pet ideas, he did so only when they did not conflict with his own
convictions . . . there is no evidence in *Macbeth* that he accepted without reservation
the Tudor doctrines of divine right and passive obedience to tyranny'.
[29] It is significant in respect of Shakespeare's (by now a 'King's Man') attitude
towards James, that the only other speech in his plays celebrating 'All Princely
Graces' is Cranmer's prophecy on the new-born Queen Elizabeth, *Henry VIII*,
v. IV, trailing off in a fulsome tribute to James I; but the scene is attributed by
many to Fletcher's hand.
[30] A. Lombardo, *Lettura del Macbeth* (Vicenza, 1969), p. 234.
[31] It should be noted that also in *Basilikon Doron* one of the 'Princely vertues' is
Humilitie'.

the advent of James I had suggested to the poet a more accom-
modating attitude) exposes in this way the fallacy of an
apparently logical process which turns out to be only a deep-
rooted mental habit: it is assumed that the great possess all the
qualities (graces) necessary to the ruler, through the mere fact
of *being* great—they are supposed to have inherited them as
part of their rank; actually this mode of reasoning should be
reversed: only those who possess 'heaven's graces' and act
accordingly ought to become great and exercise power. The
relevancy of these conflicting attitudes to current political
issues is obvious at a time when the ruler—Queen Elizabeth—
was going to die without direct descendants. The fact that
Shakespeare was rejecting the traditional attitude (virtue
depends on power) in favour of a new ethical one (power
depends on virtue), is apparent not only from *Macbeth* and
King Lear, but also from earlier plays, from *Hamlet*, and from
the great debate on honour in *All's Well*; and is the very subject
of Sonnet 121, where social and moral values are contrasted.
In Sonnet 94 it is further stressed by equating the mighty's
'inheritance' (*not* conquest) of 'heaven's graces' with their
preoccupation to secure earthly goods, to 'husband nature's
riches from expense'.

2.3. The economics of power (lines 5–6). Line 6 recalls
the economic imagery of the marriage sonnets (see ch. I. § 4
above), especially nos. 2, 4, and 6, already anticipated in
'inherit' in line 5. We may remember the praise of good
husbandry, the deploration of waste (*expence*, here as in the
opening of Sonnet 129, has this meaning); but we should also
keep in mind the unorthodox doctrine expounded there, a
materialistic interpretation of the parable of the talents,
according to which earthly riches must be made productive by
any means, usury included. Now, the two parallel syntactical
units in lines 5 and 6 are juxtaposed, producing a single
structure with interchangeable parts:

$$\text{They rightly} \begin{Bmatrix} \text{[do] inherit} \\ \text{[And] husband} \end{Bmatrix} \begin{Bmatrix} \text{heaven's} \\ \text{nature's} \end{Bmatrix} \begin{Bmatrix} \text{graces} \\ \text{riches} \end{Bmatrix} \text{from expense}$$

Heaven's graces are equated with nature's riches (or heaven's
riches and nature's graces): paradoxically, Shakespeare adopts

the Puritan doctrine according to which earthly prosperity, the result of good husbandry, is considered as a sign of divine favour.

We must make a clear distinction between: (a) Shakespeare's objective awareness of the changing values due to 'the revolution of the times'—in fact, the rise of capitalism which was radically transforming the social structures—and, (b) his mental attitude to such a change. The group of the marriage sonnets bears witness to that awareness, while a poem like Sonnet 94 is a self-exploration reflecting his mental attitude— hence its importance. In other words, lines 5–6 of Sonnet 94 imply the same objective situation represented in the marriage sonnets and its corollaries, but not necessarily its acceptance by the poet. In the same way, if we want to know the poet's real conception of marriage, we must turn not to Sonnets 1–17 but rather to Sonnet 116: 'Let me not to the marriage of true minds'. True marriage is the permanent union of two minds through a Love which is not subject to time. In Sonnet 94 Shakespeare gives us the pattern of the success of the mighty, but this does not imply his approval. His tactics in the sonnet have been based on the reversed quotation, the personal reminiscence of negative contexts, the introduction of doubtful, ambiguous, or negative elements in apparently laudatory statements. In these very lines, and thanks to the premises stated in the first quatrain discussed above, Shakespeare manages to superimpose on his objective view of things already described, his interpretation, or rather the expression of what I called before his mental attitude to it, which is essentially critical.

2.4. The Lords and the stewards (lines 7–8). The next tactical move comes in the two following lines (7–8), which I have already discussed in connection with *Edward III*. We have seen the relevance of that context to the fact that the mighty are Lords and masters not of their inner nobility, but only of external appearances. I wish to call attention, however, to the implicit contrast between masters and stewards, which mirrors exactly, in the second half of quatrain II, the contrast expressed in the second half of quatrain I, establishing, through the repetition of *others*, a perfect symmetry between the two parts of the octave. In economic terms we may recall once again the parable of the talents, already implicit, as we saw, in lines 5–6; but the emphatic *others* stresses a new fact, which calls in doubt the rightness of the whole procedure: the good husbandry of nature's riches is not exercised directly by the mighty, but is entrusted to the *others*, to the good servant who puts to 'use' the talent left in his custody.[32] The negative implications of lines 3–4, where 'moving others' is joined by antithesis with 'unmoved', associated with 'stone' and 'cold', are reflected in lines 7–8: the god-like aloofness of the mighty is mere evasion, since they *do* act, but only by proxy, and we have seen the ambiguous import of such behaviour. Once again Shakespeare takes advantage of symmetrical grammatical structures to make his point: of their faces / of their excellence. *Excellence* mirrors *faces* and in so doing inherits the hollow quality that we saw expressed in that word. Excellence means power, supremacy, superiority, and carries a positive connotation within the sub-codes used in the octave of the sonnet: chivalrous, political, social, and economic. But are these really the supreme and only standards of human perfection? The clever placing of *faces* has already undermined this belief, indicating how all this belongs in fact only to the world of appearances, to the exclusion of the moral world of truth and reality, the reality of (human) nature.

Up to now the poet has apparently adopted the different *objective* codes, according to which *They*, the mighty, are certainly not found wanting. But all the time, through subtle insinuations and inverted quotations, through the play of associations of such words as 'show', 'stone', 'cold', 'slow' in quatrain I, through the antithesis They/Others in both quatrains, he managed to convey his attitude to this state of affairs; so that, though in quatrain II there is no single word (not even 'faces' out of context) that could be picked out as having in itself a negative connotation, the cumulative effect is by no means positive. The minimal tactical moves on the lexical level that we noticed above were all subservient to an over-all

[32] And compare (or contrast) with another New Testament context, 1 Peter 4:10: 'Let every man as he hath received the gift, minister the same one to another, as good disposers [James's Bible: 'stewards'] of the manifold grace of God.' See my treatment of the Lord–servant relationship in Sonnet 146, chapter V, § 2.0 below.

strategy intended to expose the shallowness and inconsistency of the sub-codes used, and to suggest the need for another system of judgement. Quatrain II is the culmination of this process, working up to that protracted double-stressed tri-syllable, 'éxcellénce', which should have been a crowning glory, the very pinnacle of this elaborate monument, but turns out to be a hollow plaster decoration, ready to topple over when exposed to the free play of natural forces.

The Sidneyan proposition 'He that has power to hurt, / And will not hurt, / is admirable' is 'rightly' applied, but its validity is shown to be merely external, and therefore tautological; if we substitute for Sidney's objective, chivalrous (and Puritan) code, which is 'unmoved, cold, and to temptation slow', the real natural code of ethics, we get something like the proposition in *Edward III*: 'He that has power to hurt, / and will not hurt, / has power to force others to (ill) doing'.

2.5. Great creating nature (lines 9–10). We see now the reason for the sharp and at first sight unbridgeable break between octave and sestet, and at the same time we see why another full line from the *Edward III* context has been borrowed for the close of the sonnet. After working his way through the codes of chivalry, politics, society, and economics, and finding all of them wanting, the poet, like Warwick in the play, forsakes them in favour of the code of nature, with its specific ethical overtones. As we saw in § 1.4 above, the sestet is closely knit together by the repetitions of key words: $_{9.9}Summer$; $_{9.11}flower$ / $_{12.14}weed$; $_{11}base$ + $_{12}basest$ / $_{9}sweet$ + $_{13}sweetest$, all of them strictly connected with great creating nature and connecting it in turn with the moral world. An antithetical relation is established with 'nature's riches' of line 6 above, where nature was merely the purveyor of economic prosperity, instrumental-ized and carefully husbanded, the blind Goddess of the evil Edmund in *King Lear*. In the sestet, on the other hand, the natural imagery (nature is never directly mentioned but evoked through its products and life-cycle—'live and die') is functional to the ethics of nature. Line 9, 'The summer's flower is to the summer sweet', insisting on the cycle of the seasons, the life and death and rebirth of nature through the repetition of 'summer,' sets the tone, while the limitative clause in line 10 'Though to

it self it only live and die'[33] reflects back on the octave, making
explicit what was implied there: the self-sufficiency of the
flower is equated to that of the mighty men who 'are the Lords
and owners of their faces', and, significantly enough, is shown
to need justification. That means that such self-sufficiency is in
itself a fault (selfishness, pride). And indeed the justification is
readily provided for the flower: even if essentially asocial, it
perfumes the summer, it contributes to the general life of the
season. No similar function was assigned on the other hand to
the mighty, who moved others only in so far as the others were
their stewards who had to carry out their orders. The mighty
are implicitly condemned by this lack of contribution to the
community, a condemnation that Shakespeare had expressed
in Sonnet 1 with another flower metaphor (lines 9–12):

> Thou that art now the worlds fresh ornament,
> And only herauld to the gaudy spring,
> Within thine owne bud buriest thy content,
> And tender chorle makst wast in niggarding:

The mighty are like the miserly spring flower, while the
summer flower, full-blown, fulfils a useful function.

2.6. Warwick speaks again (lines 13–14). A reconsideration at this point of Warwick's speech in *Edward III*, ii. i, where
the line on 'lillies that fester' occurs, may well serve to show the
principles behind Shakespeare's strategy in Sonnet 94: a
strategy which seems to have been suggested by that dramatic
context, where it is fully declared, while in the sonnet it is
simply applied, eliminating the logical transitions between its
successive moments. As we saw (§ 2.0), in *Edward III* Warwick
had been trying, very half-heartedly but in duty bound, to
induce his daughter, the Countess of Salisbury, to become the
King's mistress. When she rejects with horror and disgust this
'Unnatural beseege' (ii. i. 412) by proxy to her natural honour,
Warwick is relieved, and begins his final speech (lines 430 ff.):

---

[33] The argument from nature against self-sufficiency is paralleled in Venus'
speech to seduce Adonis, 'Things growing to them selves, are growths abuse'
(line 166); see chapter I, § 4 above. Philip Martin (op. cit., p. 32) is inclined to
treat the line as parenthetical, but reminds us that '"onely" ("one-ly") means
"singly", and points to the infertility of the flower'.

Why, now thou speakst as I would have thee speake:
And marke how I unsaie my words againe.

These lines make explicit what is implicit in the open gap between the octave and the sestet of the sonnet; the poet's determination to 'unsay' what he had been saying in the octave (where he used, like Warwick, the language of 'policy') is not stated, but firmly implied in the sudden complete change of the lexical code, and of the metaphoric system employed. In Warwick's speech in *Edward III* the transition, instead of being sudden, is fully explained and followed up through a catalogue of metaphors and maxims ('A spacious field of reasons', as Warwick puts it in line 447), some of which are quite relevant to the moral context of Sonnet 94. He says (II. i. 434-5, 438-44):

> The greater man, the greater is *the thing*,
>   [cf. Son. 94, lines 2 and 13]
> Be it good or bad, that he shall undertake: [. . .]
> The freshest summers day, doth soonest taint
> The lothed carrion that it seemes to kisse:
> Deepe are the blowes made with a mightie Axe:
> That sinne doth ten times agrevate it selfe,
> That is committed in a holie place:
> An evill *deed*, done by authoritie,
>   (cf. Son. 94, lines 2-4 and 13]
> Is sin and subbornation:

The rhythm of the imagery becomes faster in the closing lines (449-53)

> That poyson shewes worst in a golden cup;
> Darke night seemes darker by the lightning flash;
> *Lillies that fester smel far worse then weeds*;
> And every glory that inclynes to sin,
> The shame is treble by the opposite.

Sonnet 94 is determined to make exactly the same point, but employing a tighter structural pattern, so that instead of moving through easy transitions, it adopts the drastic measure of changing its lexical code. The two patterns are shown side by side in fig. 3.

2.7. True and false syllogisms. The argument developed in the more than one hundred lines of *Edward III* is concentrated in the fourteen of the sonnet. The latter is formed by two

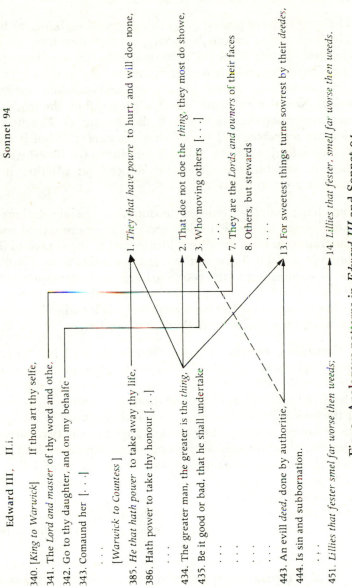

Fig. 3. Analogous patterns in *Edward III* and Sonnet 94

separate syllogisms, the first (the octave) false, the second (the sestet) true. Here is the octave:

1) The mighty have power to do things (good or bad), 2) but refrain from acting except by proxy, 3) therefore they are in full control of their outward behaviour. Hardly a syllogism— rather a tautology, which is effective according to the codes of politics, economics, social behaviour, and possibly ancient chivalry. Now let us apply to this proposition the code of nature, replacing the mighty with the flower: 1) The flower (which has no power and stands alone) is sweet: 2) but it may meet with infection, which makes it inferior to the basest weed; 3) *Ergo* its sweetness and standing depend on whether it is infected or not (on its *deeds*).

The change of code (politics—economics—social relations—chivalry versus nature) is underlined on the grammatical level by the transition from the plural forms used in the octave to the exclusively singular forms in the third quatrain: from a rather vague generalization to the concrete example from nature. The final couplet employs once again only plural forms, but here the sense of vagueness has been dispelled—it is rather a general theorem extracted from a single demonstration.

2.8. Changing codes. I have already pointed out (§ 1.2) how line 13 links back, on the lexical level, to line 2 of the sonnet, establishing the mirror structure of the poem. I need not go into the further implications of this relation, but wish only to stress that the lexical links between octave and sestet are of an anti-thetical nature, so that, while holding together the two parts of the sonnet, they emphasize the opposition between them. Or rather, they stress the fact that the sestet, far from being a wholly separate unit, is essentially a turning inside out of the argument contained in the octave.

Furthermore, while in the octave the lexical codes coincided with the metaphoric meanings, leaving no space for other implied semiotic systems, in the sestet the lexical code of nature, and the associated garden metaphor, does not ignore but on the contrary implies and subsumes the systems of meanings appertaining to the lexical codes of the octave. Fig. 4 sets out these changes.

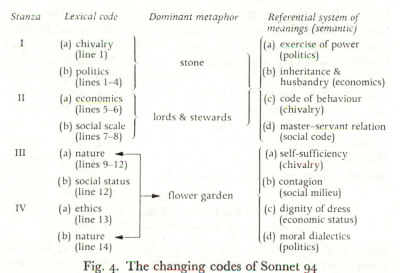

Fig. 4. The changing codes of Sonnet 94

The semantic referents of the sestet reproduce the code of the octave, while the semantic referents of the octave are not reproduced in the code of the sestet, but only in that of the octave itself. So the first part of the poem turns on itself, unmoved, cold, like the metaphorical stone of line 3. But as soon as the sestet is put beside it in antithetical tension, the apparent self-sufficiency of lines 1–8 is exposed as mere self-limitation, lacking the vitality of nature-processes and ethical dialectics; it is actually transcended and absorbed by the second part of the poem which alone provides the reasons for the existence of the first part.

2.9. The dignity of dress (line 12). Reverting now to the sestet, two separate lines (12 and 13) must be taken into consideration, since at first sight they may seem intrusions in the unified lexical code of the whole section, so firmly centred on nature. Line 12

> The basest weed out-braves his dignity:

though connected through *weed* to the nature-world, carries a completely separate overtone, centering on the same word. 'Weed' in Shakespeare also very frequently means 'dress', and it is easy to take the whole line as meaning: 'the poorest dress

looks richer than the splendid finery of the flower'. There is no
need to point out how often Shakespeare uses 'brave' in connection with 'finery' or 'garment', while 'dignity' is as frequently associated with 'outer fair' as with 'inward worth'.[34]
The dignity of dress is the most obvious sign of social distinction
and economic status, and these concepts apply exactly to the
context of the sonnet, which is run through by the theme of the
contrast between appearance (wealth, social rank) and real
substance. A theme which is obviously also present among
Warwick's *sententiae* on the corruption of greatness in *Edward III*,
quoted in part above; see II. i. 444–6:

> Decke an Ape
> In tissue, and the beautie of the robe
> Adds but the greater scorne unto the beast.

Line 12, therefore, introduces by implication into the code of
nature that of social status, and, through the dress metaphor, the
semantic suggestion of economic rank.

2.10. Deeds and weeds in Sonnet 69. The dominant
nature code, in the next line (13), though continued by
sweetest (linked with 'sweet' = 'perfumed' in line 9), is once
again in abeyance, momentarily overpowered by that of moral
judgement—a criterion underlying the whole sonnet but never
emerging into the open before now:

> For sweetest things turne sowrest by their deedes,

We have already seen the supreme relevance of this line both
for its parallelism with the argument of the *Edward III* context
(cf. § 2.6 above) and for its antithetical symmetry with line 2
of the sonnet (cf. §§ 1.2 and 2.8 above). Nothing remains but to
point out its ethical import, and this can best be done by
reference to another sonnet: 69, lines 9–14:

> They [thy judges] looke into the beauty of thy mind,
> And that in guesse they measure by thy deeds,
> Then churls their thoughts (although their eies were kind)

---

[34] More frequently their colour is considered as the 'dress' of the flowers; I
would not therefore adopt the emendation of *weare* into *were* in line 11 of Sonnet 98,
a passage which is quite relevant to the sonnet now under discussion: 'Nor did I
wonder at the Lillies white, / Nor praise the deep vermillion of the Rose, / They
weare but sweet, but figures of delight: / Drawne after you, you patterne of all
those.'

> To thy faire flower ad the ranke smell of weeds,
>> But why thy odor matcheth not thy show,
>> The soyle[35] is this, that thou doest common grow.

The nature imagery matches very accurately that of Sonnet 94, insisting on the sinesthetic effect of the rank smell of the flower infected by its mixing with commonness. The meaning in Sonnet 69 is unequivocal in so far as the poet is dealing in personal terms with a private matter, and the tone is hortatory, like that of the marriage sonnets (note the absence of first person pronominal expressions contrasted with the heavy stress on the second person, as in Sonnets 1–9). There is no questioning of the ethical purpose served by the specific language used here. A comparison between this and Sonnet 94 throws into sharp focus by contrast the characteristic tone of the latter: neither dramatic, like the parallel *Edward III* context and so many of the sonnets, nor hortatory, like Sonnet 69 and for that matter Sonnets 1–17, but *meditative*. This implies a transcendence of the particular case, the private persons, and the specific circumstances, in order to reach out towards first principles, to the roots of human motivations, to the general condition of humanity—I am loath to use the word philosophy, since a poet is not a philosopher; but he is certainly a man who grapples with reality and inquires into its implications (like a philosopher or a mystic) through the direct testimony of his senses, his imagination, and his creative power. The particular case, the dramatic relationship with the 'lovely boy', may have provided one imaginative stimulus for this meditation on the nature of power:[36] but to assume, as nearly all critics do, by analogy with other sonnets where the poet's friend is identified with a flower or more specifically a rose, that the single flower in the sestet of Sonnet 94 is *tout court* the boy—and to interpret the Sonnet merely in that key—is preposterous. I say *merely*

[35] I adopt the obvious emendation for the misprinted *solye* of Q.

[36] I am inclined to agree with E. K. Chambers (see chapter I, § 4, note 28 above) who sees in the so-called Sonnet 126 (actually a sequence of six rhymed couplets), not the envoy of all the first 125 sonnets to the Friend, but rather the closing rhyme of the marriage group, with which it shares the hortatory tone, the insistence on the second person, the self-effacement of the first person (only one *my*), and some of the imagery. I would tentatively suggest that the conceit of the Boy's power over Time (lines 1–2: 'O Thou my lovely Boy who in thy power, / Doest hold times fickle glasse, his sickle, hower') may have set off the meditation on power, its nature, and the nature of those who wield it.

because such an interpretation is in fact possible on an essentially psychological level, especially when handled by such skilful and subtle interpreters as Empson, Landry, or Booth; but it has a limited validity because it presupposes the general private context of the rest of the sonnets (or of most of them). The flower is not the young man, but rather the emblematic expression of the dominant metaphor of the sestet: not the garden flower but the flower garden.[37]

In fact, Sonnet 94 (like Sonnets 121, 129, and 146) claims independent attention, and all Shakespeare's skill has been employed in placing it outside the context of the rest of the sonnets. Necessarily, some of the lexical, semantic, and metaphoric materials are the same, and comparisons with other sonnets, as we have seen, are useful, but the total semantic arrangement, the way in which its 'signs' are used, is radically different. We have examined it before, and noticed Shakespeare's subtle strategy, based on a sequence of tactical moves intended to dislocate meanings, reverse traditional contexts, play the lexical codes and semantic sytems against each other; the dialectics created in this way suggest the tortuousness of meditation, an attempt at reconciling a mass of contradictions.

2.11. The Garden-State and Richard II.[38] In the sestet

[37] I wish to clear up one perplexing point in connection with the flower and the lilies of the last line. Hallet Smith (*Elizabethan Poetry*, p. 190) surmised that the lilies may be a recollection of another famous verse in the Sermon on the Mount (Matthew 6:28): 'And why care yee for rayment? Learne, howe the lilies of the fielde doe growe; they labour not, neither do they spinne'—and I would add the next verse: 'And yet I say unto you, that even Solomon in all his glorie was not arayed like one of these' (cf. the clothes-imagery in line 12 of the sonnet, § 2.9 above, and chapter V below). This text, according to Smith, establishes the self-sufficiency of the flower, maintained in lines 9–10, as against the necessity for husbandry celebrated in the octave and in the marriage sonnets. Apart from the fact that in my opinion the last line comes directly from a precise context in *Edward III*, we have already seen the ambiguous use of the principle of husbandry in lines 5–6 (see § 2.3 above) and its negative connotations. But besides this objection to Smith's argument, there is the biblical specification—lilies *of the field*: they grow in the common field and therefore, as Shakespeare has been at pains to suggest, they may well be subject to 'base infection', so that, in the terms of Sonnet 69, by 'growing common', to the fair flower is added 'the rank smell of weeds'. See for this chapter III, § 1.2 below and remember the current saying found in Lodge's *Rosalynde* (1590): 'Lillies are fair in show but foul in smell'.

[38] Arthur Mizener's admirable essay, 'The Structure of Figurative Language in Shakespeare's Sonnets', now available in a revised form in *A Casebook on Shakespeare's Sonnets*, ed. G. Willen and V. B. Reed (New York, 1964), pp. 219–35, with

of Sonnet 94 Shakespeare is advancing an argument parallel to the famous contrast, in Sonnet 54, between the 'canker' or dog-rose which grows wild, and the 'sweet' or garden rose, which survives and fulfils a function thanks to its perfume. That the poet, in Sonnet 94, is thinking of the garden flower and not of the wild one, is made clear by the insistence on its sweetness, i.e., perfume. The flower which 'is to the summer sweet' (line 9) thanks to its perfume, is by no means useless to the summer garden, even if 'to itself, it only live and die' (line 10), like the odourless canker blooms of Sonnet 54 (line 11) which 'die to themselves'. But the latter 'live unwoo'd, and unrespected fade' (Sonnet 54, line 10) while, the flower in Sonnet 94, by being 'sweet', can survive its physical death, like the garden roses in Sonnet 54 (lines 11–12):

> Sweet Roses do not so,
> Of their sweet deaths, are sweetest odours made:[39]

Shakespeare's fear is not that the flower should 'unrespected fade', but that it should be contaminated by the weeds that grow also in the best-kept garden, and which may overcome even the 'sweetest things', taking advantage of their weakness.

In other words, Shakespeare is afraid that the garden flower, through its own deeds of weakness, should follow the same fate as Richard II, a weak sovereign 'eaten up' by 'the weeds that his broad-spreading leaves did shelter' (*Richard II*, III. iv. 50), so that the rebel Lancastrians, in Hotspur's words (*1 Henry IV*, I. iii. 175–6), were able to

> put downe *Richard*, that sweet lovely Rose,
> And plant this Thorne, this Canker *Bullingbrooke*.

I have just referred to the Gardeners' scene in *Richard II* (III. iv.), and I think that its context is very relevant to the sestet of Sonnet 94. The iconic analogy is obvious. The Gardener proposes to

its extremely perceptive discussion of Sonnet 124, including references to *Richard II* and Sonnet 94, and an exploration of the meaning of 'State', is very relevant to this section.

[39] For the 'summers distillation', the extraction of essence which becomes the flower's posthumous life, see Sonnet 5: 'But flowers distil'd though they with winter meete, / Leese but their show, their substance still lives sweet.'

root away
The noysome Weedes, that without profit sucke
The Soyles fertilitie from wholesome flowers, (lines 37–9)

and his Servant compares the 'firm estate' of the garden to that
of Richard's ('the wasteful king', line 55) England:

our Sea-walled Garden, the whole Land,
Is full of Weedes, her fairest Flowers chokt up. (lines 43–4)

The Garden is the readiest metaphor for the State, amply
used before Shakespeare. I need only refer to the documentation provided by Peter Ure in his introduction to the New
Arden edition of *Richard II*,[40] and point out the two main
aspects of the garden metaphor: the Utopian, or ideal state of
the prelapsarian Garden of Eden, the Golden Age, and
Arcady; or the more strictly political one, where the garden is
seen as a living natural commonwealth of plants, and flowers,
and weeds. It is significant that as we approach the end of the
sixteenth century, in the Utopian metaphors stress is also
placed on their fall and corruption. John of Gaunt (*Richard II*,
II. i. 42–4) calls England

This other Eden, demy paradise,
This Fortresse built by Nature for herself
Against infection, and the hand of warre:

only to remind us that this ideal state (lines 59–60)

Is now Leas'd out [. . .]
Like to a Tenement or pelting Farme.

Present political and economic preoccupations impinge on the
Garden of Eden, paving the way for the complexities of
Marvell's gardens and Milton's *Paradise Lost*.[41]

In the same way, Sidney's *Arcadia* is not that of the Golden
Age, of Virgil's *Bucolics*, or Sannazzaro, but, as Christopher Hill
remarks, it 'contains a grim reminder of social realities: for the
pastoral existence of his ruling-class heroes and heroines is in
continual danger from the irruption of *real* peasants, with very
different manners. *Arcadia*, appropriately enough, was com-

40 London, 1956, pp. li–lvii.
41 See Empson's treatment of Marvell and Milton in *Some Versions of Pastoral*.

posed in a park made by enclosing a whole village and evicting the occupants'.[42]

But this is beside the point, and I went into it only in order to stress the social, political, and economic consciousness that had entered the traditional metaphor of the garden at the time when Shakespeare was writing Sonnet 94. The context of this sonnet is obviously closer to *Richard II*, III. iv, the garden as commonwealth or state, beset by weeds, rather than as Eden (even with its serpent). Or rather, what Richard Altick has rightly called the 'symphonic imagery' of the whole play of *Richard II*[43] is an unlimited expansion of the iconic structures of Sonnet 94, in the same way as the sonnet itself may be considered a distillation of some scenes of *Edward III*. The examples are many, from the insistence in *Richard II* on the concept of *stewardship* (II. ii. 59; III. iii. 79; IV. i. 126; cf. line 8 of the sonnet and § 2.4 above) to the obsessive repetition throughout the play of *face, outface* etc. (at least 26 times; cf. line 7 of the sonnet and § 2.0 above), implying the contrast between outward appearance, or 'office', and the real 'person'.[44] And there is no other play in the canon where the words *base* and *sour* (in constant opposition with *sweet*) are repeated so many times, reproducing on a much larger scale the iconic antinomies of the sestet of Sonnet 94, supported by the frequent recurrence, in *Richard II*, of such terms as *flower, summer* (with reference also to the other seasons) and by the presence of the *infection–fester–corruption* word-cluster.

The sonnet could be taken as the imaginative core of a much wider dramatic structure centring on Richard, the passive leader, a projection into English history of the responsibilities

[42] Chr. Hill, *Puritanism and Revolution* (1958, repr. London, 1968), pp. 61–2; this contains a brief but illuminating excursus on the myths of the Fall, the Golden Age, Arcadia, Midas, and the Noble Savage (pp. 58–64). For another perceptive religious-political interpretation of *Arcadia* see F. Marenco, *Arcadia puritana* (Bari, 1966). The later development of the idea of death in Arcady is illustrated by E. Panofsky, 'Et in Arcadia Ego': Poussin and the Elegiac Tradition', in his *Meaning in the Visual Arts* (1955), pp. 295–320.

[43] R. D. Altick, 'Symphonic imagery in *Richard II*', *PMLA*, lxii, 1947, included in the excellent Casebook *Richard II*, ed. Nicholas Brooke (London, 1973), pp. 101–30.

[44] See Philip Edwards, 'Person and Office in Shakespeare's Plays', *Proceedings of the British Academy*, lvi, 1970 Annual Shakespeare Lecture. On the meaning and imagery of *Richard II* see too N. Brooke, *Shakespeare's Early Tragedies* (London, 1968), and A. R. Humphreys, *Shakespeare: Richard II* (London, 1967).

of 'They that have power', and the debate on the implications of the exercise of power.

2.12. The meaning of the form. This, I feel, goes beyond Empson's view of this sonnet, neatly summarized in the sub-title of his essay: 'Twist of Heroic–Pastoral Ideas into an Ironical Acceptance of Aristocracy'.[45] I hope that my analysis has revealed greater complexities in Shakespeare's basic attitude: the chivalric code is set against the new economic code of nature, which is in itself contradictory. A point that even a very perceptive critic like J. W. Lever seems to have imperfectly grasped when he says that Sonnet 94 'stands back from the group [on the Friend's fault] much as a contemplative soliloquy does from the dialogue of a play. Like the soliloquy it provides a generalized consideration of themes elsewhere stated from an individual viewpoint'.[46] So far so good—but he draws from this premiss a questionable conclusion: 'To understand the poem as a whole we must consider it as part of the group'. I would take issue with this statement; all that I have said before goes to prove that Sonnet 94, like Sonnets 121, 129, 146, is a soliloquy in so far as it has to *get away* from the *private* context of the surrounding poems, and to debate, before the sessions of the poet's silent thought, matters of general concern. It is not a case of personal experience projected on to a universal level, but of a reconsideration of basic principles in order to clear away the deformations in thought brought about by private passions. The very structure of the poem, insisting on the generalized 'They', proves that Shakespeare's attitude in the sonnet is the one I have described. Current interpretations within the context of the Sonnets are therefore misleading. Even Empson, when referring to the 'ironical acceptance of aristocracy', is thinking in terms of Shakespeare's personal relation to the aristocratic Mr. W. H.—projected in the figure of Prince Hal. So that, not finding a clear statement about the relation with the 'boy', the sonnet is felt to be somewhat unsatisfactory and unsuccessful.

My plea is in favour of taking the poem on its own terms, following the suggestions of the language it uses and of the codes

[45] W. Empson, *Some Versions of Pastoral*, p. 87.
[46] J. W. Lever, *Eliz. Love Sonnet*, pp. 216–17.

it applies. They establish it as a 'political' poem—not, as Lever says, the repetition of 'political commonplaces' applied to a private context, but a genuine and successful attempt at reconsidering such commonplaces on their own merits in order to expose their inner contradictions. In this the poem is perfectly successful. Its real context is not represented by the group of sonnets that surround it, but is infinitely wider; it is the whole changing culture of Elizabethan England. I hope that this analysis, by concentrating on the systems of signs peculiar to this poem, and on their arrangement, has managed to throw light on its consistency, on the purposeful progression of its basic metaphorical units (stone → lords and stewards → garden-state), on the effortless but subtle balancing of all its component parts, so as to produce out of a mass of antitheses not a temporary feat of equilibrium, but a harmonious permanent structure.

121

Tis better to be vile then vile esteemed,
When not. to be, receiues reproach of being,
And the iust pleasure lost, which is so deemed,
Not by our feeling, but by others seeing.
For why should others false adulterat eyes
Giue salutation to my sportiue blood?
Or on my frailties why are frailer spies;
Which in their wils count bad what I think good?
Noe, I am that I am, and they that leuell
At my abuses, reckon vp their owne,
I may be straight though they them-selues be beuel
By their rancke thoughtes, my deedes must not be shown
    Vnlesse this generall euill they maintaine,
    All men are bad and in their badnesse raigne.

CHAPTER III

'TIS BETTER TO BE VILE:
SONNET 121 AND THE
ETHICS OF SOCIAL BEHAVIOUR

0.1. From 94 to 121. While one of the main obstacles to a reading of Sonnet 94 was the impression that it fitted into a closed group of sonnets concerned with one specific moment of Shakespeare's relation with the 'lovely boy', Sonnet 121 offered no such problem, and has been recognized as standing relatively apart from the main sequence. Samuel Butler,[1] for instance, who was anxious to rearrange the sonnets in order to reconstruct a love-story, did not even suspect that no. 94 was incorrectly placed; but when he came to 121 he felt that it did not belong there, and moved it forward, between Sonnets 32 and 33, as portending a 'catastrophe' in the relationship between Shakespeare and his friend. The obvious fact is that Sonnet 121, like 94, 129, and 146, is *not* a love-poem and does *not* address a specific interlocutor, a 'thou' (Butler was forced to move Sonnets 129 and 146 to an appendix in his edition, as 'occasional' poems); it is, like those I have just mentioned, a meditative poem, and shares with them some formal characteristics. I take it in connection with 94 because, like 94, it explores a moral ambiguity in terms of general human behaviour, though with a double change of focus:

(a) The ethics of power of Sonnet 94 are replaced by the ethics of social behaviour and possibly sex, moving towards the problem treated in Sonnet 129, which some critics have connected with this one.

(b) While Sonnet 94 insisted on the contrast between two patterns of behaviour—They versus Others—, Sonnet 121 is based on the dialectics of society versus individual, so that They and Others are grouped together at one pole, while the opposite pole is represented by the 'I' of the poet.

[1] S. Butler, *Shakespeare's Sonnets Reconsidered* (1899; new ed. London, 1927), pp. 310 and 312.

0.2. The sonnet out of context. On the whole, Sonnet 121 has received in recent times less critical attention than Sonnet 94, though it is also considered a 'difficult' poem—the definition is generally accepted by the critics, mainly concerned with extracting *one* unequivocal meaning from the obvious (and to me obviously deliberate) syntactical ambiguities of the text. As typical treatments of the sonnet I would quote G. Wilson Knight[2] who is aware of the complexity of the theme (it deals 'with something more subtle and less easily definable than any specific action and more than morality; and it is with this core of the personality that our sonnet is primarily concerned'), or Hilton Landry, who provides a careful analysis quoting previous interpretations in order to show it as an attack against too cynical an attitude.[3] Both critics, though, seem to agree on the futility of previous attempts to include this in the wider context of some group of sonnets (the self-accusing ones), in spite of Landry's remark that 'it may also serve as a kind of generalizing conclusion to a group of poems beginning with Sonnet 109'.[4]

Indeed, Sonnet 121 has to be taken on its own merits as a personal statement, not so much 'out of sequence', but rather 'out of mood'. I propose therefore to examine in the first place its formal organization. Two features emerge immediately: (a) The sonnet is dominated by *one* rhetorical figure, antithesis, which emerges at all levels from the very first lines; (b) The logical and metrical structures of the poem are fully coincident and integrated—from the structural point of view, indeed, this is one of the most perfectly constructed sonnets of the sequence.

1.0. Antithesis.[5] The figure of antithesis, most forcibly ex-

---

[2] G. W. Knight, *The Mutual Flame* (London, 1955), p. 52.

[3] H. Landry, *Interpretations* etc., pp. 87–96.

[4] Ibid., p. 87.

[5] C. Schaar (*Sonnet Problem*, pp. 133–6) remarks that the figure of antithesis is extremely frequent in Shakespeare's Sonnets and is found in serial form; but, rather surprisingly, he does not include no. 121 among those showing particularly elaborate series of antitheses, while nos. 94 and 129 are included in that group. The antitheses and the semantic areas illustrated in this and in the next paragraph coincide with Hamlet's famous dilemma in his soliloquy (III. i) 'To be or not to be'; a perceptive discussion of the ethical implications of the choice between 'being' and 'not being' as well as 'acting' and 'not acting'—relevant also to the moral world of Sonnet 94 (see chapter II, §§ 2.1, 2.2 and *passim*, above)—is to be found in Eleanor Prosser, *Hamlet and Revenge*, pp. 163–6.

pressed in the first line, *be vile* versus *vile esteemed,* as well as in the ninth, *I* versus *they,* provides the means of isolating and contrasting the two main semantic areas of the sonnet, one connected with *being* and *I,* the other with *esteeming* (or *seeming*) and *they* (or *others*). Once again, the basic contrast is between reality (the reality of the *I,* the inner personality of the speaker), and appearance (the outer world of *them,* the *others*).

All the antitheses are placed within single lines neatly distributed in the two hemistichs or at most within two consecutive lines, as follows: line 1—be vile versus vile esteemed; line 2—not to be versus being; line 4—our feeling versus others' seeing; lines 5–6—others' . . . eyes versus my . . . blood; lines 7–8—my frailties versus their wills; line 8—[they] count bad versus I think good; line 9—I versus they; line 10—my abuses versus their own [abuses]; line 11—I . . . straight versus they . . . bevel; line 12—their . . . thoughts versus my deeds.

It will be noticed that this neat play of antitheses stops short of the final couplet. The significance of this will appear later.

1.1. Semantic areas.   We can now define the two semantic areas I have hinted at above (§ 1.0), one linked with reality and the pronouns or pronominal expressions in the first person, the other with appearances and the pronouns or pronominal expressions in the third person plural (they, their, others):

Areas: BEING. OUR. I. MY ↔ SEEMING. OTHERS. THEY. THEIR.

$_1$to be	↔	$_1$esteemed, $_3$deemed
$_2$being	↔	$_2$not to be
$_4$feeling	↔	$_4$seeing
$_6$blood	↔	$_5$eyes
$_7$frailties	↔	$_8$wills
$_8$think good	↔	$_8$count bad
$_{11}$straight	↔	$_{11}$bevel
$_{12}$deeds	↔	$_{12}$rank thoughts

At this point we may be deceived into classifying the I-area as positive and the THEY-area as negative, and this opinion can be reinforced by two considerations: (a) Shakespeare's usual identification of reality (the I-world) with truth, and of appearance (the others' world) with deception; (b) the final couplet where $_{14}$*bad* and $_{14}$*badness* are associated with $_{13}$*they* and $_{14}$*their*. It is true that the inner world of the self is a world of actual $_{1-2}$*being* and $_{4}$*feeling*, of passionate ($_{6}$*blood*) action ($_{12}$*deeds*), where in spite of minor failings ($_{7}$*frailties*) and $_{10}$*abuses*, things are what they are and therefore $_{11}$*straight* and $_{8}$*good*. While the world of the others, the outside world, is a world of $_{2}$*not being*, of outer forms perceived by deceptive senses ($_{4}$*seeing*, $_{5}$*eyes*), deformed and distorted ($_{11}$*bevel*) by $_{12}$*rank thoughts* and uncertain apprehensions ($_{1}$*esteemed*, $_{3}$*deemed*) that tend to consider everything in a negative light ($_{8}$*count bad*).

1.2. Deeds and rank thoughts (line 12 and Sonnets 69 and 94). But we should take into account the words that belong to both areas: $_{1}$*vile*, and $_{10}$*abuses*: and the deliberate word-play in line 7, where *my frailties*, apparently an extenuating definition of a minor fault included in the I-area, is traduced to the THEY-area with an utterly negative connotation in *frailer spies*.[6] The world of subjective reality is by no means untainted, and the extent of its corruption is glimpsed in the extremely subtle ambiguity of line 12, the closing line of quatrain III:

By their rank thoughts my deeds must not be shown.

The surface-meaning is of course, 'my actions must not be interpreted in the light of the deliberate misconstructions that the corrupt minds of the *others* place upon them'; but, considering that the most common acceptation of *deeds* in Shakespeare is *misdeeds*,[7] deeds of darkness,[8] the line may well sound: 'I don't want that by the malevolence of their corrupted minds my crimes should be exposed'—reflecting on the previous line 11, which does not state 'I *am* straight', but merely 'I *may be* straight'.

The ambiguity of line 12 will appear even more clearly as

---

[6] The figure is called by Puttenham, *The Arte of English Poesie* (1589), ed. G. D. Willcock and A. Walker (Cambridge, 1936), *tranlacer*, in Latin *Traductio*, 'which is when you turne and tranlace a word into many sundry shapes as the Tailor doth his garment, & after that sort do play with him in your ditty'; in other words, a repetition of the same root with different affixes. For the use of this figure in Shakespeare's and Daniel's sonnets see Schaar, *Sonnet Problem*, pp. 123–7.

[7] Cf., e.g., the whole context of *deeds* in Sonnet 94, discussed in chapter II.

[8] 'Deeds of darkness' had of course a sexual connotation; cf. *Pericles* (1609 Q), v. iv. 34: 'If shee'd doe the deedes of darknes'.

the expression of an ethical position by setting it side by side
with another context containing a similar placing of the adjective 'rank'[9] and the noun 'deeds'. This is found in Sonnet 69,
lines 9–12:

> They looke into the beauty of thy mind,
> And that in guesse they measure by thy deeds,
> Then churls their thoughts (although their eies were kind)
> To thy faire flower ad the rancke smell of weeds,

Here there is no doubt that the young man's deeds, by which
the others judge his 'mind', are misdeeds, and that his judges'
(the others') thoughts are 'rank' in so far as his deeds are such—
quite apart from the malicious inclination of the world to 'add
the rank smell of weeds' to the fairest flowers. On a previous
occasion I quoted the same lines of Sonnet 69 in connection
with the closing lines of Sonnet 94, pointing out the identity
of the ethical positions in the two passages (cf. ch. 11, § 2.10).
Sonnet 69 is the link between 94 and 121, revealing the consistency of the moral conceptions in the meditative sonnets—
a consistency no less real for the ambiguity that Shakespeare
discovers in the ethical world.

1.3. Reigning frailties (line 14 and Sonnet 109).   Line 12,
then, casts a deep shadow on the soundness of the passionate
inner world defended in the previous lines and prepares us,
through its ambivalence, for the final couplet, introduced by
an *Unless* which calls into question the whole imaginative structure: the operative expressions symmetrically arranged here are
$_{13}$*general evill*, $_{14}$*All men* and $_{14}$*raigne*. In its turn *evil* reflects ana-
grammatically *vile* in line 1, establishing a close correspondence
between the beginning and the end of the sonnet by way of
this evident paronomasia. In the last line the world of the 'I'
so proudly affirmed at the beginning of the sestet ($_{9}$*I am that I
am*—with its God-like overtone[10]) is swallowed up and sub-
merged by the world of *all men*, the true kingdom:

> All men are bad and in their badnesse raigne.

The main difficulty in this line, though, is in the final word

---

[9] Note that the adjective *rank* is used in the Sonnets only in these two cases,
nos. 69 and 121.
[10] See the later sections of this chapter, especially § 3.4.

raigne which has perplexed commentators. Butler had recourse
to his usual desperate remedy, emendation, and adopted the
reading 'feign', paraphrasing: 'all men are bad, but pretend
to be better than they are'; but could not help adding: 'I am,
however, by no means confident that I understand the passage'.
Or, to take a recent interpreter, who has scrupulously examined
all the suggestions of previous commentators, these are the conclusions reached by Hilton Landry, after quoting the use of
'reign' in biblical and lay texts:[11]

> I suggest that Shakespeare's general intention in the last line of
> Sonnet 121 is to present the preposterous antithesis of this traditional
> view of man's nature and his place in the universe. Instead of
> reigning by virtue of his excellence, whether actual or potential,
> man rules the world in and by its badness. Since it is unthinkable
> that the poet's slanderers could actually maintain such a generaliza-
> tion, it serves to destroy the case against him by reducing their
> position to the absurd.

The fallacy of this attitude is once again that of assuming
that Shakespeare has a personal axe to grind. True, he is
speaking about himself, but his purpose is not that of producing
an apology, but rather of taking a step back and looking objectively at his position, assuming his personal predicament as
emblematic of that of Everyman. I feel that it is wiser to
consider the use of *reign* as a verb in other contexts in the
Sonnets. It occurs only twice. In Sonnet 31, line 3, it is absolutely conventional (in the friend's bosom 'there raignes Love'),
but the usage in Sonnet 109 seems to me relevant:

> Never beleeve though in my nature raign'd ⟨,⟩
> All frailties that besiege all kindes of blood,
> That it could so preposterouslie be stain'd,
> To leave for nothing all thy summe of good: (lines 9–12)

This is indeed a personal and private approach to the problem
of human personality, but the lexical analogies are revealing.
The frailties of the human blood are those mentioned in
quatrain II of Sonnet 121, where 'my sportive blood' was
maliciously saluted by the 'false adulterate eyes' of the others—
and 'my frailties' were counted bad by even frailer observers.

11 H. Landry, op. cit., p. 95.

In Sonnet 109, however, they are 'all frailties' of mankind and of 'all kinds of blood' reigning in the single nature ('my nature') of the speaker. There is an interesting exchange of adjectival and possessive terms in the two sonnets:

109 line 10: *All* frailties → 121.7: *my* frailties
109 line 10: *all* . . . blood → 121.6: *my* blood
109 line 9: in *my* nature → 121.14: in *their* badness [of *all* men]

The exchange works as an identification by opposition: Sonnet 109 suggested that the negative attitudes of the others may have been subsumed in the nature of the one subject 'I'; Sonnet 121 implies, in quatrain II, that the faults for which the subject is reproached may well be those of the others, hypo-critically alternating the two roles of accomplices and censors. In both contexts 'reign' is the operative word; but in 109 it is found in its right position within the context (frailties and blood *reign* in the subject's nature), while in 121 Shakespeare operates a deliberate misplacement, moving it right to the end of the sonnet, in a more ambiguous syntactical position. Not 'all frailties' but 'all men' *reign*; and their domain is not 'in my nature' but 'in their badness'. We had been informed, however, that 'All men' shared the 'frailties' that besieged 'my sportive blood', and we had been made aware of the 'badness' of their nature. Therefore the last line of Sonnet 121, by misplacing the verb 'reign', confirms the merging of the speaker's 'I' with 'all men', and of his nature with 'their badness'. It is indeed the choice of this verb as the closing active word of the sonnet that establishes beyond doubt the completion of the unconscious psychological process by which the 'I', the individual, is absorbed in the indiscriminate mass of 'All men', the vile and proud community of mankind.

1.4. What peece of worke is a man. The semantic pattern of the poem can be summarized in fig. 5.

Apart from the paronomasic link between lines 1 and 13 represented by the anagram *vile/evil*, there is a symmetrical correspondence between the repetition in the first line (*vile . . . vile*) and that in the last (*bad . . . badness*), repetitions whose function seems to be that of reconciling the two antithetical semantic areas that form the body of the sonnet. They frame

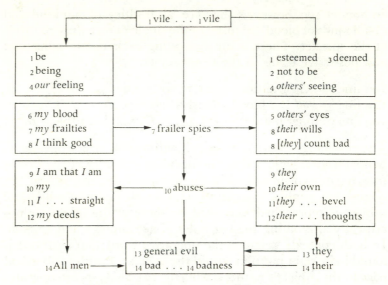

Fig. 5. Semantic pattern of Sonnet 121

and enclose the semantic pattern of the poem,[12] but the
repeated connotative words tend to unbalance it in the direction
of the THEY-area: the exploration of the nature of the self
reveals from the first a basic ambiguity, which in the end tends
to push over the jealously defended individual personality
(assumed to be the only *real* one) into the indiscriminate mass
of generalized mankind, which had been conceived at first as
the alien world of the *others*, of mere appearances. The central
affirmation ₉*I am that I am*, equating the speaker with God
and placing him apparently once and for all above the 'others',
is undermined by the doubtful and ambiguous expressions of
lines 11–12 (see § 1.2 above), while the closing couplet, by
suppressing altogether the first person singular, suggests its
merging into and identification with ₁₄*all men*: I am not
Jehovah, but a man—and as such undistinguished from 'them',
the 'others'; my reality is not above, but inside the world of
deceptive appearances, of 'their badness', of 'general evil'—
perhaps. It should be stressed, though, that the couplet is a

[12] Stephen Spender, 'The Alike and the Other', in *The Riddle of Shakespeare's
Sonnets* (London, 1962), pp. 91–128, has put this more imaginatively. I shall quote
and discuss his views in § 3.4 below.

hypothetical sentence: the debate on the nature of the human ego is by no means settled: 'What peece of worke is a man, how noble in reason, how infinit in faculties, in forme and moving, how expresse and admirable in action, how like an Angell in apprehension, how like a God: ... and yet to me, what is this Quintessence of dust': (Q2, sig. F2; II. ii. 315–21).

2.0. Metrical and logical structures.   This interpretation must now be verified against the admirably coincidental metrical and logical structures of the poem. There is hardly any need to stress that the established scheme of the Elizabethan sonnet with its rhymes (abab, cdcd, efef, gg) is fully respected— the only doubtful rhyme for us, $_6$*blood*–$_8$*good*, was perfect in sixteenth century pronunciation. The Quarto punctuation emphasizes the structure, clearly identifying the three quatrains and final couplet; the only emendation required is the omission of the semicolon at the end of line 7, while I feel that the fairly strong punctuation introduced by nearly all modern editors at the end of line 11 is misleading, since lines 11 and 12 are parallel, and form a single logical unit.

2.1. The functions of the rhyme-words.   A consideration of the rhyme-words confirms the extraordinary solidity of the sonnet structure: the opening and closing strophes have verbal rhyme-words, but with a subtle variation. Those in the first quatrain are all participles, alternating past and present, while those in the final couplet are in the present tense. The sonnet is enclosed in this grammatical scheme, echoing the semantic arrangement (see § 1.5 above); the frame is uniform but more ambiguous in the opening stanza than in the final one. Within the frame, the two central stanzas show a specific progression. The rhymes of quatrain II are perfectly uniform: all nouns except the last ($_8$good), where an adjective used in a predicative position acquires a noun-function. Quatrain III is an epitome of the rhyme-functions of the whole sonnet: the first and last rhyme-words are verbs, inverting the functions of the rhyme-words of the first and last stanzas of the whole poem, since we find in line 9 a present tense and in line 12 a past participle; the middle rhyme-words (lines 10–11) are adjectives, the second in a predicative position like the rhyme-word of line 8. The

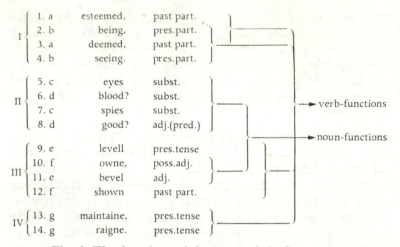

Fig. 6. The functions of rhyme-words in Sonnet 121

absolute balance of this arrangement and its significance are best seen in fig. 6.

In stanzas I and IV, then, the grammatical functions of the rhyme-words exactly match the arrangement of the rhyme-scheme. In stanza II they act as a constant ground bass to the alternating rhymes. In stanza III they create a counterpoint to it, supporting alternation with framing.

2.2. Finding a centre. Turning now to the unified logical and syntactical pattern, we find it a model of simplicity. Each metrical unit, or stanza, is a complete self-contained logical unit as well, with a different syntactical structure characterizing it. Stanza I is a double statement; stanza II a double question; stanza III is again a double statement, emphatical in the first two lines, with a dubitative note in the next two; stanza IV, the couplet, is a single hypothetical sentence. For the first three stanzas I mentioned double statements or double questions. This means that each of them is comprised of two sentences taking exactly two lines each and matching each other in syntactical and logical construction. I feel that it would be hard to find another poem where the binary structural principle is so punctiliously and effortlessly applied. The questions in stanza II are the direct consequence of the statements in stanza I, while the hypothetical sentence in stanza IV, opening with the word *Unless*, follows up directly the arguments advanced in stanza III. The stanzas therefore form two groups of two, each with a marked break after line 8. This corresponds precisely to the structure of the Petrarchan sonnet, with its division into an octave and a sestet. The whole movement of the octave builds up its sequence of indignant statements and questions towards a climax. This is reached in the exclamative statement in the first hemistich of line 9, 'No, I am that I am,' the logical and emotional centre of the poem. From that point on the sestet moves downward towards its ambiguous ending.

The centripetal movement of the octave is nicely balanced by the centrifugal movement of the sestet. As we already noticed in observing the semantic pattern of the poem (§ 1.4), the whole sonnet describes a perfect parabola from the ambiguity of the first line to the central cry of self-affirmation (line 9), to the more complex ambiguity of the final couplet. It very nearly ends where it began, but not quite, since in the process it has acquired a new wealth of experience, the sonnet itself being the experience—from impersonality to the recognition of individual subjective personality and back again, not to indiscriminate impersonality but to the consciousness of belonging to the very imperfect world of 'all men'. The structure, binary and based on the figure of antithesis, by beginning and ending on a note of ambiguity, establishes a perfect circularity of thought—and the circular verbal organism which is the poem finds its centre in the first hemistich of line 9, where the unambiguous repetition *I am . . . I am*, balances the two amphibolic repetitions of the outer circumference: *be vile . . . vile esteemed* in line 1, *bad . . . badness* in line 14. Alternatively, we can look at the sonnet as a see-saw, with the two repetitions in lines 1 and 14 as its two ends, and that in line 9 as the balancing-point.

2.3. The progress of pronouns. Before looking more closely at the central hub, the still point of the turning world of the sonnet—I am that I am—it is better to consider the movement of the two halves of the see-saw, and how it is suggested and achieved. I am not trying to make out that Shakespeare was the perfect engineer or mathematician, calculating at his drawing board the stresses and counter-stresses in the building he was going to put up for posterity—but he certainly was an architect of genius, who intuitively found the means to hold together harmoniously structures made up of contrasting materials. The see-saw effect communicated by the poem is achieved not only by the repetition of antithetical constructions in nearly every line or couplet, but also, and I should say principally, by the choice and placing throughout the sonnet of the pronouns and pronominal adjectives: *It, our, others', my, their, I, they*. There is a steady progress in their movement which seconds the logical progress of the sonnet itself, underlying the parabolic movement which I have discussed before (see § 2.2 above). Let us take each stanza in turn.

Quatrain I opens with the neuter pronoun in the third person singular—*'T*is, with the usual impersonal connotation; the starting-point is, then, a general statement of universal validity, referring to mankind at large, and the next three lines confirm this impersonal, nearly abstract tone: the only two pronominal expressions are found in the last of them, line 4, and are two possessive expressions: *our*, a plural which generalizes and de-personifies the individual experience, and *others'*, a pronoun in the genitive case with possessive value, which avoids the person-al implications of the adjectival 'their'. Quatrain I, then, is characterized by impersonality in the use of pronominal ex-pressions, and these are introduced with some caution, though a movement is indicated, from the neuter, utterly impersonal 'it' of the first line to the generalized possessive adjectives (*not* pronouns!) of the last.

Quatrain II starts where quatrain I left off: line 5 picks up the genitive (possessive) *others'* from the end of line 4 and counters it, this time, not with the general plural *our* but with the more specific singular *my* in line 6: the sequence of the possessives is inverted, and the poet takes advantage of this inversion to introduce for the first time the first person singular: but the approach to the individual personality of the 'I' is indirect: what is introduced is not the pronoun itself but its possessive adjective. The second half of the quatrain repeats the process with a new symmetrical inversion: line 7 picks up and repeats the *my* of line 6, but line 8 does not repeat mechanic-ally the impersonal genitive *others* from line 5, but substitutes it with something closer to 'my', the possessive adjective *their*, still generalized, still indirect, but a definite step forward in the direction of identification. What is more, in the very last hemistich of this quatrain, the real thing, the personal pronoun in the first person singular, the 'I' of the poet, finally makes its appearance. But it appears as yet unobtrusively, as the subject of a relative clause within the frame of an interrogative sentence: its syntactical placing prevents any emphatic power of statement. In the octave, then, the progression of the pronominal words has been as follows: $_1$It/$_4$our → $_4$others; $_5$others → $_6$my; $_7$my → $_8$their/$_8$I.

There is no doubt that, with the appearance of the 'I', we have reached the centre and the turning-point of the poem. The opening hemistich of quatrain III confirms it, most emphatically this time. The tentative questions asked in the previous quatrain (a 'merciful indirection', as Henry James would have said) are answered with a firm negative—No—, immediately followed by the thundering affirmative direct statement, *I am that I am.* The 'I' is, for a moment, utterly triumphant; we realize that the careful movement of the octave was a spiral progress by narrowing circumvallations (to borrow again from James) towards this central point of consciousness, the implications of which I propose to consider in the last section of this chapter. It was a constant centripetal motion underlined by the careful spacing and sequence of the personal pronouns. But the central point, as I said, is also a turning-point; once reached, the progression is over, the reverse process begins. It began, indeed, in the very same line (line 9), where the proud iteration of 'I' is tentatively (at first) counterbalanced in the second hemistich by the first appearance in the sonnet of the pronoun in the third person plural, *they*— the deuteragonist in this struggle between the one and the many, the individual and society, the poet's ego and common humanity. In line 10 the conflict is already reduced to that same level of possessive adjectives that we recorded in lines 7–8: *my* versus *their*. The stone hits the water, and after the impact the circles widen. The movement is centrifugal. Line 11 propounds a new direct statement, but (as we saw in § 1.2 above) the power of the initial *I* is weakened by the dubitative verbs (*may be*), and is contrasted in the second hemistich by the emphasis put on *they* by the reinforcing addition of the reflective *themselves*. Indeed, *I* is overpowered and will not appear again in the sonnet; its possessive adjective, *my*, in the very next line 12, is postponed, with a significant inversion, to its counterpart, *their*.

Inevitably, the centrifugal motion continues in stanza IV, the final couplet, a hypothetical sentence exalting the element of doubt which had emerged in the last two lines of the previous quatrain. The ripples become indistinct: no trace of the first person is left, the pronoun *they* appears in line 13 and is toned down to the adjective *their* in the last line—a possessive adjective which no longer refers, as in the octave, to the *others*, the common men different from and antagonistic to the dominating ego of the poet; its referent now is *all men*, the whole of undifferentiated humanity, by which that individual ego has been absorbed and obliterated.

2.4. The structural pattern.   What we are left with, as a testimony of the greatness of that poetic *I*, is a superb work of art, Sonnet 121. Its formal perfection is graphically represented by the structural pattern summarized in fig. 7.

3.0. The logic of meaning.   But the recognition of the formal perfection of this poetic structure (which could be confirmed by an analysis of the sound-pattern) would be nugatory if, to the impeccable logic of its semantic arrangement, did not correspond an equally compact logic of its meaning, when we place the sonnet within its social and ideological context. As a matter of fact, previous exegetical work on this sonnet has been directed mainly to extract the ethical meaning within the framework of Shakespeare's life and times; but I feel that its basic fallacy was that in so doing it overlooked the semantic and structural patterns in which such meaning was grounded. I shall try instead to repeat the search keeping in mind all the time what has been revealed by the formal organization which I examined: the antithetical union of the two worlds of the 'I' and the 'others', of reality and appearance; the progress from the impersonal to the individual and back to the general; and the movement from ambiguous statement through questioning to affirmation, and then back to doubt and a final hypothesis apparently rejected but subliminally accepted—accepted at least as the statement of a position that cannot be ignored or discounted.

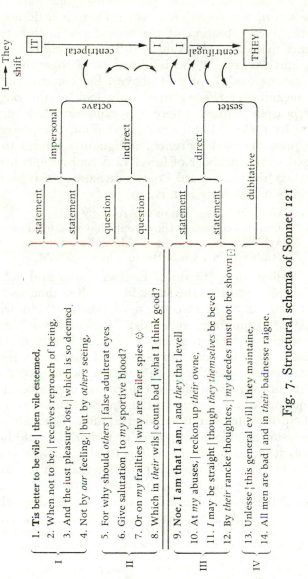

Fig. 7. Structural schema of Sonnet 121

3.1. Talbot's scorn.   The first line has suggested to many
critics a social context: the profession of the actor, with its
servile status, was considered 'vile'. There is little doubt that
the primary acceptation of the second *vile* in line 1 is with
reference to social rank. 'Vile' and 'base' are equivalent in this
sense, and we saw all the implications of 'base' and 'basest'
in Sonnet 94 (see chapter II above). For confirmation of the
basic meaning of *vile* we need only look at the only other
Shakespearian context where the expression 'vile esteemed'
occurs. In *1 Henry VI*, the valiant Talbot, overpowered and
taken prisoner by the French, indignantly refuses to be ex-
changed with a prisoner of lower rank and accepts his release
only when 'the brave Lord Ponton de Santrayle' is his ransom.
He relates to Salisbury in 1. iv. 29–32:

> But with a baser man of Armes by farre,
> Once in contempt they would have barter'd me:
> Which I disdaining, scorn'd, and craved death
> Rather then I would be so vild[13] esteem'd.

Brave Talbot, the paragon of English valour and nobility, at
whose heroic death on the stage in 1592 'ten thousand specta-
tors at least', in Nashe's words, 'new embalmed' him with their
tears,[14] is no quibbler on words; 'base' and 'vile' have only
one meaning for him: of low rank and low birth. Talbot's
scorn is born of his consciousness of belonging to a rigid hierarchical system—and thus is right within the context of a history
play celebrating the dynastic values and the embodiments of
national pride. But the subject of the Sonnets is not England,
but the private man and/or universal man. The scale of values
of the histories no longer applies; or rather, it would be wrong
to apply it to the new context. The trouble is that it *is* applied,
and Shakespeare in Sonnet 121 (or, for that matter, in Sonnet
94) is reacting to this. He is rebelling against the pinning-down
of human personality to man's position on a rigid social scale.[15]

---

[13] The quotation is from Folio, except for the universally accepted emendation
of the nonsensical reading *pil'd* into *vil'd*; all modern editors go further, adopting
Pope's spelling *vile-esteemed*, but I do not see any need for hyphenation.

[14] Th. Nashe, *Pierce Pennilesse his Supplication to the Divell* (1592), sig. H2.

[15] Cf. L. C. Knights, 'Shakespeare's Sonnets', p. 155; 'The sonnet is a protest
against the rigidly imposed moral scheme that the majority see fit to accept, a
protest on behalf of a morality based on the nature of the writer.' I find this an
excellent description of the octave of the sonnet—but I shall try to show that in
the sestet this alternative kind of morality is questioned in its turn.

So far so good: but it would be wrong to think that his reaction should be confined to the statement, 'since I am classed among the vile, let me actually *be* so'. This is putting the case on too personal a level, while it is clear that the greatest preoccupation of the first quatrain is that of stressing the impersonality of its statements. Even if it were demonstrated that the poet was thinking specifically of the stage-profession (we can accept this for the purposes of demonstration, but it is far from proven), his concern is with the ethical implications of the social definitions, and his attitude is that of turning to the higher rungs of the social ladder and of discovering there worse moral faults than those imputed to the lower *only because* they are lower. In other words, the poet is playing (in dead earnest) with two sub-codes at once, social and ethical, revealing a terminological confusion: where the social code considers 'vile' a certain class of people, the term is taken also to apply automatically on the moral level. The untruth of this assumption and its implications is shown in quatrain II, and the one way of getting over this ambiguity—reflected in the semantic pattern of the poem, where *vile* belongs both to the area of reality and to that of appearance—seems at first to be the substitution of the antithesis reality versus appearance, or rather, moral versus social, with a different antithesis: individual versus society, or, I versus others.

3.2. The lustful eyes.   Within this context, I have already pointed out (see § 1.3 above) the relevance of the 'frailties' of 'blood' in lines 6–7. Both words are placed in the I-area in a polemical effort to contrast the current morality which would condemn them (the frailty of the flesh, the erotic passion)— though according to the same false moral code, they are condoned when found among the 'others', the people of higher rank and birth. If this is kept in mind, it is possible to clear the difficulties that most critics have found in the first two quatrains of the sonnet. They have been disconcerted by two facts: (1) the multiplicity of possible interpretations of some words and lines, arising in some cases from the uncertainty about the referents of some specific terms (e.g. *so* in line 3); (2) the introduction of references to sexual ethics, beginning with *pleasure* in line 3 and becoming obvious in *sportive blood* in line 6. Lines 3–4 have been real cruces, since their syntactical and semantic organization can be decoded in at least three different ways: (a) we lose whatever honest (=just) gratification we may receive because it is considered vile (=so) not by the way we feel but according to the others' point of view (seeing = conventional morality) ; (b) we lose the pleasure of being honest (just pleasure = pleasure of justice) because in judging honesty we must submit not to our way of feeling about it, but to the others' way of looking at it (in this case the referent of *so* is *just pleasure*) ; (3) we lose that pleasure to which we are entitled (just = right), and which we consider just, because it is seen as vile (=so) by the others who judge by external appearances.

I do not see why these three basic interpretations—and all their possible combinations—cannot coexist and be accepted as all being valid at the same time. The two lines are deliberately semantically ambiguous because they want to communicate a moral ambiguity which remains unaltered whichever specific line of interpretation we choose to adopt. The basic contrast is between a 'pleasure' (whether of the senses or of the mind and feelings makes no difference) which is within reach of us, that is to say of Everyman, independent of social status—and a moral standard of judgement which is heavily conditioned by social prejudice. The implication is that this standard of judgement is not a real moral code, but merely a social code of behaviour. The operative word is *seeing*—not inner vision but external appearances. The sense of sight is emblematic of the lack of real vision. What the eyes see is merely the surface, the exterior.

Now, lines 3–8 are dominated by sight imagery: *seeing* in line 4, *eyes* in line 5, *spies* (with its voyeuristic implications) in line 7. And there is also a progression in the use of this imagery —always referring to the 'others', the cynical and apparently detached onlookers, from their assumed superior positions, of 'our' actions, like the privileged gentlemen in the lords' rooms of the public theatre. But the way of looking of the 'others' eyes' is not constant: there is a subtle shift of attitude in each pair of lines:

lines 3–4: the attitude is merely critical: the 'others' pass judgement on the 'pleasures' of their inferiors (like the 'unmoved movers' of Sonnet 94) applying their own exclusive code.

lines 5–6: the eyes of the others—who owing to their social status can afford to be thoroughly corrupt—hypocritically pretend to condone in their inferiors the sensual failings in which they themselves indulge. They maliciously 'salute'[16] them: the only kinship they acknowledge with the actor-poet is their common sexual indulgence. The adjectivation used, though, goes to show how indignantly Shakespeare rejects this suggestion of secret complicity in sin: the others' eyes are false and adulterate, that is, hypocritical and indiscriminately lecherous, while his blood, his sexual passion is 'sportive', the expression of irrepressible vitality. The scornful tone is similar to that of Talbot's speech, but while in *1 Henry VI* it was motivated by pride of place and military 'virtù', here it is transferred from the social to the ethical level. The poet can feel himself as much above the others morally, as they feel superior to him by reason of their rank. The confusion between the social and ethical codes is further exposed and deplored here, and the reference to the sexual domain, where such confusion is most common, appears particularly appropriate.

lines 7–8: The others' eyes, critical on the social level, maliciously conniving on a negative ethical level, reach an extremity of meanness—they spy on those frailties that they not only share, but exceed by far. In spite of the fact that 'frail' belongs, as we noticed, both to the THEY- and I- areas, the moral distinction made in the preceding two lines holds good. Actually it is further stressed in line 8, where 'bad' and 'good' are the two poles of morality. The action of spying is self-condemning, and here the perversion of the ethical code is complete: the despicable spies sit in judgement, and their scale of values is established not by an absolute moral code, but by 'their wills'. The choice of this last word (balancing 'my frailties' in the previous line) is carefully calculated to convey the arbitrariness of their criteria: not mind, the rational feeling, but will, the determination to exercise their superiority. Further, another current meaning of 'will', especially in Shakespeare

---

[16] I feel that, in spite of Landry's objection (op. cit., pp. 91 and 162) to a specifically sexual implication, *give salutation* here has the same value as Ann Boleyn's 'Salute my blood' in *Henry VIII*, II. iii. 103.

and more specifically in the Sonnets, is 'lust': the prying eyes which pretend to decide what is good or bad in what they see, are governed by their lusts.

Seeing → false adulterate eyes → frailer spies: through this imagery of sight, *They* have moved from the false assumption of the social for the ethical code, to the adulteration of the latter and finally to its application in reverse. The poet's defence consists in opposing to the corrupt social world that judges by perverted standards, his individual personality—No, I am that I am, comes at this point (line 9) as the only possible reaction, the rejection of the world of false appearances and values.

3.3. The new Machiavelli. The affirmation of the absolute and unrepeatable (and therefore undefinable) nature of the individual personality has one drawback. While exposing the falsity of ethical standards based on social superstructures, it does not provide a real alternative, a universally valid criterion of moral judgement. Hence the growing uneasiness in quatrain III, culminating in lines 11–12, whose ambiguity I have had occasion to point out more than once (see especially § 1.2 above). We need only consider the inverted semantic parallelism of the last lines of stanzas II and III, symmetrically placed on either side of the central point of the sonnet:

> 8. [they] count bad what I *think* good
> 12. By their rancke *thoughtes*, my deedes must not be shown

The process of 'thinking' is transferred from the I- to the THEY-area, from positive to negative, from *good* to *rank* (an epithet which invariably carries in Shakespeare a connotation of physical, mental, and moral corruption, with strong sexual overtones).[17] In other words, the very validity of thought is called in question: human thought does not provide a ratio of judgement. In the same way, when Rosencrantz denies that Denmark is a prison, Hamlet replies:

> Why then 'tis none to you; for there is nothing either good or bad, but thinking makes it so: to me it is a prison. (II. ii. 255–7)

And this leads him to talk of ambition and the unreality of earthly greatness, the paradoxical conclusion being that beggars

---

[17] The clearest example is Posthumus' speech against woman in *Cymbeline*, II. iv. 24: 'Lust, and ranke thoughts, hers, hers'. See Interchapter, § 2 below.

are bodies while monarchs are only beggars' shadows. Like all
Shakespeare's paradoxes, this one also, pronounced by Hamlet
acting the fool, is an essential truth: the only reality is the body,
while the privilege of rank is mere appearance, and the subjective human mind contemplating both is incapable of objective discrimination between reality and appearance as well
as between good and bad.

The parallelism by opposition between lines 8 and 12 that
I have just noted (think/thoughts) is repeated, along an outer
circle, in the parallelism by anagram of lines 1 and 13: vile/evil
—'vile' was still ambiguous, being operative within two separate
codes at once, the social and the ethical in sharp contrast with
each other; in line 13 this saving ambivalence which left room
for debate, or even mystification, is denied—the moment 'vile'
is transformed into 'evil', it allows only one interpretation: the
ethical code condemns it. With this subliminal pun, the poet
has burnt his last bridge.

The final couplet of the sonnet sees the complete disappear-
ance of the individual personality, absorbed in the indiscriminate community of 'all men' (see §§ 1.3 and 2.3 above). I have
described this as an unconscious process of reabsorption, since,
ostensibly, the poet is merely expressing, in hypothetical form,
a position different from and possibly diametrically opposed
to his own: not I, but they maintain 'this general evil'.

Once again I must turn to the thorough and perceptive
commentary of Hilton Landry, who takes for granted the latter
position. After his remarks on the reading of 'reign', which I
discussed in § 1.3 above, he concludes:

there is no place in Shakespeare's range of values for a kind of
cynicism that Elizabethans associated with the realistic Machiavelli:
'whoever desires to found a state and give it laws, must start with
assuming that all men are bad [rei = guilty], and ever ready to
display their vicious nature [usare la malignità dello animo loro =
lit. use the badness of their minds], whenever they may find occasion
for it'.[18]

It is true that Shakespeare almost certainly had no direct
knowledge of Machiavelli's *Discourses on the first ten books of
Livy*, whence the quotation comes, and that in *Love's Labour's*

[18] H. Landry, op. cit., pp. 95-6.

Lost he seems to make fun of Raleigh and the other English Machiavellians;[19] but the evidence of the history plays, of crowd-behaviour in *Julius Caesar* and *Coriolanus*, of 'they that have power' in Sonnet 94 and in the great tragedies, points to the fact that he was fully aware of the implications of these doctrines. The cynicism is not inherent in them but in their application as the foundations of 'policy', in the exercise of power. Shakespeare may reject Machiavellian policy, but must take the doctrine itself into account when considering man's ethical predicament. This is what he does in the closing couplet of Sonnet 121: after exploring the possibility of establishing an ethic of utter individuality, and finding it unsatisfactory, he reverts to the ethics of social behaviour. Within its domain one proposition stands out, and he offers it as an opinion that cannot be ignored: all men are bad and prevail through their badness. This is the alternative to the affirmation 'I am that I am'. Shakespeare does not make a choice; he simply puts the alternative before us, and suggests that there is no third way out of the dilemma. He does not state this in so many words. The renunciation of the individualistic third way is perhaps not even fully conscious: it emerges very clearly, though, from the structural patterns we examined before. As I. A. Richards said apropos of another sonnet of Shakespeare's,[20] the analysis of the formal features of a poem may result (is meaningful if it results) in the identification of its subliminal structures. The most obvious structure of this kind in Sonnet 121 is the parabolic movement from the impersonal through the highly individual to the anonymous and inclusive 'all men'; from an ambiguous statement through a shrill affirmation to an open doubt. The poet's function is not that of solving problems, but of apprehending and communicating them imaginatively. This is what Sonnet 121 does: in the octave it exposes and clears away the confusion between social and ethical values; in the sestet it restates the contradictions and tensions met in the attempt to reconcile the social and ethical spheres.

[19] See the commentaries on *Love's Labour's Lost*, iv. iii; and for Machiavelli see M. Praz, 'The Politic Brain: Machiavelli and the Elizabethans', in *The Flaming Heart* (New York, 1958), pp. 90–145; F. Raab, *The English Face of Machiavelli* (London, 1964); and N. W. Bawcutt, 'Some Elizabethan Allusions to Machiavelli', *English Miscellany*, xx (1969), pp. 53–74.

[20] I. A. Richards, 'Jakobson's Shakespeare'.

3.4. Shakespeare's God. I have been moving all the time back and forth through the sonnet from end to end, or round and round its circumference and its several concentric circles. I have passed and repassed by and over its central point, but have never really stopped there. I have merely spoken of a loud, proud, shrill affirmation of utter individualism. What makes one wary in approaching what is undoubtedly its centre is the identity of the sentence 'I am that I am' with the famous verse of Exodus 3:14: 'And God answered Moses: I AM THAT I AM', as the Geneva Bible translated it. Those five words are the very name of God, the Being,[21] Jehovah, the existing one. Even if the most recent tendency is to discount this as mere coincidence, it seems necessary to look more closely at the implications of Shakespeare's use of the expression. As representative of two widely diverging critical attitudes towards this central point of the poem, we can take the comments of Stephen Spender and of Hilton Landry.

Spender[22] paraphrases: 'But whatever I do I remain what I am and therefore my deeds may not be twisted to make me look as if I am the same as they'. And comments:

One has the sense of concentric circles of bad and less bad, the outer circle of which is the proposition 'all men are bad'. But at the center of all, that which maintains him is 'No, I am that I am', the final inviolable fortress of an awareness of his own being, separate from the actions which he shares with all, and therefore not at all to be condemned or fixed down by others' opinion because forever escaping into unscathed, ever-renewed, and renewing existence.

This position has many points in common with the one I have been outlining, but I would question the inviolability of the fortress of 'being': it does not take into account the centrifugal movement which is so obvious in the rest of the sestet, by which it appears that the 'I' cannot help 'sharing' with all

---

[21] Vulgate, 'Ego sum qui sum'; I am aware that the real meaning of the scriptural words is somewhat different, 'indicating', as R. Young says in his *Analytical Concordance*, 'rather the *unsearchableness* of God, than his mere *existence*, as commonly supposed'; but what matters is the interpretation current at the time, which identified the sentence with 'my name is Jehovah', in Exodus 6:3. Compare as well the opposition *Being/I* versus *not being or seeming/others or they* in Sonnet 94, discussed in chapter II.

[22] S. Spender, 'The Alike and the Other', pp. 108–9.

men, that the fortress is not really a fortress, but a mirage, a momentary delusion of security, or, like Kafka's castle, a place to get lost in. Spender goes on to speak of Shakespeare's aristocratic view of life, meaning by Aristocracy 'original being which has purity and integrity'. This I believe is true, but it means merely a recognition of the wrongness of social distinctions— and the awareness that such distinctions have brought corruption and maintain it by confusing ethical values with the position in the social scale. This is why Shakespeare can speak of 'this vile world';[23] on the other hand, the individualistic position is untenable because in its attempt to reject the false values imposed by an unjust social hierarchy, it ignores the true community of being, of all men, which is a 'general evil' only because of the artificial, adulterate standards of judgement superimposed on it. To affirm one's private individuality is to identify oneself with an abstract Being, instead of true mankind —is an escape into Godhead, a desertion of Man. And we know that Man and his nature is always the centre of Shakespeare's poetic world.

It is significant that the only characters in Shakespeare's plays who pronounce similar statements, shutting themselves up in the fortress of their individuality, are either haters and destroyers of men, like the inhuman and deformed monster, the Duke of Gloucester, the future Richard III, who towards the end of *3 Henry VI* (v. vi. 83) exclaims: 'I am myself alone', or despicable, subhuman windbags, like the ineffectual liar Parolles who says (*All's Well*, IV. iii. 369): 'Simply the thing I am shall make me live.' Both place themselves outside humanity, against and below it.[24]

In the plays Shakespeare had to be outspoken and direct, suiting the action to the word, the word to the action, and not overstepping the modesty of nature. In the sonnets written for careful perusal he could afford to be subtler and more cryptic, for his own sake even more than for that of his 'under-

[23] In Sonnet 71, line 4; cf. *Antony and Cleopatra*, v. ii. 317, and see chapter IV, § 0.2 below.

[24] Is it at all significant that Mr. Jones, the villain in Conrad's *Victory*, says of himself 'I am he who is'? Conrad's ethical stand is more truly Christian than Shakespeare's: the title of the novel refers to the Pauline doctrine, 1 Corinthians 15:52–6 (O grave, where is thy victory?), which I shall discuss with reference to Shakespeare's Sonnet 146 in chapter V, § 1.4 below.

standing readers'. Instead of placing a declaration of individualism (and selfishness) on the lips of inhuman villains, he words
it in biblical terms, repeating the formula that expresses the
name of God. Whether the adoption of this particular wording
was conscious or subliminal makes little difference: what
matters is the placing of individualism once again outside
humanity—this time not against or below it, but *above*. Whether
this use of the name of God reflects Shakespeare's conception
of Godhead, is too early to discuss.

We must turn rather to the other current attitude towards
the central statement of Sonnet 121—bent on playing down
its metaphysical implications. The attitude is exemplified by
Hilton Landry's comments.[25] He objects to those readers who
'are led by the Biblical context of "I am that I am" to see it
as a proud declaration of absolute freedom in which Shakespeare announces that, like God, he is a law unto himself, or,
in Wilson Knight's phrase, "beyond good and evil"'. Of
course, the position here suggested is an extreme one; I have
been at pains to point out that, if the biblical reference is
deliberate, it is there not as a statement to be appropriated by
the poet, but rather as a warning against losing touch with
humanity. Landry's objection, however, is on quite different
lines:

If it is a kind of declaration of independence, it is also moderate
and relative, perhaps no more than the condensed equivalent of,
I know what I am far better than my slanderers do, and my standards are different from and probably higher than theirs, hence their
accusations are irrelevant and unwarranted.

I find this too much of an anticlimax after the build-up in
the octave; Landry is treating the sonnet as if it were a logical
continuum from the first to the last line, so that for him line 9
is merely a link in the chain: the most elementary structural
analysis reveals instead a progressive–regressive pattern that
places a very heavy emphasis on that line, and an arrangement
of the various members of the sonnet functional to this central
statement. Landry speaks of 'condensed equivalent', but does
not seem to realize the psychological connotation of the adjective he is using: condensation is a single unconscious repre-

sentation, the concentrated expression of the point of intersection of several chains of associations; he is following instead
only one associative process, and, in my opinion, not the most
relevant.

It must be acknowledged, though, that Landry produces at
least two apparently solid pieces of evidence in support of his
restrictive interpretation. One is that, unlike Crookback and
Parolles, Shakespeare's arch-villain, Iago, reverses completely
the statement contained in the sonnet; underlining the difference between his appearance ('my outward action') and his real
nature ('the native act and figure of my heart') Iago states
(*Oth.* i. i. 15): 'I am not what I am'. But this frank admission
by Iago of his duplicity is in its turn a trap to catch Roderigo
and make him subservient to his evil designs. He is merely
saying that he is wearing a disguise like Viola disguised as
Cesario, who uses an identical phrase in the course of a banter-
ing exchange with Olivia, who, deceived by her masculine
attire, has fallen in love with her (*Twelfth Night* iii. i. 155). The
negative use of the sentence is just an ironical play on a common
stage-situation, not an attempt by the speaker to set himself
or herself apart from the rest of mankind. This is instead
emphatically the case with the affirmative use of the sentence
by Richard, which I quoted before:

> And this word (Love) which Gray-beards call Divine,
> Be resident in men like one another,
> And not in me: I am my selfe alone.[26]

On the whole it can be said that Iago's (and Viola's) negative
version of the statement is irrelevant to its understanding.

The second analogue, suggested by Landry, deserves closer
attention, since it is, as Landry says, 'a more obvious gloss on
the assertion' contained in line 9 of the sonnet. This is an
untitled forty-line poem by Sir Thomas Wyatt, not published
during the sixteenth century, but circulating in manuscript.[27]
What matters is not whether Shakespeare knew it or not, but
rather the fact that its subject and mood seem, at first sight,

[26] *3 Henry VI*, v. vi. 81–3; Iago, on the other hand, in the lines immediately
preceding his statement, has just been saying: 'These Fellowes have some soul, /
And such a one do I professe my selfe', identifying himself with the *others*.

[27] It is only included in the Devonshire MS; see Wyatt, *Collected Poems*, ed. K.
Muir (London, 1949).

perfectly coincidental with those of Sonnet 121—so that it could be said that the latter is, after all, only a repetition of a poetical commonplace: let people say what they like, and judge me as they wish, I will not change my nature for that. The poem is too long to be quoted in full, but here are the most relevant quatrains:

> I am as I am and so wil I be,
> But how that I am none knoith trulie,
> Be yt evill, be yt well, be I bonde, be I free,
> I am as I am and so will I be.
> . . .
> Dyvers so judge as theye doo troo,
> Some of plesure and some of woo,
> Yet for all that no thing theye knoo,
> But I am as I am where so ever I goo.
>
> But sins judgers do thus dekaye,
> Let everye man his judgement saye;
> I will yt take yn sporte and playe,
> For I am as I am whoso ever saye naye.
> . . .
> Yet some there be that take delight
> To judge folkes thought for envye and spight
> But whyther theye judge me wrong or right,
> I am as I am and so do I wright.
>
> Prayeng you all that this doo rede
> To truste yt as you do your crede,
> And not to think I change my wede,
> For I am as I am howe ever I spede.
> . . .

There is no doubt that, at the conceptual level, Sonnet 121 is modelled on the same lines and is meant to express the same attitude. But the tighter form of the sonnet in comparison with Wyatt's loose sequence of quatrains, makes for compression, which means (on the next, the psychological level) condensation: the associations connected with human individuality, with the judicial faculties, with the ethical standards, with thinking and knowing, with appearance and reality, are not treated serially, as in Wyatt's poem, but packed into a single representation. This, at first, obscures and confuses the meanings by compounding them: censorship (in psychological terms) has intervened to push down to a deeper level of consciousness those arguments that Sir Thomas Wyatt enunciated in a care-free mood. Writing more than half a century later, when social consciousness had matured through a sequence of historical events that were transforming the religious and economic foundations of English society, Shakespeare could not share that mood. He was consciously appropriating a theme belonging to the lyrical poetry which had been produced by an aristo-cratic cultural élite; he was an outsider, a middle-class actor-poet using literary forms of expression outside and above his social range—poaching in the preserves of Sir Thomas Wyatt, the Earl of Surrey, Sir Philip Sidney, the initiators of the sonnet vogue in England.[28] Surely, the anecdote about deer-poaching in Sir Thomas Lucy's park at Charlecote, is not simply apocryphal but emblematic of Shakespeare's early liter-ary activities. Shakespeare was overstepping an age-old barrier —I discussed this when speaking of Stephen Spender's remarks on the poet's aristocratic view of life—and it meant that he must be cautious, it meant setting up all his mental defence mechanisms. What on the psychological level is censorship and condensation, becomes, on the aesthetic level, pregnancy—not a loss but a gain in formal ordering and in meaningfulness—indeed, the very core of Empson's notion of poetic ambiguity. The process of compression becomes a generative process: whatever Dr. Johnson might have thought of it, what he called the yoking-together of heterogeneous ideas—ideas that the traditional or enlightened poet would have merely arranged in a correct sequence, developing each one with the appropriate figures of simile, comparison, etc.—is in fact a *coupling-together*. They fertilize each other, and the result is not merely their sum, it is something more and something new.

This is the fundamental difference in the treatment of the same theme by Wyatt and Shakespeare. The intervening his-torical and social factors, and their psychological corollaries, have brought about a radical reconsideration of the theme itself, and therefore its transformation into something much richer and more strange. Eliot would perhaps have spoken of tradition and individual talent—but Shakespeare's genius is

[28] See my discussion of this point in chapter I, § 2 above.

certainly motivated also by the consciousness of historical
change. And Sonnet 121 becomes the exploration of the ethics
of social behaviour in a new context: Wyatt could discount the
judgement of the others because they were at most his equals,
if not his inferiors—Shakespeare, on the other hand, must
question judges who are socially his superiors by reference to
the condition of the individual and of humanity as a whole.

It is within this context that we must consider why Shakespeare has chosen to echo precisely the biblical words, I AM
THAT I AM, rather than use the more natural expressions
'I am *what* I am' (cf. Iago) or 'I am *as* I am' (cf. Wyatt). The
latter expressions allow of only one meaning each: (a) I am
the thing I am, (b) I am made like that, both boiling down
to 'there is no way of changing my nature, good, bad, or in-
different as it may be, since I am an individual in my own
right' (cf. Richard's 'I am myself alone'). Now, this paraphrase
could apply also to the wording in Sonnet 121, but only as
one of several coexisting and co-active meanings. Indeed, the
primary sense of the phrase in the biblical context is quite
different. We remember that Moses had asked of his God: 'if
they [the Israelites] say unto me, What is his Name? what
shall I say unto them?' And after replying, the voice from the
burning bush had added: 'Thus shalt thou say unto the children
of Israel, I AM hath sent me unto you'. So the reply means:
'My name is I AM', with its corollaries: 'I am the one who is,
the Being, the Existing one'. Or again, 'My name is ineffable,
I have no name, what counts is the fact that I exist'.

In Sonnet 121, by adopting the identical phrase,[29] the poet
is in the first place communicating the fact of his existence,
of his being a 'being', before stating that he is an individual.
By using 'that' instead of 'what' or 'as' he stresses not (or not
primarily) the individuality of his nature, but rather the fact
that man exists *in so much as* (=that) he exists. The statement
acts on at least two semantic levels at once: (1) in a limited

[29] According to Rollins (New Variorum *Sonnets*, i, p. 306) the phrase is found in
this form (with *THAT* instead of *what* or *as*) only in two non-religious writers:
Lyly's *Euphues* (1578), ed. Bond (1902), i, p. 294, and in *Philotimus, or The Warre
betwixt Nature and Fortune*, by Brian Melbancke (1583), sig. B3v. But both authors
use it in direct scriptural quotations, Lyly in Euphues' reply to Atheos' objections,
Melbancke with reference to God, 'whose name is in Scripture I am that I am
(so incomprehensible in his maiestie)'.

sense, it implies that man exists *only* in so far and so long as he
lives; (2) as sharing God's name, man is equated with God,
and vice versa, God's and man's natures are identified. Shakespeare has moved a long way beyond Wyatt's simple notion,
'my nature is just what it is, take it or leave it'. The choice of the
scriptural wording may have been instinctive, the reminiscence
of a well-known text, but it is no less significant for that, and
testifies to Shakespeare's awareness of the pregnancy of language.

We are left now with the fact that, consciously or subliminally, the phrase 'I am that I am', with the implicit semantic
polarity I have mentioned, poses the question of man's relation
to Godhead or, reversing the terms, of justifying the ways of
God to man. It is unthinkable that the mention of the biblical
ineffable name was introduced into the sonnet as a kind of
flippant in-joke—the tone of the whole poem, earnest and
searching even in its irony, does not allow it. Now, the relation
established is that both 'I' and God find our identity in the
fact of Being—I in physical, God in metaphysical terms. The
very ineffability of His Name emphasizes the abstract nature of
His Existing. God is an abstract concept, above man and
utterly separate from him—not the comforting Presence, the
providential principle, but the idea of Godhead. It is significant
that in the plays the word 'God' is not very frequent, and it
occurs nearly always in set phrases, such as 'God forbid', 'God
bless', etc. that have lost their real meaning.[30] When Shakespeare wants to refer to metaphysical entities he speaks of the
pagan gods or the 'powers above'; and the contexts where these
appear are at times disturbing:

> As flies to wanton boys are we to th'Gods,
> They kill us for their sport. (*Lear* IV. i. 37–8)

[30] Cf. R. M. Frye, *Shakespeare and Christian Doctrine* (Princeton, 1963), p. 165:
'Most of these [references to God in Shakespeare's plays] are virtual clichés,
ranging from conventional piety to conventional expletive'. There was, of course,
an excellent reason for not mentioning the name of God in plays, more precisely
the Act of Parliament of 1606 'for the preventing and avoiding of the great abuse
of the holy name of God in stage plays', which fixed a fine of £10 for every such
mention, half of which would go to the informer; G. E. Bentley (*The Profession
of Dramatist* etc., p. 183) shows that the variants between the 1622 Quarto and the
Folio text of *Othello* are mainly concerned with the omission or substitution of
God', 'Lord', or even 'Zounds', so that, e.g., at v. ii. 270, 'O God, O heavenly
God. Zouns, hold your peace', becomes 'Oh Heaven! oh heavenly Powers! Come,
hold your peace.'

Edgar's final words of comfort to Gloucester facing death, 'Ripeness is all' (v. ii. 11), oppose to the aloofness of the cruel powers above, man's maturity reached through his suffering.[31]

If there is Godhead, it is inside man himself. The identification of I–Everyman with the name of God in Sonnet 121 confirms the centrality of man in Shakespeare's universe; man with his goodness and badness, even Parolles, Crookback or Iago. This is not a matter of religious belief; Shakespeare never denies the metaphysical level. But he finds it not in an abstract empyrean, but within man himself—as Spirit, the animating principle in Sonnet 129, or as his 'poor Soul' in Sonnet 146. Shakespeare's God is the man within.

Excursus: The geometry of iteration—a note to § 3.3.   I should perhaps try to use to some purpose the lexical code of geometry I have employed here—though I confess that I offer this more in the spirit of a concluding *burletta* than as serious exegesis.

In geometrical terms, what I called the centre of the sonnet is actually eccentrical, coming, as it does, in line 9, well beyond the middle of the poem and belonging only to the I-area; its eccentricity is further emphasized by the fact that the only other iterative unit in the sonnet that could balance 'I am . . . I am' in the opposite THEY-area, establishing some kind of symmetry, is 'bad . . . badness' in the very last line.

Also, the two circles I mentioned—the inner one whose circumference is marked by the repetition of the same root in $_8$*think* and $_{12}$*thoughts*, and the outer one characterized by the anagrammatic repetition of $_1$*vile* and $_{13}$*evil*—are not concentrical, though the first is internal to the second. None the less their study is not unrewarding, since it reveals that their respective centres are the only two other iterative expressions in the sonnet, apart from those I have already mentioned. I take of course the centre of each circumference to be in the middle line of verse between the two touched by the circumference itself; in other words, considering the lines of the poem as a series of parallel straight geometrical lines, four of them will

---

[31] The subject has been treated exhaustively and with full documentation in W. R. Elton's admirable book, *King Lear and the Gods*. His conclusions are naturally much more complex and discriminating, but my oversimplification here substantially agrees with them; for amplification see chapter IV, § 2.2 below.

be tangents to the two postulated circumferences, while two more will coincide with their respective diameters.

Taking first the inner circumference, whose tangents are line 8 (containing *think* in the I-area) and line 12 (containing *thoughts* in the THEY-area), we find that its diameter, parallel with the two tangents, is line 10: this contains in its first hemistich *my abuses*, while in its second hemistich, though the word *abuses* is not repeated, it is clearly understood as the referent of *their own*, so that 'abuses' belongs both to the I- and the THEY-areas (see the schema in § 1.4 above). It could therefore be maintained that the central position of 'abuses' in respect of the references to 'thinking' confirms the argument I have developed in § 3.3., on the non-validity of thought, which abuses and deceives the human mind and nullifies ethical judgement.

Now for the outer circumference: its tangents are line 1 (containing the iteration *vile . . . vile* in both the I- and the THEY-area), and line 13 (containing *evil*, the anagram of 'vile', which, as defined by the attribute *general*, belongs to both areas at once). The diameter parallel with these tangents is line 7, where we find the iteration of the root 'frail', with *frailties* in the I-area and *frailer* in the THEY-area. Also in this case I could refer to the discussion in § 3.3., adding that the transition from the social/ethical ambiguity in the evaluation of 'vileness' to the final moral condemnation in 'general evil', is justified by the central position of the human 'frailties': it is through their presence in Everyman that a false judgement confusing social and ethical values becomes generally true.

As for the oblique line adjoining the two iterations *I am . . . I am* in the I-area of line 9, and *bad . . . badness* in the THEY-area of line 14, it will be noticed that it intersects the vertical dividing line between the two areas at the middle point of line 12, and is a secant of both circumferences. This could be taken as a confirmation that: (a) line 12 is transitional between the affirmative tone of line 9 and the negative conclusion, as demonstrated in §§ 1.2 and 1.3; it is remarkable that line 11, contrasting *straight* and *bevel* (= oblique), reflects on the lexical level the geometrical pattern I have been delineating, with the appropriate mathematical terminology; (b) the movement in the sestet from positive to negative cuts across and links together the two semantic patterns I illustrated, concerned with human thought and judgement, and with the evil born of the confusion between social and ethical values.

So, for the edification of those who like to think of the poet as a mathematician, here is a final schema (fig. 8).

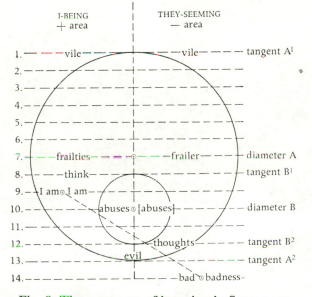

Fig. 8. The geometry of iteration in Sonnet 121

LOVE'S USE AND MAN'S HUES
IN SONNET 20

0. Spirit and Soul. Sonnet 121 is the one Shakespearian poem mentioning, albeit in cryptic form, the name of the God of the Old Testament—I am that I am—. Shakespeare's God is rather a pervasive principle in a man-centered universe; Shakespeare had no difficulty in accepting the current belief in the coexistence within the human frame of the mortal, the immortal, and the animating parts: body, and soul, and spirit— the latter being the vital agency. Soul and spirit are plurisignificant terms, and Shakespeare explores and exploits all the nuances of meaning in them. He contrasts them in turn to the body, as being the better or the nobler part of man. It is interesting to consider briefly some contexts in the few Sonnets where the words are used. The most impressive occurrence of 'spirit' is in Sonnet 74:

> When thou revewest this [poem], thou doest revew,
> The very part was consecrate to thee,
> The earth can have but earth, which is his due,
> My spirit is thine the better part of me,
> So then thou hast but lost the dregs of life,
> The pray of wormes, my body being dead, [. . .] (lines 5–10)

With its startling parallel in Ronsard rather than in Ovid:

> Je vous consacre icy le plus gaillard de moy,
> L'esprit de mon esprit, qui vous fera revivre [. . .]¹

---

¹ See J. B. Leishman, *Themes and Variations in Shakespeare's Sonnets* (London, 1961), p. 61. The relationship between body, soul, and spirit is most clearly set out in a fairly popular book which Shakespeare must have known, since he echoed it more than once in his plays and sonnets; see M. I. O'Sullivan, 'Hamlet and Dr. Timothy Bright', *PMLA*, xli. 3 (1926), pp. 667–79, and J. Dover Wilson, 'Shakespeare's Knowledge of *A Treatise of Melancholie* by Timothy Bright', published as Appendix E to his *What Happens in Hamlet* (Cambridge, 1965). Bright's *A Treatise of Melancholie*, published twice in 1586 and reprinted as late as 1613, announces in its lengthy title the inclusion of 'diverse philosophicall discourses touching actions, and affections of soule, spirit, and body'; the spirit is compared to the

Here *spirit*, though identifiable at first sight with *soul*, the immortal part, is a much more complex spiritual principle, the place where poetry originates; it goes beyond death not as an immortal entity, but as a projection of man's creative faculty. In this sense *spirit* is used also in the 'rival poet' sonnets (nos. 80, 85, 86); but elsewhere it is the equivalent of the inspirational agents, Good and Evil, Angel and Devil; for instance, in Sonnet 144, the spirits represent the two aspects of Love:

> Two loves I have of comfort and dispaire,
> Which like two spirits do sugiest me still, (lines 1–2)

Spirit is an intellectual faculty that can transfigure the apprehensions of the senses and outlive them, as well as condition one's ethical behaviour.

In the same way, *Soul* is not just the eternal and undecaying part of man. For instance, in Sonnet 107 it is *anima mundi*, the collective consciousness of mankind, 'the prophetic soul / Of the wide world'—in contrast with Hamlet's individual 'prophetic soul' (I. v. 40), which is his faculty to penetrate beyond the world of present reality. Indeed, the soul is one of the many 'parts' or faculties with which man is endowed, as in two of the sonnets addressed to a woman—nos. 136 and 151. It is surprising to find that these sonnets (two of the few in which the soul is mentioned) are among the bawdiest in the collection; in them, the most prominent other 'parts' of the human frame are, most emphatically, the male and female sexual organs, the punning *wills* of Sonnet 136:

> If thy soule checke thee that I come so neere,
> Sweare to thy blind soule that I was thy *Will*,
> And will thy soule knowes is admitted there, (lines 1–3)

or more openly, without even the conniving disguise of the pun, in Sonnet 151:

hand of the workman or of the musician, which moves the saw or the axe, or touches the lute (the workman or musician being the soul, the instrument the body); and the mutual relationship of body, spirit, and soul is defined in chapter IX (T. Bright, *A Treatise of Melancholie*, reproduced from the 1586 edition . . . with an introduction by Hardin Craig (New York, 1940), pp. 37–8): 'So then these three we have in our nature to consider distinct, for the clearer understanding of that I am to intreat of: the bodie of earth: the spirit from vertue of that spirit, that did as it were hatch that great egge of Chaos: & the soul inspired from God, a nature eternall and divine, not fettered with the bodie, as certaine Philosophers have taken it: but hand-fasted therwith, by the golden claspe of the spirit.'

For thou betraying me, I do betray
My nobler part to my grose bodies treason,
My soule doth tell my body that he may,
Triumph in love, flesh staies no farther reason,
But rising at thy name doth point out thee,
As his triumphant prize, proud of this pride, (lines 5–10)

In a sonnet addressed to the 'lovely boy' (no. 62), the balance of the 'parts' is altered:

Sinne of selfe-love possesseth al mine eie,
And all my soule, and al my every part;

The parallelism of *eye* and *soul* is more deliberate in the central and most puzzling lines of that extraordinary Sonnet 20 which Leslie Fiedler[2] sees as the crucial expression of Shakespeare's conception of the ambivalent Eros, the two 'spirits' of Sonnet 144 rolled into one:

A man in hew all *Hews* in his controwling,
Which steales mens eyes and womens soules amaseth.

---

[2] I wish to record my agreement with Fiedler's brilliant treatment ('Some Contexts of Shakespeare's Sonnets', *The Riddle of Shakespeare's Sonnets*, pp. 55–90) of the conceptual background of the Sonnets, starting with the two (138 and 144) published in *The Passionate Pilgrim*, and culminating in Sonnet 20; he rehandles the theme more briefly in his book *The Stranger in Shakespeare* (London, 1973), pp. 21–7. It is more difficult to follow him when he considers Sonnets 129 and 146 as 'a denial of love and joy' (see chapter IV, § 0.1 below), while W. H. Auden (in the already quoted introduction to the Signet edition, pp. xxix) adopts a similar approach to Sonnet 20 as 'the Vision of Eros', but overstresses the mystical aspects of the experience. Another poet-critic, Pier Paolo Pasolini ('Come Shakespeare vedeva il rapporto fra uomo e potere', *Tempo*, xxxv. 41 (14 October 1973), pp. 86–7), reviewing the present book in an earlier Italian version, reproves the author for underplaying or 'removing' the role of Shakespeare's Eros in the Sonnets. On a different level, the bawdy innuendos in Sonnets 144 and 151 have suggested to John Bayley the novel notion that the 'he' mentioned by the poet there as well as in 133 and 134 is not the 'friend' but, to use his words, the poet's '*membrum virile*, the Shakespearian penis in fact' (J. Bayley, 'Who was the "Man Right Fair" of the Sonnets?' *TLS*, 4 January 1974, p. 15; and see the *TLS* correspondence columns in the two following months, including John Sparrow's amusingly ribald suggestion for a reading of Milton's most famous sonnet, and Bayley's reply to Dame Helen Gardner, 15 February 1974). The evidence of Sonnet 151 (containing no mention of or allusion to the 'man right fair', but only of the lady to whom the poet's 'body' pays the obvious sexual compliments) cannot be used at all in the other three cases, where the love-triangle, with its sexual innuendos, is unquestionable. Bayley's *jeu d'esprit* (which I suspect was inspired by Alberto Moravia's latest novel at the time, *Io e lui*, where the 'he' is indeed the writer's own penis) may be taken as a warning for latter-day sonnet biographists, such as R. J. C. Wait and A. L. Rowse, whose recent labours are not mentioned here as irrelevant to the subject of the present book.

Here women's souls are something different from their 'parts';
they are in fact much closer to the 'spirits' of Sonnet 144, a
poem in which Shakespeare was elaborating on the view of
woman as the weaker vessel. He would not go as far as to
repeat the common saw, 'women have no souls',[3] but he would
certainly subscribe at this stage to Drayton's definition of
woman in the last line of *Idea*, Sonnet 20:

> this good wicked Spirit, sweet Angell Devill.[4]

Soul and *spirit* seem to share this polarity of good and evil,
especially through their connection and confrontation with
love. It is important to establish Shakespeare's view of love,
since love in its different aspects is a conditioning factor of his
ethical world. Beside Drayton's, I have also mentioned Shakespeare's Sonnet 20: the central lines I quoted are its core of
meaning, but they make sense only when seen within the context of the whole poem:[5]

1. A womans face | with natures owne hand painted
2. Haste thou ¦ the Master Mistris ¦ of my passion
3. A womans gentle hart | but not acquainted
4. With shifting change | as is false womens fashion,

5. An eye more bright ¦ then theirs, | lesse false in rowling;
6. Gilding the obiect | where-upon it gazeth,
7. A man in hew | all *Hews* ¦ in his controwling,
8. Which steales mens eyes | and womens soules amaseth.

9. And for a woman | wert thou first created,
10. Till nature ¦ as she wrought thee | fell a dotinge,
11. And by addition | me of thee defeated,
12. By adding one thing | to my purpose nothing.

[3] See M. P. Tilley, *A Dictionary of the Proverbs in England in the Sixteenth and Seventeenth Centuries* (Ann Arbor, 1950), item W709.

[4] This sonnet, first printed in the 1599 edition of *Idea*, and therefore later than Shakespeare's, is very closely connected with Shakespeare's no. 144—a poem so well known and circulated by that date as to be included in *The Passionate Pilgrim*. A comparison between the two is instructive: they are built with the same linguistic materials, having no less than 24 different words in common, some of which, like 'Spirit', 'Angel', 'Devil'; 'Evil', 'tempt', Despair', 'good', 'ill', are highly signifi-cant; they share some rhyme-words—despair[s], still, ill, evil, devil; and line 1 of Drayton's, 'An Evill spirit your beautie haunts Me still', parallels the grammatical structure and the sound-pattern of line 2 of Shakespeare's Sonnet 144, 'Which like two spirits do sugiest me still'. See on this especially Schaar, *Sonnet Themes*, pp. 74–8.

[5] The greater variety than usual in the possible logical and metrical breaks is due to the fact that, all rhymes being feminine, each line has an extra syllable.

13. But since | she prickt thee out | for womens pleasure,
14. Mine be thy love | and thy loves use | their treasure.

Perhaps not a very good sonnet, yet it is certainly the most interesting expression of Shakespeare's views on a number of conceptions which represent the co-ordinates of his ethical world.

1. Beauty is not Truth. As Marcello Pagnini says in the most extended and perceptive analysis of Sonnet 20 that I know,[6] the basic semantic antinomy, corresponding to and supporting the binary structure of the sonnet on the semiological level, is between 'platonic love' and 'sexual passion'. The same opposition is most clearly expressed in Sonnet 144, where the two 'loves', coexisting within the individual according to Platonic philosophy, are turned first into the Christian conception of the co-presence of Guardian Angel and Devil Tempter, and are finally personified in the figures of 'a man right fair' and 'a woman coloured ill'.[7]

But in Sonnet 20, where the antinomy is synthesized in the single figure of the Master–Mistress, there emerges a second implicit binary conceptual system, which, I feel, Pagnini has not sufficiently stressed: the implicit parallelism *beauty/truth* is very relevant to an understanding not only of this, but of many

[6] M. Pagnini, 'Lettura critica' etc.; add now to this: Silvano Sabbadini and Lorenzo Renzi, 'Grammatica e senso nel Sonetto ventesimo di Shakespeare', *Strumenti Critici*, xix (October 1972), pp. 330–7: this is an original attempt at determining, along the lines of Charles J. Fillmore's grammar of cases, the roles of Nature, the Lover, and the Poet in the sonnet's narrative. The authors find that in the four parts of the poem (the three quatrains and the couplet) the role of *agens* is filled alternatively by Nature and Lover, that of *patiens* by Lover and Poet, while *Thou* is in turn *locus*, *agens*, *effectum*, and *patiens*. This is by no means incompatible with the views of the sonnet's structure expressed either by Pagnini or by myself— but it enhances the impression that this poem suffers from an unsolved and arbitrary semiotic complexity, so that the accumulation of contradictory signs tends to smother its poetic vitality; see also on this point § 5 below.

[7] J. M. Steadman, '"Like two Spirits": Shakespeare and Ficino', *Shakespeare Quarterly*, x (1959), pp. 244 ff., finds that Sonnet 144 reflects Ficino's idea of the *gemini amores*, the two daemons intent the one upon elevating and the other upon degrading the soul. More pointedly, James Winny (*The Master-Mistress*, pp. 116–17) provides a diagrammatical representation of 'the situation in Sonnet 144' in support of the central thesis of his book: Shakespeare's divided self. He comments: 'It is the speaker, not the friend, who is then the divided self attracted and repelled by the same object; ... The friend is angelic, the lady diabolical; and the speaker to whom both moral forces belong is a contradictory figure, whose divided nature is self-opposed.'

other Sonnets. In this case the two members of the binary system are not antithetical but complementary—though still far removed from the Keatsian identification of truth with beauty. Truth for Shakespeare is in the first place genuineness, wholeness of being—and then faithfulness, honesty, and again worth, desert, virtue. Beauty in its turn is both a physical and an ethical category, fully achieved only when complemented by truth:

O how much more doth beautie beautious seeme,
By that sweet ornament which truth doth give, (Son. 54, 1–2)

Shakespeare rings the changes on truth and beauty in a number of Sonnets; in no. 101, after saying that 'both truth and beauty on my love depends', he plays on metaphors from painting:

Truth needs no collour with his collour fixt,
Beautie no pensell, beauties truth to lay: (lines 6–7)

where the pun on *colour* recalls both the 'woman coloured ill' of Sonnet 144, and the play on 'hews' (=hues) in 20. In Sonnet 105 he tries to transform the pair into a triad, with the addition of kindness to truth and beauty:

Kinde is my love to day, to morrow kinde,
Still constant in a wondrous excellence,
Therefore my verse to constancie confin'de,
One thing expressing, leaves out difference.
Faire, kinde, and true, is all my argument, [. . .] (lines 5–9)

but this sonnet, a monotonous sequence of deliberate variations on 'three theams in one' ('in this change is my invention spent'), has a false ring, due to the conventional use of the word kindness (=generosity, courtesy, the granting of favour by the lady) in love-poetry. By placing *kind* between *fair* and *true* the poet tried to work out a proportion—fair : kind :: kind : true—which can be accepted only as an elegant conceit, soon exhausted.

Something similar is found in the marriage sonnets, confirming the impression that they were mostly written to order:

As truth and beautie shal together thrive
If from thy selfe, to store thou wouldst convert: (Son. 14, 11–12)

And again, with wisdom replacing truth:

Herein lives wisdome, beauty, and increase,
Without this follie, age, and could decay, (Son. 11, 5–6)

The economics of sex intrude in the presentation of the 'whole man', introducing an adventitious element in the perfect balance between beauty and truth.

2. The woman's part. Sonnet 20, at least at one level of interpretation, is meant to restore this balance, by exorcising once and for all the 'additions to my purpose nothing', that is to say sex and courtly 'kindness'. A reading of the sonnet that keeps this in mind reveals another intellectual pattern, a further decoding grid that, when superimposed on the semiological structure illustrated by Pagnini, exalts—though somewhat laboriously—those very qualities of symmetry and harmony of parts that this critic considers as the poet's highest achievement.

I suggest that, side by side with Pagnini's model, proceeding by sub-multiples (8 = octave, 4 = quatrain III, 2 = couplet), there is a centralized organization of the semantic values of the sonnet, that yields a very different pattern: a central nucleus formed by lines 7–8, and two isomorphic sections on either side, each of which can be subdivided into three pairs of lines. The central section is characterized by the fact that the word *man* (and *men*), the real subject of the poem, appears *only* there. In the rest of the sonnet the subject is described and defined only by analogy and/or contrast with the other sex—*woman/women*; these words appear altogether six times in the poem, or rather seven, if we take into consideration the possessive pronoun *theirs* in line 5 that stands for *women's*. More specifically: four times in section I (two in the singular and two in the plural): $_1$*a woman's face*, $_3$*a woman's gentle heart*, $_4$*false women's fashion*, $_5$*theirs* [false eyes]—once (plural) in section II: $_6$*women's souls*— twice (one singular, one plural) in section III: $_9$*for a woman*, $_{13}$*for women's pleasure*. It is quite clear that the stress is constantly put on the physical and emotional aspects of woman, with a more marked derogatory connotation when the word is in the plural, and therefore referring to the whole sex. The poet seems to share Posthumus' attitude (*Cymbeline*, II. v. 19 ff.):

> Could I finde out
> The Womans part in me, for there's no motion
> That tends to vice in man, but I affirme
> It is the Womans part: be it Lying, note it,
> The womans: Flattering, hers; Deceiving, hers:
> Lust, and ranke thoughts, hers, hers: [. . .]

but Posthumus' antifeminist tirade is occasioned by the evil Iachimo's deception; Innogen, his woman, is a paragon of innocence.

Now, taking first the singular use of *woman* in Sonnet 20: in section I the word is associated with outward appearance (₁*face*) and the show of courtly emotional 'kindness' (₃*gentle heart*), and in section III with the work of doting nature—in all three cases, then, woman stands for the paradigm of external beauty and conventional emotional behaviour. When in the plural, *women* are associated in section I with false appearances (₄*false women's fashion*, [their eyes are] ₅*false in rolling*) with strong implications of crude sensuality; and in section III (line 13) with frank and stark sexual pleasure; these associations indicate that, in the words ₈*women's souls* in section II, *soul* must be understood not as the spiritual principle but as 'the seat of emotions'.[8] Woman, in the sonnet, is equated with beauty but opposed to truth. Two reasons are given for considering her as beauty without truth, one implicit in section I: her conventional 'kindness' is emotionally unstable (*acquainted with shifting change*); the other in section III: she is the personification of sex itself.

A formal and semantic link between sections I and III—one way of establishing their parallelism—is to be found in the opening lines of each of the sections, 1 and 9–10: in both *woman* is connected with *nature*. In section I nature is the 'painter' of woman's face, appropriately enough since the lines deal with her external beauty; in section III nature—personified in the feminine, herself a woman—falls *adoting* on her creature, and this 'love-dotage' fully accounts for the crude sexual paronomasiae of the following lines.

3. The symmetry of the dual Eros.   The two outer sections are parallel in their openings, but they are also symmetrical in specular form: taking the lines in pairs, the initial pair of section I corresponds to the terminal pair of section III through the coincidence between ₂*Master Mistress*,[9] the union

---

[8] M. Pagnini, op. cit., p. 4, note 1.

[9] The normal metrical caesura in the line would fall exactly between the upbeat and the downbeat of the third (middle) foot, but it is impossible to separate *Master* from *Mistris*, at the cost of taking 'Mistris of my passion' to be a mere appositional clause of 'Master'. We are forced therefore to read the line with two very unusual

of masculine and feminine principles (= platonic love + sexual passion), and ₁₄*thy love and thy love's use*, which reflects exactly the same antinomic union. But there is more: if we consider the middle line between the symmetrical extremes 2 and 14, i.e. line 8, we find:

Which steals men's eyes | and women's souls amazeth

which, as Pagnini's careful analysis shows, represents the basic antinomy of the sonnet; there the current acceptations of the key words, *eyes/souls*, are reversed: *eyes*, the seat of physical sensual attraction (in line 5 *women's* eyes are said to be 'false in rolling', lascivious and deceptive[10]) in connection with *men* become the purest among the organs of the five senses,[11] a metaphor for the platonic love of pure moral beauty; while *souls*, normally belonging to the spiritual sphere, here, in association with *women*, are taken to refer, as we have seen, to the emotional, sensual parts of female nature. This semantic exchange confirms the centrality, the pivotal function, of lines 7–8, and establishes beyond doubt that the main theme of the sonnet is the ambivalence of love—the dual Eros—and the celebration of the Platonic conception which, while condemning sexual passion, sees the whole man as the synthesis of both forms of Eros.

Lines 7–8 are the turning point of the sonnet: the double switchover in line 8 from physical to spiritual and from spiritual to physical accounts both for the antinomic sequence in line 1–6, where man's qualities are described in terms of woman's faults, and for the paronomasic sequence of lines 9–14, where sexual love originates a series of bawdy puns, which many critics have found disconcerting and rather repulsive.

breaks, after the downbeat of the first and the upbeat of the fourth foot, with the effect of placing an extraordinary emphasis on 'the Master Mistris'. My reading is not meant to contradict any of the interpretations offered for this expression, including the recent one by Martin B. Friedman ('Shakespeare's "Master Mistris"': Image and Tone in Sonnet 20', *Shakespeare Quarterly*, xxii. 2 (Spring 1971), pp. 189–91) who discovers in the first part of the poem images from bowling (Master Mistris = the jack) and in the second part from archery (*prick* being the peg at the centre of the target), with amusing if obvious Freudian implications.

[10] For the eyes as the seat of lechery, punished with blindness, see the rich contemporary documentation provided by W. R. Elton, *King Lear and the Gods*, pp. 107–12.

[11] The use here corresponds to the definition given in Achilles' words in *Troilus and Cressida*, III. iii. 106–7: 'the eye itself, / That most pure spirit of sense'.

The most cryptic line remains line 7: Pagnini rightly notices its triadic structure on the phonological level (in *hew* all *Hews* in *his*), but sees it as the completion of the octave, a sequence of four pairs of lines which he describes as a kind of ladder where each rung is one of the young man's 'parts':

> the FACE, in lines 1–2, leads to the HEART, in lines 3–4; the Heart to the EYE, lines 5–6; then the eye, to the whole of his APPEARANCE (*hues*), lines 7–8.[12]

The critic is therefore forced to translate, or paraphrase, line 7 as follows: 'A man who in his appearance is the model of all other appearances'. Though there is no question of the centripetal sequence from the parts to the whole, the paraphrase provided is surely only one, and a rather limited one, of the possible readings of the line. The limitation is due to the view of the poem as structured on the Petrarchan model, with an octave followed by a sestet; in this way the careful balance between the two outer, centripetal and centrifugal sections of six lines each is lost sight of. I think that a better understanding of the all-important line 7 and especially of the very puzzling expression 'all hues in his controlling' can be gained from a different approach to the organizing principles of Sonnet 20.

4. All Hues: the pattern of convergence.   In spite of the testimony of punctuation, which indicates the major breaks after lines 8 and 12, the structural organizations we have so far examined point in another direction, to a centralized arrangement of the sections of the poem, contradicting the conventional prosodic pattern. There is *parallelism* and *symmetry* between the two framing 6-line sections; moreover, unbroken *continuity* is provided by the fact that all rhymes are feminine, a feature shared with only one other sonnet (no. 87), and obviously significant in a poem emphasizing throughout the man–woman polarity and defining man only by contrast with woman.

But there is a fourth and perhaps even more marked structural feature: *convergence*. The framing sections converge into the middle not only through the reflection of the specular extremes (line 2 and 14) in the central line 8, but also when we

---

[12] See Pagnini, op. cit., p. 5; I have translated the rather ambiguous Italian 'sembiante' as 'appearance'; but see the discussion of *hewe* in Hoby's *Courtier* at the end of note 15 below.

look at them as separate sequences of three pairs of lines each.
Section I: lines 1–2 are concerned with the *beauty* of the face—
natural and therefore true beauty as opposed to the 'painted'
beauty of false women—the particular use of the verb is
significant and sets in motion the chain of implicit antinomies
in the sonnet, since in most Shakespearian contexts painting
means falsity;[13] here instead it is nature who has played the
painter, like the poet's eye in Sonnet 24:

> Mine eye hath play'd the painter and hath steeld
> Thy beauties forme in table of my heart, [. . .] (lines 1–2)

so that the painting, like the face, is genuine and true. Lines
3–4 deal with the *truth* of man's heart, similar to woman's in its
gentleness (see § 1 above for the discussion of 'kindness' in
connection with beauty and truth), but opposed to it in so far
as hers is fickle, and therefore *false*, while his is constant, and
therefore true. The first two pairs of lines have defined in turn
the *Master Mistris'* beauty and truth; lines 5–6 effect the synthesis expressing, to borrow the words of Sonnet 101, '*truth in
beauty dy'd*': here man's eye is not only contrasted with woman's,
but in its turn, like nature in line 1, it plays the painter, 'Gilding
the object whereupon it gazeth'. The metaphor from painting
is repeated, with the same positive value: man is endowed with
an even greater power than nature, since what his eye colours is
ennobled and made richer.

At this point the discussion on the meaning of 'man in hue' in
line 7 becomes supererogatory. The usage of *hue* here in no way
differs from that in the other sonnets, where it constantly means
'colour, shade', with the occasional metaphorical implication
of 'aspect, appearance'.[14] 'A man in hue' carries over from
section I to section II the painting metaphor, and means 'a
man in his natural and genuine colours'—one in whom the
native hue of resolution is not sicklied over by the pale cast of
thought, like Castiglione's ideal courtier:

The Courtyer therefore, beside noblenesse of birthe, I wyll
have hym to be fortunate in this behalfe, and by nature to have not
only wytte, and a comely shape of persone and countenance, but

---

[13] The most obvious is *Hamlet*, III. i. 142 ff.: 'I have heard of your paintings too,
well enough; God hath given you one face, and you make your selves another.'
[14] Cf. Sonnet 82, line 5: 'Thou art as faire in knowledge as in hew.'

also a certayne grace, and (as they saie) a *hewe*, that shal make him at the first sight acceptable and lovyng unto who so beholdeth him.[15]

The contrast 'false painting versus living hue = artificial versus natural' is confirmed by Sonnet 67, where it appears in conjunction with the theme of 'truth in beauty dy'd':

> Why should false painting immitate his cheeke,
> And steale dead seeing of his living hue?
> Why should poore beautie indirectly seeke,
> Roses of shaddow, since his Rose is true? (lines 5–8)

Attention should be paid in this quotation also to the contiguity of 'steal' and 'seeing' (= eye): while false colouring robs the natural living hue and leaves only a dead appearance for the eye to see, in Sonnet 20 the man who has a true colour (*in hew*) conquers (*steales*) the living eyes of other men.[16] But the puzzle of the second part of the line (*all Hews in his controwling*) remains.

I am not going to deny off-hand that *Hews* may be here a homonymic pun on the surname Hughes; I shall only say that, for a reading of the poem, the actual existence of a Willie Hughes, boy-actor or merchant sailor, is absolutely irrelevant. A pun is a play on words of the same sound but different meanings; when one of them is a proper name, the only meaning poetically valid is that of the other word, the common

---

[15] B. Castiglione, *The Book of the Courtier*, done into English by Sir Thomas Hobye (1561). The passage is quoted, in connection with Master Mistris of Sonnet 20, by T. W. Baldwin, *On the Literary Genetics of Shakspere's Poems and Sonnets* (Urbana, 1950), p. 165. He quotes also a passage from the last book of *The Courtier* (Bk. iv, § lxii): 'Therefore whan an amiable countenance of a beautiful woman commeth in his sight, that is acompanied with noble condicions & honest behaviours, so that as one practised in love, he wotteth well that his hewe hath an agreement with herres, assoone as he is ware that his eyes snatch that image & carie it to the heart . . .' Baldwin compares the central lines of Sonnet 20 and comments (p. 166): 'Shakspere is fully conscious that he is here giving the doctrine of "souls" a twist. Since the master-mistris is for beauty *all in all, and all in every part*, he controls "all hues in his", for both men and women.' In both quotations Hoby translates most appropriately with *hewe* Castiglione's peculiar usage of the word *sangue* (blood), on which Vittorio Cian annotates (Castiglione, *Il libro del Cortigiano* (Firenze, 1947), pp. 41–2) that in this sense it is unrecorded in dictionaries, and corresponds to the Latin *os*, or to Dante's *colore* (colour).

[16] A case could be made for considering 'seal-eye-hue' a subliminal image-cluster to be analysed by the psychologist; see Sonnet 104, lines 9–12: 'Ah yet doth beauty like a Dyall hand, / Steale from his figure, and no pace perceiv'd, / So your sweet hew, which me thinkes still doth stand / Hath motion, and mine eye may be deceaved.'

noun,[17] and the pun degenerates into a cryptogram. The non-cryptographic meanings of the second hemistich of line 7 have been decoded in several ways. One of them I have already quoted: 'a model for all other appearances'; other possibilities, all equally acceptable on the level of Empsonian ambiguity, are: 'dominating, well above all other men for handsomeness' (the youth as Ganymede); 'setting the rules of beauty for everybody' (the youth as Paris in his arraignment); 'conquering all women, whatever their colour' (the youth as Adonis).[18] Another difficulty is that in the Sonnets the verb 'to control' is generally used in its original sense of 'to keep count, to check (esp. accounts)'[19]—see Sonnets 58 line 2, 66 line 10, 107 line 3—rather than 'to restrain, to overpower'.

Before facing these further complications of section II, I propose to look at the semantic structure of section III, symmetrical with section I, and see if it can throw any light on the central passage. The opening pair of lines (9–10) has already been discussed: nature, no longer the painter of true colours, is personified as a woman, and as such she is subject to gross sensuality; great creating nature becomes Edmund's adulterous Goddess, doting on her creatures. Lines 9–10, then, are concerned, with love as *dotage*, the irrational sexual passion; balancing dotage, we find in the last pair of lines (13–14) love as physical ('women's') *pleasure*, sexual satisfaction. The whole of the last section has as its subject sex or sexual passion, as opposed to platonic love, in its two aspects: folly and enjoyment. It is appropriate that the middle pair of lines (11–12) should be ruled by the allusion to the sexual organ,[20] that addition

---

[17] Not so when the proper name has a symbolic value, as with Petrarch's Laura = L'aura.

[18] See Sonnet 53, lines 5–6: 'Describe *Adonis* and the counterfet / Is poorely immitated after you.' The whole of this sonnet, where the youth is both Adonis and Helen, is relevant to the 'Master Mistris' idea in no. 20; the relevance of the Adonis figure is pointed out by James Winny, op. cit., pp. 152–4 (on Sonnet 20), and *passim*, and that of the androgynous or epicene figure (Helen–Adonis/Hermaphroditus) by Leslie Fiedler, *The Stranger in Shakespeare*, p. 22.

[19] See Dover Wilson's note in his edition of the *Sonnets*, p. 118.

[20] The obscene innuendo repeats those in Sonnet 144 and, even more closely, in 136 and 151, which I quoted above. The technique—the shock produced by the juxtaposition of the crudest representation of the sexual act in contexts ruled by such words as 'angel', 'spirit', 'soul'—is identical. Note that while Sonnets 136 and 151 were addressed to a woman (the soul being rather hers than the poet's), in no. 20 the allusions are reversed: the recipient is a man, the souls are those of all women.

which to the poet's 'purpose', his search of truth in beauty dy'd expressed in section I, is indeed 'nothing' (see § 2 above). But if sex is nothing to poetry, it is something to the 'lovely youth', emblematic of the whole man, in whom 'love' must be united to 'love's use'.[21] The sexual passion of section III as well as the poetical passion of section I (see line 2, where 'passion' is both love and the love-poem, the sonnet itself) converge in the 'Man in hue' of section II. If beauty and truth in him can 'steal men's eyes', his sexual potency 'women's souls amazeth' (see § 3 above).

And here we come to *all Hews*. The youth is 'a Man in his natural colour'—but that colour is made up of many 'hues', all the shades of colour that nature can confer, both as the painter of outward beauty and of inner truth in beauty dy'd, *and* as the doting female lover, who adds an extra touch, useless for the sonneteer but essential for her own pleasure. What matters is to establish a balance of nature's gifts, beauty, truth, sex; in fact, to keep count of and to be able to check all these gifts, the hues,[22] the nuances of his native colour. Such is Shakespeare's young friend, *A man in hew all* Hews *in his controwling*.

5. More matter, with less art.   Only by unravelling the various structural layers of the sonnet has it been possible to reach a core of meaning. The resulting structural schema (fig. 9) may serve as a compensation for the labours undergone. Its very elaboration, the complicated play of correspondences, make it look more like the painstaking conjectural reconstruction by a deluded treasure hunter of the map of a buried labyrinth, than the reproduction of the original ground-plan of a surviving monument. The fact is that Sonnet 20 is an overloaded structure, in its determination to be original and witty at all costs. In this attempt, it breaks down the lucid and simple basic organization of the sonnet-form (a simplicity containing in itself numberless opportunities for variations), and sets about

[21] There is little doubt that the expression 'love's use' carries its justification in the economics of love and marriage, and is a further apology for the forced arguments of the generation sonnets: see, e.g., Sonnet 6, lines 5–8: 'That use is not forbidden usery, / Which happies those that pay the willing lone; / That's for thy selfe to breed an other thee, / Or ten times happier be it ten for one.'

[22] A phonemic correspondence between line 7 and line 14 confirms that sex is part of the 'hues' in man's control: the phonic sequence *l.ius* in ₁₄*loves use* (= the sexual act) is an echo of that in ₇*all Hews*.

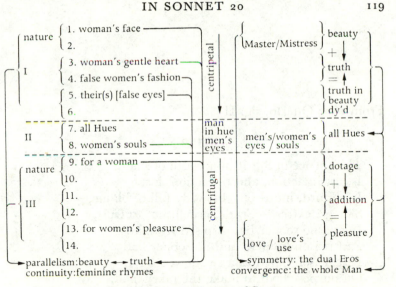

Fig. 9. Structural schema of Sonnet 20

reconstructing on the same foundations an infinitely more complicated structure. Oddly enough, the superimposed pattern fulfils Roman Jakobson's requirement of a 'contrapuntal symmetrical trichotomy' $(6+2+6)$ in the sonnet,[23] but is an unfortunate example of it, since it manages only to conceal the original groundwork underneath a wealth of supersubtle elaborations. The result is cumbersome as well as composite, like the minor paintings of the later Mannerists. No doubt, Sonnet 20 is an extremely 'important' poem, especially from an ideological point of view: in its circumvolutions it contains the basic thematic motifs of most of the Sonnets; and it reveals an exceptional ingenuity and consciousness of the linguistic medium. But it can be called a work of art only if the latter word is taken in the worst of its Shakespearian acceptations: artifice—the art not of Prospero, but of Polonius.

[23] See the discussion of Jakobson's theory of the sonnet-form in chapter IV, § 0.4 below, and especially note 23.

From 1609 Quarto, sig. H3ᵛ

129

Th'expence of Spirit in a waste of shame
Is lust in action, and till action, lust
Is periurd, murdrous, blouddy full of blame,
Sauage, extreame, rude, cruell, not to trust,
Inioyd no sooner but dispised straight,
Past reason hunted, and no sooner had
Past reason hated as a swollowed bayt,
On purpose layd to make the taker mad.
Made In pursut and in possession so,
Had, hauing, and in quest, to haue extreame,
A blisse in proofe and proud and very wo,
Before a ioy proposd behind a dreame,
    All this the world well knowes yet none knowes well,
    To shun the heauen that leads men to this hell.

CHAPTER IV

TH'EXPENSE OF SPIRIT: SONNET 129 AND THE ETHICS OF SEX

0.1. Occasionals: Sonnets 129 and 146. The digression on soul and spirit, and the dual Eros, in Sonnet 20—the equivalent of the 'spirits who suggest' in Sonnet 144—seemed necessary to provide some kind of intellectual background for the last two of the meditative sonnets which I propose to consider, nos. 129, 'Th'expense of spirit', and 146, 'Poor soul, the centre'. I see them as sharing the same qualities of intellectual tension that characterized Sonnets 94 and 121, moving on from the sphere of human behaviour (the exercise of power, the application of social criteria to moral judgement) to that of emotional and spiritual motivations, from the outer to the inner life of man.

Most critics have not connected these two sonnets with nos. 94 and 121, but have seen instead a close link between the two of them. This is because both 129 and 146 come in the second general section of the collection—the 'dark lady' sonnets—but their tone is different from the other twenty-six in the section. The connection was made most recently by Brents Stirling in his attempt to establish the order of Sonnets 127–54;[1] his rearrangement received the distinction of the full support of the late John Dover Wilson, who found it 'the more convincing' in so far as it was based on a theory which 'is bibliographical rather than stylistic'.[2] As a matter of fact, the bibliographical evidence is not unimpeachable, and the new order relies mainly, as do those proposed by Acheson, Bray, etc., on subject-matter and word-links; and nos. 129 and 146, being in that respect unrewarding, are lumped together at the

---

[1] B. Stirling, 'Sonnets 127–154', in *Shakespeare 1564–1964*, ed. E. A. Bloom (Providence, R.I., 1964), pp. 134–53. The attempt is extended to the whole sequence in the same author's *The Shakespeare Sonnet Order: Poems and Groups* (Berkeley and Los Angeles, 1968), where Sonnets 129 and 146 form Group v. E.

[2] *Sonnets*, ed. Dover Wilson, pp. 242–4.

end of the supposed sequence as expressing and concluding 'a
theme already apparent'. The attitude is not very original—it
goes back to at least Samuel Butler (1899), who, not finding a
place for these sonnets in *his* sequence, confined them to an
appendix as *occasional* sonnets, 'not having any reference' to
Mr. W. H.[3] Patrick Cruttwell associates them with each other
as showing 'a moral tone far fiercer and deeper, and a self-
examination more searching, than anything before', and
attributes this to Shakespeare's perception that 'the lady is a
whore'.[4] In the same way, but on sounder ground, J. W. Lever
places them firmly at the close of the 'Mistress' group of sonnets,
as 'familiar palinodes'; the analogy he establishes between these
two poems and the closing pair of Sidney's *Certain Sonnets* appended to the 1598 *Arcadia*, is particularly inviting: 'Desire is
castigated in similar terms, and the contrast between sensual
and divine love marked with the same antithetical phrases'.[5]
In fact the rejection of worldly passion (Sidney's 'Thou blind
man's mark') and the invocation to Eternal Love are the obvious formal close of many a sequence of love-poems—and see
Petrarch in the first place. If Shakespeare's two sonnets were
only that, as Yvor Winters seems to think, we could agree with
him when he says that 129 and 146 (to which he adds no. 23)
are 'good poems [. . .] which do not achieve at any point the
greatness of certain lines from sonnets which fail'.[6] The idea of
the two sonnets as formal palinodes is taken up again by Leslie
Fiedler, who rightly connects them with the dual conception
of love in sonnets 144 and 20;[7] Northrop Frye instead underlines their polarity: they are the two ends of the axis on which
the experience of the Sonnets revolves, 129 representing the
nadir, and 146 the zenith.[8]

Most of these interpretations rely far too much on the
private 'experience' expressed in the Sonnets: they see it in
terms of the love-triangle poet–boy–mistress, rather than as the

[3] S. Butler, *Sonnets Reconsidered*, p. 130.

[4] P. Cruttwell, *The Shakespearean Moment*, p. 12.

[5] J. W. Lever, *Eliz. Love Sonnet*, pp. 180–1.

[6] Y. Winters, 'Poetic Style in Shakespeare's Sonnets', originally in *Four Poets on
Poetry*, ed. D. C. Allen (Baltimore, 1959), now in *Discussions of Shakespeare's Sonnets*,
ed. B. Herrnstein (Boston, 1964), p. 113.

[7] L. Fiedler, 'Some Contexts' etc., p. 89; and, more dogmatically, in *The
Stranger in Shakespeare*, p. 32.

[8] N. Frye, 'How True a Twain', in *The Riddle of Shakespeare's Sonnets*, pp. 23–53.

experience of the duality of human nature. They notice the connection between the two poems, but fail to place them within the context of a wider search for the essential nature of man, rather than of Mr. Shakespeare or of Master W. H. It has hardly been noticed that these sonnets, like nos. 94 and 121, are among the few non-dialogical in form, in sharp contrast with the rest of the collection.

0.2. Critical hunting-ground.   The four sonnets 94, 121, 129, and 146, are dramatic meditations (see ch. I, § 5 above). No. 129 is the one that has received most attention; but, to my knowledge, while many critics have seen its relation to no. 146, only Hilton Landry[9] has linked it not with 146 but with 121. This is because he finds that 121 and 129 have in common the theme of *contemptus mundi*: together with no. 66 (whose connection with 129 we shall see in a moment), they repeat Cleopatra's dying question, 'What should I stay', which Charmian completes: 'in this vile world?'[10] As a matter of fact, Sonnet 66 provides a highly conventional reply to the question: 'to dye I leave my love alone', so that the link with the opening of no. 121, ''Tis better to be vile than vile esteemed', is more apparent than real. Landry is too preoccupied in finding 'contexts of interpretations' for the sonnets he considers,[11] and we saw how his treatment of the 'unique' no. 94 suffers from his taking it as part of a group.[12]

But Sonnet 94 has been associated with 129 by other critics. L. C. Knights says that Sonnet 94 'forms an interesting complement to the more famous Sonnet 129',[13] while Northrop Frye finds that while 'Sonnet 94 explains in a bitterer context [that] the youth causes but does not produce love', Sonnet 129 generalizes the experience of the unrequited lover at its lowest

9 H. Landry, *Interpretations* etc.; see his chapter IV, p. 81–104.

10 *Antony and Cleopatra*, v. ii. 317. The expression is used more conventionally in Sonnet 71, where the 'surly sullen bell' warns that 'I am fled / From this vile world with vildest worms to dwell', and in Clifford's exclamation on seeing the dead body of his father (*2 Henry VI*, v. ii. 40): 'O, let the vile world end.'

11 H. Landry, op. cit., p. 132.

12 See chapter II, § 0.1 above; Landry sees the only point in common between Sonnets 94 and 129 in the fact that they share the quality of 'uniqueness' with nos. 66, 121, and 125. But in a later footnote (op. cit., p. 168) he extends the definition also to Sonnet 146: 'Some sonnets, however, are independent and virtually unique (66, 129, 146 for example)'.

13 'Shakespeare's Sonnets', p. 147.

level (both share the thematic word 'expense'), describing 'what a life completely bound to time is like, with the donkey's carrot of passion jerking us along its homeless road'.[14] Also in this case the critic sees the link, but is over-anxious to 'contextualize' the Sonnets on the basis of a private love-story.

The difficulty in approaching Sonnet 129 is of a different kind. Most critics have interpreted it as a definition—and condemnation—of lust. The extraordinary number of detailed commentaries and *explications de texte* it has provoked is due to subtler points of interpretation, connected with problems of emendation and structure. In fact, from Malone onwards, at least three major emendations have been suggested and nearly universally adopted; and a number of commentators have noticed that the poem does not conform to the usual pattern of the Shakespearian sonnet: though prosodically impeccable, the logical structure does not fall easily into the received scheme of three quatrains and a couplet, or octave and sestet. That is why it had the good, or bad, fortune of being taken as a test case by those who intended to suggest new and even revolutionary critical approaches to the Sonnets—so that it is the subject of at least two essays which will remain, for better or worse, as milestones in the history of sonnet-criticism.

In 1927 Laura Riding and Robert Graves took it as the most obvious example of the misinterpretations produced by indiscriminate emendation and modernization of Shakespeare's text: their essay 'William Shakespeare and e. e. cummings'[15] induced a new awareness of the need for a deeper understanding of sixteenth century usage in punctuation and spelling, and for a sounder philological approach to Shakespeare's text. In 1970 Roman Jakobson and Laurence Jones selected this sonnet for a demonstration of the importance of structural linguistic analyses to literary criticism and evaluation;[16] their brilliant work on the sonnet was taken a step further in a long review

[14] N. Frye, op. cit., p. 44. The approach of James Winny (*The Master-Mistress*, p. 112) is similar: 'The particular authority of Sonnet 129—and, in the sequence, of Sonnet 94—seems to result from a break in the narrative which allows the poet to discard his role, and to make a much bigger kind of pronouncement over the heads of his characters'.

[15] In *A Survey of Modernist Poetry* (London, 1927), pp. 49–82. The essay, with extensive revisions, was included in R. Graves, *The Common Asphodel* (London, 1949), pp. 84–95, from which I take the text.

[16] *Shakespeare's Verbal Art* etc.

by I. A. Richards,[17] who pointed out the subliminal relevance of the linguistic structures.

The methodological importance and the innovative value of both the Graves–Riding and the Jakobson–Jones + Richards approaches is such that no reconsideration of Sonnet 129 at this date can ignore them.

The Graves–Riding proposal to go back to the original text and punctuation of the sonnet, rejecting Malone's emendations that had unchallenged currency, was hailed as an extremely important contribution to Shakespearian criticism—but succeeding editors, after paying lip-service to it, brazenly adopted most of Malone's emendations, so that, by 1965, Richard Levin could confidently state:

There is no need to linger here over the Riding–Graves argument. Based as it was upon a wholly unwarranted reverence for the text of Thorpe's quarto, and upon the dogma which now sounds so old-fashioned, that the best interpretation of a poem is the 'one embracing as many meanings as possible', it only succeeded in destroying some of Shakespeare's most striking antitheses and parallels, and reducing most of the poem to grammatical and emotional incoherence.[18]

The charge is serious and the more unfair since Levin, in his essay, is trying to demonstrate the dramatic quality of the sonnet, and provides some valuable insights in this direction, showing the displacement of the time-sequence in the sonnet, and its emotional parallelism with Hamlet's third soliloquy ('O, what a rogue', at the close of II. ii). Levin does not seem to realize that the dramatic quality of this sonnet is in fact due to the co-presence of as many conflicting meanings as possible, and what he calls incoherence is merely the ambiguity of feeling and expression, the contradictoriness of the speaker's position. True, the Empsonian search for polivalence of meaning can be pushed to silly extremes, but if the text presented only one unequivocal interpretation, where would its 'drama' be?

0.3. Emendations: Malone to Graves–Riding.   It is more relevant to consider the Malone emendations which Graves–Riding invite us to reject. Malone introduces two verbal

---

17 I. A. Richards, 'Jakobson's Shakespeare' etc.
18 R. Levin, 'Sonnet CXXIX as a "Dramatic" Poem', p. 176.

changes: in line 9 he reads 'Mad' for 'Made', and in line 11 instead of 'and proud [obviously = prov'd] and very wo' he reads 'and prov'd, A very woe'. The punctuation is radically altered, ostensibly to 'conform to modern standards'; most of the changes are of no real importance, except that they weaken the directness of impact produced by the economical use of punctuation in the original Quarto, but in two cases they affect the interpretation: (a) In line 3, the introduction of a comma between 'blouddy' and 'full of blame' separates the two parts of what in the original appears as a single forceful expression— it reduces to two items, in a list of nine predicative attributes, the single central unit, the pivot on which the breathless arraignment of 'lust till action' revolves; in the same way in Hamlet's invective against the lustful King, quoted by Levin in this connection, the first expletives are strictly joined together in a single logical and phonetic unit—'bloudy, baudy villaine,' (bl.d.b.d.v.ln), before moving on to the list of indictments in the next line: 'Remorselesse, trecherous, lecherous, kindlesse villaine';[19] the alliterative tight knot of consonantal sounds in this hemistich of line 3 confirms this impression of close unity and singleness (*bl*.d.*f.l.vbl*.m). (b) In line 10 Malone moved the third comma from after 'quest' to a position between 'have' and 'extreme', so as to make the latter word, at the end of the line, symmetrical with 'Mad' (substituting the Quarto's 'Made') at the beginning of line 9, and both of them—the only two adjectives to appear twice in the poem, in lines 4 and 6 respectively—the defining elements of the three stages of lust, 'Had, having, and in quest to have', or 'In pursuit and in possession'. I do not deny that there is method in this mad lust for emendation—the restoration of the original punctuation can be defended only by taking into consideration the whole semiotic structure of the sonnet, and this I am going to do later; for the time being it should be noticed that even Dover Wilson[20] agrees for once with Graves–Riding in reading 'to

---

[19] This is true if we accept Q2's reading, *plus* the modern editors' punctuation, which starts a new sentence here, and peppers it with exclamation marks and such-like 'expressive' decorations. The Folio reading firmly separates *bloody*, which refers to *offal* in the previous sentence, and starts anew with *a Bawdy*: 'I should have fatted all the Regions kites / With this Slaves Offal, bloudy: a Bawdy villaine, / Remorselesse, Treacherous, Letcherous, kindles villaine!'

[20] Edition quoted, p. 248.

have extreme' without a comma, as meaning: to feel the extremes [of lust] in all three stages (had, having, and in quest).

0.4. Structural deception: Jakobson–Jones. It is surprising to discover that, more than forty years after the Graves–Riding plea for fidelity to the original, Jakobson and Jones, though preserving the Quarto punctuation, adopt Malone's two major word-emendations in lines 9 and 11; and even in the case of the commas in lines 3 and 10, they consider the original punctuation metrical rather than logical, so that in their view the commas are introduced in the Quarto only to indicate caesurae in the middle of the feet, and are omitted where the logical break coincides with the end of the foot. In fact, for the purposes of logical structure, we can read 'Had, having, and in quest, to have extreame,' as if it were 'Had, having, and in quest to have, extreme'. This agreement with the 'received' views of eighteenth- and nineteenth-century editors seems to me in contrast with the modern critics' attempt to demonstrate that 'an objective scrutiny of Shakespeare's language and verbal art, with particular reference to this poem, reveals a cogent and mandatory unity of its thematic and compositional framework',[21] and with their determination to make short work of the interpretations (like those of C. W. M. Johnson and R. Levin[22]) of the sonnet as an expression of post-coital melancholy or revulsion—and even more of those who find that the sonnet lacks logical organization.

An analysis which is forced to rely on the very readings that have induced other interpreters to pass wrong judgements on the poem, must raise some perplexity. In fact, the Jakobson–Jones analysis is an example of the limitations as well as of the uses of structural linguistics when applied to literary criticism. Its insights on the level of pervasive features, sound-patterns, and phonetic organization, are extremely valuable; but they become critically relevant only when placed within a wider referential semantic context.

The fallacy, in this case, consists in Jakobson's determination to demonstrate that Sonnet 129 also conforms to the principle

[21] Jakobson and Jones, op. cit., p. 32.
[22] C. M. W. Johnson, 'Shakespeare's Sonnet 129', *The Explicator*, vii (April 1949), item 41; and R. Levin, op. cit.

he repeatedly maintained—on the basis of a number of examples from Dante to Baudelaire and Hopkins—according to which a sonnet is a perfect poetic unit only when, side by side with the obvious asymmetrical structure of octave + sestet (8 + 6) or even three quatrains + couplet (4 + 4 + 4 + 2), it allows the co-existence of a contrapuntal organization based on the opposition of the two central lines to the first and the last six, so as to create a centralized symmetrical pattern: 6 + 2 + 6. Jakobson and Jones, therefore, spend a tremendous amount of ingenuity to show, in order to defend Sonnet 129 from the accusation of formlessness, that it has a perfectly symmetrical structure, implying a double centripetal and centrifugal movement and an identifiable centre, corresponding to the mathematical or geometrical centre of the poem, lines 7–8. In so doing they do not seem to realize: (1) that the accusation of formlessness is hardly worth considering, in view of the nature itself of the sonnet-form; (2) that the existence, or rather co-existence, of a converging centralized pattern, far from being a prerequisite of formal perfection, can result at times in a merely formal elaboration, disruptive of the very structure of the sonnet and of its unified effect; this, I feel, was the main implication of my analysis of Sonnet 20—a poem which conforms only too well to Jakobson's requirements of contrapuntal patterning (see Interchapter, above). In other words, the criteria that apply to Baudelaire's *Les Chats*—Jakobson's first great exploration of the structure of a sonnet—are not necessarily valid for Shakespeare's Sonnet 129.[23]

[23] C. Lévi-Strauss and R. Jakobson, '"Les Chats" de Charles Baudelaire', *L'Homme*, ii. 1 (janvier 1962), pp. 5–21, now included in the splendid volume edited by Tzvetan Todorov: R. Jakobson, *Questions de poétique* (Paris, 1973), pp. 401–19. Jakobson has taken advantage of this reprint to reply, in a 'Postscriptum' dated January 1973, to the very many critics who had taken exception to his approach to Baudelaire's poem (he lists some thirty of them), notably to the extremely thorough critique of Michael Riffaterre, 'Describing Poetic Structures: Two Approaches to Baudelaire's Les Chats', *Yale French Studies* (October 1966), pp. 200–42, reprinted as *Structuralism*, ed. J. Ehrmann (New York, 1970), but more readily accessible, with additions, in D. Delas's French translation: M. Riffaterre, *Essais de stylistique structurale* (Paris, 1971), pp. 307–64. In his postscript, Jakobson invokes the authority of Gerard Manley Hopkins (together with Baudelaire, one of 'les grands maîtres du sonnet dans la poésie du siècle dernier') in support of his theory of a centralized structure of the sonnet: 'Étant donné le nombre inégal des vers dans les quatre strophes du sonnet, on y remarque souvent une tendance à opposer au moyen d'un système de correspondances et contrastes le septième et huitième vers, c'est-à-dire le centre du poème, aux six vers du début

1.0. The careless workman. I shall therefore start from
scratch, that is from the Quarto text in its pre-Malone state, and
consider first the negative criticisms, those accusations which
are partly responsible for Jakobson's reaction. The most typical
is Yvor Winters's dogmatic statement that Sonnet 129 'is powerful in phrasing, but repetitious in structure—as Douglas
Peterson has shown (*Shakespeare Quarterly*, v. 4), it derives its
structure and much of its matter from a passage in Wilson's
Arte of Rhetorique—and appears to be a forceful exercise on a
limited topic'.[24] One looks up with awe Peterson's definitive
discovery of 'A Probable Source for Shakespeare's Sonnet
CXXIX',[25] only to find that Wilson, in his treatise, lists some
of the rhetorical figures applied by Shakespeare in the sonnet
(Puttenham, of course, does the same), and as an example of
'regression' ('when we repeat a word eftsome that hath bin
spoken and rehersed before', e.g., 'Men must not live to eate,
but eate to live', cf. lines 2 and 13) he quotes:

> If man do any filthy thing, and take pleasure therein
> The pleasure goeth away, but the shame tarieth still.

which Peterson candidly takes to be the very and only point of
the sonnet in question. That Winters should credit such a
disingenuous oversimplification is hardly credible—except that,
in his determination to be iconoclastic in respect of the Sonnets,
he echoes the words of an authoritative predecessor in the same
line, John Crowe Ransom. In order to maintain that 'struc-
turally, Shakespeare is a careless workman', Ransom says that,
apart from 'a large minority'(!), in most Sonnets 'we can find

et aux six de la fin. Suivant les termes de Hopkins, cette trichotomie symétrique
et distincte de l'arrangement des strophes peut être définie comme un *contrepoint*,
accoutumé dans la composition du poème.' (Op. cit., p. 495.) Also Jakobson's and
Jones's analysis of Sonnet 129 has stimulated a number of counter-analyses, the
most cogent of which seems to me that of Helen Vendler, 'Jakobson, Richards and
Shakespeare's Sonnet CXXIX', in *I. A. Richards: Essays in His Honour*, ed. R.
Brower, H. Vendler, and J. Hollander (New York, 1973), pp. 179–98; this came
too late for me to be able to give it the space that it deserves, but I wish to underline the adroitness with which Professor Vendler points out the basic confutation
of some parts of Jakobson's analysis in Richards's review-essay, and the attention
she pays, in the wake of R. Levin's article, to the time-element in the sonnet (cf.
§ 2.0 below). A different interesting approach to the sonnet is that of B. F. Skinner
in an essay, 'Reflections on Meaning and Structure', included in the same volume
in honour of Richards, pp. 199–209.

[24] Y. Winters, op. cit., p. 113.
[25] *Shakespeare Quarterly*, v (Autumn 1954), pp. 381–4.

the standard metrical organization, and then some logical organization which clashes with it. At least twice we find only fourteen-line poems, with no logical organization at all except that they have little couplet conclusions: in 66 [. . .] and in 129.'[26]

1.1. The forward thrust: the sound-pattern. Ransom merely repeats in a censorious tone what Beeching thirty years earlier had stated more neatly, concisely, and dispassionately: '66 and 129, unlike the rest of the sonnets, are not written in quatrains, though the rhymes are so arranged.'[27] The two sonnets (which, as Landry points out, are thematically linked)[28] lack neither structure nor organization: they have a different structure from the rest, an unbroken sequence of twelve lines, closed by a final couplet. A form by no means unknown to other sonnet-writers, from Sidney to Donne. There is no reason for scandal or concern. For once the chosen subject has suggested to Shakespeare a different treatment of the sonnet-form—tentatively in 66, where the repetition for eleven consecutive lines (2–12) of an identical antithetical pattern held together by ten anaphorae is indeed monotonous,[29] and the symmetrical link between line 1 and the final couplet appears forced and too artful; more maturely and skilfully in 129, where the unquestionable continuous progress from line 1 to line 12 is much more articulated, so as to leave room for the precise individuation of the three quatrains, or even the octave and the sestet, while the symmetrical correspondences between lines 1–2 and the final couplet are much more subtly worked out.

To superimpose on this a centralized converging pattern, as Jakobson and Jones endeavour to do, is mistaken. Any consideration of the structure of the sonnet must start from the recognition that this is a case where there *is* a prevailing feature; and this is not 'Center Against Marginals' (6 + 2 + 6 as in Sonnet 20), but 'Couplet Against Quatrains' (12 + 2). The other symmetries pointed out by Jakobson and Jones ('Odd Against Even', 'Outer Against Inner', 'Anterior Against

---

[26] J. C. Ransom, *The World's Body*, p. 275.
[27] Quoted in Dover Wilson's edition, p. 247.
[28] H. Landry, op. cit., chapter IV.
[29] But Shakespeare meant to produce a deliberate effect of weariness, as expressed in the very first hemistich of the sonnet: 'Tired with all these'.

Posterior') are variously relevant, but all subordinate to the 12 + 2 scheme. A much better approach is that of Stephen Booth,[30] who produces this as the best example of 'the forward thrust in the sonnets':

Sonnet 129, whose subject is unstoppable energy, is itself unstoppable[. . .] The forward motion[. . .] is partly achieved in its sound. In the first quatrain the convoluted and contorted relationships of the nouns to one another are vouched for by a succession of *s* sounds frustrated by stopped consonants[. . .]. The pattern in *sp* and *st* sounds in *expense, spirit,* and *waste* in line 1 is picked up in *lust* in line 2. [. . .]the pattern in *s* plus consonant continues in *Is perjured* and *murd'rous, bloody.* A pattern in *rd,* holds *perjured* and *murd'rous* together; the *d* reappears in *bloody,* which in turn begins a new yoking pattern in *b* and *l* in *bloody full of blame.* Such interlinked sound patterns and repeated words and rhythms continue throughout the poem. They preclude any sense of pause, and their principal effect is to carry the reader forward[. . .]

This type of sound-analysis is carried on more thoroughly by Charles Rosen, in an extensive review of the Jakobson–Jones pamphlet.[31] While Jakobson, impressed by the closely knit phonetic texture of the first line, suggested an anagrammatic interpretation (the stressed sounds of *expense, spirit, shame*—ksp, spir, sha—producing the name Shakspeare), Rosen rightly notices that 'the four consonants of *Spirit* dominate the first twelve lines', and lists the relevant words in each line, characterized by the obsessive repetitions of plosives (p/b) and dentals (t/d) in combination with sibilants and fricatives, emphasized by phonetic symmetries within the lines or in consecutive ones (the most remarkable being the exchange in the consonant sequence in *sooner* and *reason,* —s.n/.r—r./s.n—repeated in lines 5–6, and 6–7). But still more interesting is the stress that he places on the sharp contrast between the pervasive presence of these phonetic features in the quatrains and their absence in the couplet:

[30] S. Booth, *An Essay* etc., pp. 148–50. A similar positive approach is that of Philip Martin (*Shakespeare's Sonnets,* p. 57), who underlines the rhythmical and syntactical elements: 'to create a sense of urgency the poem develops a powerful momentum of rhythm and syntax, driving over the line-endings and the quatrain-divisions in one long inexorable sentence'.

[31] Ch. Rosen, 'Art Has its Reasons', *New York Review of Books,* xvi. 11 (17 June, 1971), pp. 32–8.

In the last two lines [. . .] this particular nexus of sounds disappears, and the contrast of sonority is striking. The final couplet has no 'p', only one 'r' [in *world*, where, incidentally, it is not voiced] and its three 't's' are all on weak beats [. . .] The dominant sounds of the last two lines are the alliterations on 'w', 'n', 'th', 'h', the occurrence of 'l', 's', and 'n' in final position, and the prominent 'sh' of *To shun*, a remarkable concentration of aspirates and soft consonants. Jakobson and Jones remark on the density of texture in the final couplet but not on its hushed quality and on the almost complete absence of the explosives that pervade the first twelve lines. If one were to construct anagrams, it might justly be said that *Spirit* determines the sonority of the quatrains, and *shame* of the final couplet.

A similar change is apparent in the vowel sounds: in the quatrains the short and long *a* sounds (/æ/ and /ei/) are repeated no less than twenty-one times, frequently emphasized by rhymatic or punning collocations (see for instance the rhyme-system of quatrain II), while they disappear completely in the couplet, where the dominant sound is ε, hardly present in the quatrains.

This analysis of the sound-pattern confirms the structural originality of the sonnet. It is the opposite case from what we saw in Sonnet 20, where an apparently progressive pattern $(8+4+2)$ turned out to be centralized. The structure of Sonnet 129 is unconventional and anomalous, in the same way as, on another level, this sonnet is different from all others by being the only one that contains *no* pronoun or pronominal expression in either first, second, or third person. This establishes the fact that it is indeed the most 'depersonalized' among Shakespeare's Sonnets: there are no actors in it, not even the speaker—it all takes place within the poet's mind and consciousness.

The separation between the quatrains and the couplet is further emphasized by the fact that the latter is phonically self-enclosed, through the inverted parallelism of its first two words in line 13 and last two in line 14: All this (.l/ðis)—this hell (ðis/.l). Besides, the indication of *Spirit* and *shame* as the governing sound-principles of respectively lines 1–12 and 13–14, suggests the way in which the two parts of the sonnet are both differentiated and held together. We shall come back later to this point, when considering the rhetorical, syntactical, and semantic organization of the sonnet.

1.2. The progress of caesurae: the rhythmic pattern. From the point of view of rhythm, another interesting pattern emerges, based on the breaks within the lines, and suggesting that the headlong rush of the verse, stemmed only by the couplet, is not without method. Jakobson and Jones, by a clever manipulation of the possible placing of the breaks, managed to separate the sonnet into two equal halves. According to them, in all the first seven lines the break falls in the middle of the line, after the fifth of its ten syllables. Here the difficulty comes in line 4, where there are two spondaic substitutions for the first and third iamb:

Savage, extreame, rude, cruell, not to trust,

Jakobson–Jones confidently place the caesura after 'rude', to make the line uniform with the three before and the three after it. But it is enough to read aloud the line to realize how illogical it would be to pause at that point: (a) the stress on 'rude' is necessarily strong, the more so in so much as it is irregular for dramatic effect; (b) in the previous line 3 the pause came after the first two adjectives, so it would be logical also here to take breath after the first two corresponding adjectives, that is to say after *extreame*; (c) *extreame* is assonant with the rhyme-word of line 3, *blame*, and a break at this point underlines it, as in lines 7–8 there is a half rhyme between *bayt*—the rhyme-word of 7—and *layd*, closing the first hemistich of 8 and occupying exactly the same position as *extreame* in line 4; (d) by placing the caesura after *rude*, instead, we lose the near-alliteration ru/kru in *rude, cruel*, which should dominate the second hemistich, in the same way as the alliteration *blouddy/blame* dominates the second half of the previous line.[32]

If we let the break in line 4 fall in its natural place, at the end of the second foot, the Jakobson–Jones argument for a division of the sonnet into two equal halves does not hold. We have instead an octave formed by two quatrains in which the metrical breaks are perfectly parallel: in each of them the first

[32] And compare the play of assonances elsewhere in the poem, e.g., peri*urd*/murd*rous* in the first hemistich of line 3, *make*/*take*r in the second hemistich of line 8.

three lines have a caesura in the middle of the third foot, while the last line is broken at the end of the second foot. It is perhaps unfair to quote the rest of Jakobson's argument: 'To this feminine, caesural break between the upbeat and the downbeat of the third, middle, foot the seven centripetal [meaning 'centrifugal'] lines oppose a masculine, diaeretic break marking the beginning and/or the end of the middle foot.'[33] As a matter of fact, we must take into account not the *seven* last lines, but more simply the sestet; and we shall discover that to the parallel arrangement of the breaks in the octave, there corresponds a symmetrical one in the sestet, the breaks falling at the beginning of the middle foot in the first and last lines, and at the end of the same foot in the remaining four lines. Jakobson's and Jones's laborious system of double breaks, on the contrary, succeeds only in breaking up some perfect logical and sound-units, and deliberate alliterations or assonances within self-contained hemistichs: see e.g., line 8, where they would separate '*make*' from '*taker*', line 11 where '*in proofe*' cannot be taken apart from '*and provd*', or line 13, with the inseparable sequence '*world well* knows'. (See the breaks marked in the structural schema, § 1.8 below.)

1.3. Lust's bliss and woe: the logic of sound and rhythm.
A study of the sound- and rhythm-pattern of Sonnet 129 reveals, then, a forward-moving structure, expressed in the consistency of the phonic organization throughout the quatrains in opposition to the subdued sonority of the final couplet: this forward movement is counterbalanced by the rhythmical pattern, which proceeds by parallel pauses in the lines of the octave and symmetrical pauses in those of the sestet, accounting in this way for the full stop at the end of line 8, a graphic mark of rhythmic change, which reminds us of the basic principle of the sonnet-form, the antithetical correlation of octave and sestet.[34] One danger of this type of analysis is that of losing sight, for the sake of the formal pattern produced, of the logical sequence of thought and, ultimately, of meaning. Formal analysis should be made subservient to that end. The fact is

[33] Jakobson and Jones, op. cit., p. 11.
[34] Jakobson and Jones (op. cit., p. 25) maintain that 'among the three types of interstrophic correlations the opposition of the anterior [octave] to the posterior [sestet] strophes plays a subaltern, third-rate role in Sonnet 129'.

that sound- and rhythm-patterns are but instinctual sensuous arrangements of thought- and meaning-patterns, they share the same logical movements—and to talk of metrical in contrast to logical breaks is nonsense. Here, for instance, the break in line 11 after 'provd', is conditioned by the rhythmic movement of the previous and the following lines: 'A bliss in proof and prov'd' reproduces the basic rhythm of the first hemistich of line 10, 'Had, having, and in quest' (where the function of *and* as a necessary link in the rhythmic unit is emphasized by its being a downbeat); and anticipates that of the first hemistich of line 12, 'Before a ioy proposd' (where the chiming past participles 'provd' and 'proposd' act as half-rhymes ending their respective half-lines). Rhythmic arrangements and pauses merely reflect logical arrangements; in this case, then, *prov'd* is to be taken together with *in proof* as both referring back to *A bliss*. The line is to be interpreted then as '[lust is] a bliss both when experienced and after the experience'. The second hemistich 'and very woe', refers as well to both stages of the experience, completing the meaning: 'and at the same time [lust] produces pain'. The rhythmic and phonic values (see the previous paragraph) confirm the inconsistency of the universally adopted emendation of the line: 'A bliss in proof, and, proved, a very woe', which would suggest the meaning '[lust] is a bliss when experienced, *but* a woe afterwards', with the hackneyed implications of post-coital sadness. The placing of the metrical pause, by the logic of rhythm, *after* instead of *before* 'and prov'd' radically alters the interpretation of the poem, restoring to it a much subtler meaning than Malone's emendation suggested. Shakespeare may well have had in mind (as Peterson suggests),[35] Petronius' famous epigram:

> Foeda est in coitu et brevis voluptas
> Et taedet Veneris statim peractae,

or its current abbreviated form, *post coitum triste*, with its infinite variations in all Western languages; but he did not mean Sonnet 129 to be simply a repetition of the ancient saw; rather, he wanted to call it in question, in order to confront the reader with the essential ambivalence of man's attitude to lust in all its stages: always a bliss (volumes of love-poems

[35] D. Peterson, op. cit., p. 383.

had emphasized this point) and at the same time always a woe.

This basic meaning needs further corroboration, by taking into account two subsidiary structural features which I have touched upon only in passing: (a) the logic of grammar and syntax, with special reference to the sequence of the parts of speech,[36] and (b) the 'time'-sequence in the consideration of the three stages of lust.

1.4. The world of men: the testimony of nouns.   Attention has been called to the peculiarities of the grammatical categories in Sonnet 129 by the fact that this is the only Shakespearian sonnet lacking all personal pronouns or pronominal expressions. Of the other two meditative sonnets I have considered, no. 94 had only third person pronouns, establishing a dialectical opposition between THEY and OTHERS, the mighty and their stewards; while in no. 121 the two antithetical semantic areas were ruled by I, the existing one, and THEY, the social world of appearances. If it is true that the absence of personal pronouns—only *none*(!) in the last line could be considered such—implies on the one hand the suppression of the personal 'I' of the man Shakespeare, on the other hand it does not portend wilful ignorance of human personality, but rather the intention to get inside it, to consider its inner dialectics, the emotional powers at play in 'the man within'. Hence the insistence on abstract nouns throughout the quatrains[37] (the only animate noun—*taker* in line 8—being deverbative and confined, together with the only concrete inanimate, $_7bayt$, to the one rhetorical figure of simile, the one 'expendable' part of the sonnet). The quatrains–versus–couplet pattern, already noted apropos the sounds of the sonnet, is confirmed as soon as we look at the four nouns in the last two lines: $_{14}heaven$ and $_{14}hell$ are far from abstractions, and while in the quatrains the plural number was never used, here we find a collective, $_{13}world$ (with a collective pronoun: $_{13}none$), and a plural, $_{14}men$. We need only look back at the final line of Sonnet 121,

---

[36] Jakobson and Jones consider these functions only in respect of rhyme-words.
[37] Quatrain I has 9 (1 of them, *in action*, with participial function), quatrain II 3 (*Past reason, Past reason, On purpose*, all with adverbial functions), quatrain III 8 (4 of which, *In pursut, in possession, in quest, in proofe*, with participial functions), for a grand total of 20.

'All men are bad, and in their badness reign', and at its significance,[38] to realize what has happened. The enclosed world
of individual personality, with its inner conflicts, ruling lines
1–12, is suddenly confronted in lines 13–14 with the larger social
world of all men, in which it must be absorbed.

1.5. Abstract nouns versus adjectives. Having established the coincidence of sound-pattern and basic grammatical
features, the latter must be further explored to determine their
progress in the quatrains. They claim attention since each
quatrain is dominated by one or more specific categories. In
quatrain I the first two lines are completely ruled by abstract
nouns: eight of them, neatly situated, two in each of the four
hemistichs:

> Th'*expence* of *Spirit* | in a *waste* of *shame*
> Is *lust* in *action,* | and till *action, lust*

Spirit, shame, action, lust receive special emphasis as the terminal
(rhyme-) words of each half-line.

In lines 3–4 we find a parallel arrangement, but the eight
abstract nouns are substituted by eight adjectives (*periurd* is of
course a past participle but obviously functioning only as an
adjective in the context):

> Is *periurd, murdrous,* | *blouddy full* of blame,
> *Savage, extreame,* | *rude,*[39] *cruell,* not to trust,

Also in this case there are two in each hemistich, but they are
crowded round the central break, with an effect of breathless-
ness enhanced by the appositional function of *bloudy* in respect
of *full of blame.* This last word (*blame*) is the only abstract noun,
recalling the dominant feature of the previous two lines, while
a link between the two halves of the quatrain is established
(apart from the rhymes) also by the repetition of the identical
opening word (*Is*—the only finite verbal form) in lines 2 and 3.
Finally, the very last words of the quatrain, *to trust,* establish a
continuous grammatical link with the other three strophes of
the poem, in each of which there is one (and only one) in-

---

[38] Or remember the sudden shift from singular to plural in the couplet of
Sonnet 94.
[39] *Rude* is used as an attribute of desire (=lust before action) in *Lucrece*, line
175: 'brainsicke rude desire'.

finitive form, with a different logical function: ₈*to make*, ₁₀*to have*, ₁₄*to shun*.

1.6. The progress of past participles. Quatrain I is formed by two closely joined blocks of grammatical categories, the first dominated by abstract nouns, the second by adjectives. Quatrain II has a completely different grammatical structure, announced by its very first word: the past participle, which had appeared only once before, and merely as an adjective, dominates the strophe:

> *Inioyed* no sooner | but *dispised* straight,
> Past reason *hunted*, | and no sooner *had*
> Past reason *hated* | as a *swollowed* bayt,
> On purpose *layd* | to make the taker mad.

The change of the dominating grammatical features is so marked as to seem due to design rather than chance. Of the two adjectives in this quatrain one is in its turn a past participle (like *periurd* in line 3) and the other (₈*mad*) is a complement, renouncing both the attributive and the predicative functions characteristic of its grammatical category; also the only three abstract nouns lose their grammatical characteristic as being part of adverbial expressions (₆*Past reason*, ₇*Past reason*, ₈*On purpose*). A structural parallelism with quatrain I is provided by the repetition of the same features at the beginning of the central lines of each quatrain, but in this case it is not used to hold together two blocks of different grammatical categories, but rather to underline the grammatical continuity between the first and the second half of the strophe; a continuity which is given purposefulness by the steady progress of the past participles. The opening *Inioyd* in line 5 is balanced by *dispised* in the second hemistich; the other four past participles (*swollowed* cannot be taken into consideration as being an adjective) are placed serially, as 'rhyme'-words for their respective hemistichs, with ₆*had* as a kind of consonantal sound-bridge between ₆*hunted* and ₇*hated* (for the chime ₈*layd*/ ₇*bayt* see § 1.2 above). The serial arrangement of the past participles throughout the strophe places an extra emphasis on the only hemistich, the last, where they do not appear, compensating in this way for the weak syntactical and semantic position of the sentence, a dependant clause within a formal comparison, the only extended rhetorical figure in the sonnet; *mad* acquires in this way an exceptional importance, and it is understandable that it should have been thought that a word, placed in such a strong position as the last of the octave, should be repeated straight away as the first of the sestet.

1.7. A mad world, my masters: past participles versus abstract nouns. But as soon as we turn to quatrain III it appears clearly, keeping in mind the pattern of grammatical categories so far, that in spite of editorial practice from Malone to Dover Wilson, and in spite of Jakobson's arguments in its favour, the emendation of *Made* in line 9 to *Mad* ought to be rejected. Apart from Graves–Riding, the rejection is advocated by Hilton Landry, who maintains that *Made . . . so* means *made mad*, and that nothing is lost of the meaning,[40] and by I. A. Richards,[41] who enlarges on the same point: 'Why not *Made* with a supplied *mad* and a merely auditory full stop following it? The added emphasis by double echo of *make* and *mad* [in line 8] is worth weighing; and the capital *I* of *In pursut* could be so explained. It is one thing to become mad; it is another to have been deliberately *made mad* [. . .]'. The phonic pun *mad/made* is not rare in Shakespeare (as even Jakobson–Jones acknowledge on Kökeritz's authority); it should be added that the phonic gap between short and long *a* (æ and ei) must have been narrower then than now; hence Shakespeare's fondness for the word-play *mad/mated*, twice repeated in *Comedy of Errors* (III. ii. 53, and v. i. 281) and once in *Taming of the Shrew* (III. ii. 246); a word-play which is punctually repeated in lines 6–7 of Sonnet 129, substituting *h* for *m*: *had/hated*. The vocalic exchange is picked up by $_8$*mad*/$_9$*made* in the next two lines of the sonnet, and used to join together quatrains II and III not by identical repetition or anadiplosis,[42] but by the variation of the inner sound, implying both continuity and change, in fact a new start on the same lines.

The necessity of keeping the original *Made* as the opening

---

[40] H. Landry, op. cit., p. 101.

[41] 'Jakobson's Shakespeare', op. cit.

[42] The figure of anadiplosis (for Puttenham, *Arte of English Poesie*, p. 200, the Redouble, when 'with the word by which you finish your verse, ye beginne the next verse with the same') is uncharacteristic of Shakespeare, while it is very frequent in Daniel. Schaar (*Sonnet Problem*, p. 140) cannot find a single perfect anadiplosis in the whole sequence.

word of quatrain III is even more apparent when we consider
the pattern of grammatical categories in this strophe:

> *Made* In pursut | and in possession so,
> *Had,* having, and in quest, | to have extreame,
> A blisse in proofe and *provd* | and very wo,
> Before a ioy *proposd* | behind a dreame.

The structure is more elaborate than in the previous quatrain,
and is based on a complex play of grammatical functions. The
pre-eminence of past participles, joining this quatrain to the
previous one (both begin with a past participle), is subtly contrasted with that of the abstract nouns, linking quatrain III
with quatrain I, of which they were the dominant feature.
The past participles are arranged with perfect symmetry in the
first hemistichs of each of the four lines: twice as the opening
words in lines 9–10—another good reason for maintaining that
Made and not *Mad* was meant, considering also the continuity
of the vowel-sound pattern (/ei/æ/) between the initial words
of these lines and the terminal rhyme-words of the previous
quatrain, b*a*yt, m*a*d; twice as the closing words of the first
hemistichs in lines 11–12. To the pattern of continuity of the
past participles corresponds the re-emergence of the abstract
nouns, in serried array. Four of them are complements indicating past or present action and are arranged in antithetical
pairs, past against present: ₉*In pursut* versus ₉*in possession*; ₁₀*in
quest* versus ₁₁*in proofe*; their semantic function is essentially
temporal, comparable to the adverbial use of *before* and *behind*
in line 12, except that here the contrast is between 'before'
and 'now', lust 'till action' and lust 'in action', leading us back
to line 2: in other words, they indicate the complex mental
pattern of the 'times' of lust, which I propose to discuss later.
The other four abstract nouns, *blisse, wo, ioy, dreame*—all expressing emotional states and attributes of 'lust'—are symmetrically arranged one in each hemistich of lines 11–12, a simplified
reproduction of the arrangement of the abstract nouns in lines
1–2, where there were two in each hemistich. This is further
testimony of the close links between the quatrains, a complete
sequence forming a unified block, leaving out of the scheme the
final couplet. As in quatrain II the second half of line 8, 'to
make the taker mad', received special emphasis from the

absence of the pervasive grammatical features of the quatrain, so in quatrain III the second hemistich of line 10, 'to have extreame', receives the same distinction: *extreame* becomes a key word, like *mad* in line 8, referring to all three stages of lust, before, in action, and after; and it fulfils, like *mad*, a complemental function. In fact, *to make . . . mad* and *to have extreame* are parallel clauses, depending on past participles, *layd* in the first case, *Made* in the second. Lust is a bait placed in order to make mad those that take it, but it is in its turn made mad when $_6$*hunted* (=*In pursut*) and $_5$*Inioyed* (=*in possession*), and is made in such a way (=*so*) that it can be had only in an extreme degree, with no middle measures; in other words, lust, in all its stages, is mad excess,[43] both bliss and woe, irrational extremes. Accepting the emendation to *Mad*, we would be confronted with an insufferable logical and syntactical difficulty: *Mad* could refer only to *taker* in the previous line, so that the subject of the quatrain would be not 'lust' but 'the lustful person', and to think of a person as 'a joy' or 'a woe' is manifestly absurd. *Made* instead, with its subtle phonic implication, makes the transition possible: it recalls the madness of the luster, but, by analogy with all the other past participles, reminds us that the subject is lust and not its 'taker'.

1.8. Grammatical categories versus rhetorical figures.

The final couplet ignores the grammatical categories dominating the quatrains ([1–2] abstract nouns + [3–4] adjectives → [5–8] past participles → [9–12] past participles + abstract nouns), and exhibits an independent, though solid, grammatical pattern. Instead of abstract, concrete nouns ($_{13}$*world*, $_{14}$*heaven*, $_{14}$*hell*); instead of past participles, finite verbal forms ($_{13}$*knowes*, $_{13}$*knowes*, $_{14}$*leads*); the infinitive ($_{14}$*To shun*) is in a more emphatic position than those in the three quatrains; finally, I have already called attention (see § 1.4 above) to the significance of the single personal noun, $_{14}$*men*, in the plural, connected with the collective value of *world* and *none* in the previous line. The structure revealed by the succession and arrangement of grammatical

---

[43] Excess is merely implicit here; the word itself is used only in one sonnet, no. 146, with reference to the pampering of the body (lines 7–8): 'Shall wormes inheritors of this excess, / Eate up thy [the soul's] charge?' See my comment in chapter V, § 2.0, and *Love's Labour's Lost*, v. ii. 73, where excess is characteristic of 'the blood of youth'.

categories is perfectly coincident with the sound-pattern (see
§ 1.1 above) and with the logical pattern which begins to
emerge in the poem. It is once again couplet versus quatrains,
the world of men versus individual lust. But the break between
lines 1–12 and 13–14 is not unbridgeable. The poet is careful
to establish, with the contrast, a balanced parallelism between
the beginning and the end of the poem. This is done through a
correspondence not of grammatical functions, but of rhetorical
figures between lines 1–2 and the final couplet. Lines 1 and 14
propose an identical antithesis, or rather antithetical parallelism: $_1$*Spirit*/ *shame*; $_{14}$*heaven*/ *hell*. These are the sonnet's four
'imagin'd corners', enclosing the 'round earth' of lust; and that
they are merely 'imagin'd' will be clear when we discover that
the four nouns share one common metaphorical meaning; like
Phoenix and Turtle, the two antithetical couples have

> the essence but in one:
> Two distincts, division none,
> Number there in *lust*[44] was slain. (26–8)

But this requires a more elaborate explanation (see §§ 2.1 and
2.2 below). The other rhetorical figure linking the opening and
closing lines of the sonnet is more rare and therefore more
striking. Wilson calls it 'Regression' (see § 1.0 above) and
Puttenham, more learnedly, '*Epanalepsis*, or the Eccho sound,
otherwise the Slowe Returne'.[45] Here it is in line 2:

> lust in action, and till action, lust

and again in line 13:

> the world well knowes yet none knowes well

The same figure is applied to completely different grammatical

---

[44] I have taken the liberty of substituting *lust* for *love*: Sonnet 129 reveals the
equivalence of the two terms.

[45] Puttenham, ed. cit., p. 200: 'Ye have an other sorte of repetition, when ye
make one worde both beginne and end your verse, which therefore I call the
slow retourne, otherwise the Eccho sound, as thus: *Much must he be beloved, that
loveth much,* / *Feare many must he needs, whom many feare.*' Schaar (*Sonnet Problem*,
p. 136) lists these under the figure of Antimetabole (see Puttenham, op. cit.,
pp. 208–9, Antimetabole or the Counterchaunge), but there is no doubt that the
definition of Epanalepsis in this case is more correct. Schaar considers also line 11
an Antimetabole, because he adopts the reading 'A bliss in proof, and proved a
very woe'. The recurrence of the same rhetorical figure in lines 2 and 13 is noted
also by J. Winny, op. cit., p. 113.

categories (two nouns in the first case, verb and adverb in the second), but there is no possibility of missing the parallelism in construction.

So, the two lines of the couplet send us back, in perfect reverse symmetry, through their rhetorical figures, to the first two lines of the sonnet, 14:1::13:2. The forward rush of the quatrains is checked by the couplet 'like as the waves make towards the pebbled shore': if it is true that the movement of the lines, the figures, the sounds and rhythms, the parts of speech, can be described in the words of Sonnet 60:

> Each changing place with that which goes before,
> In sequent toile all forwards do contend,

it is also true that, upon reaching the shore of the final couplet, they ebb back, retracing the initial design; the cycle is complete, at least for a moment, and the sonnet is a form perfectly achieved. In spite of its unusual structure, Sonnet 129 is not merely 'a fourteen-line poem': it has an extremely precise, rather than elaborate, formal organization, which supports an even more consistent logical organization. Taking into account the elements so far considered, its formal structure can be schematized, as shown in fig. 10.

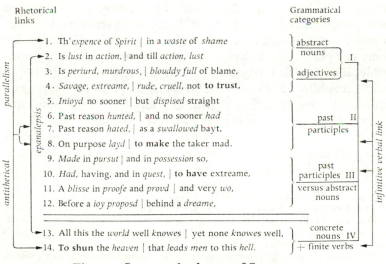

Fig. 10. Structural schema of Sonnet 129

2.0. The times of lust.[46]   One outstanding aspect of the
structural organization of the sonnet is the treatment of the time
element: a study of it may well show the coincidence of the two
patterns, formal and logical. The opening lines are clear:
they define lust *in action*. They establish an ideal (or historical)
present—*Is*—which is the moment of action—in fact the
sexual act. But the rest of the sonnet, after taking that moment
as its starting-point, moves all the time backward and for-
wards from it. The four abstract nouns in line 1 establish the
abstract 'now' of the poem, further emphasized by $_2$*in action*,
which, like the similar expressions in quatrain III ($_9$*In pursut*,
$_9$*in possession*, $_{10}$*in quest*, $_{11}$*in proofe*), acts as a temporal definition.
But the second hemistich of line 2, reversing the first, effects a
temporal displacement, so that the eight adjectives in lines 3–4
refer to lust 'before' its enjoyment, the effects of the unsatisfied
sexual impulse. In quatrain II the temporal function is entrusted to the serried array of past participles: $_5$*Inioyd* evokes
once again the 'now', the moment of enjoyment, but the
second hemistich of line 5 and the next two lines (with a
momentary throw-back in the first half of line 6—*hunted*) deal
with the 'after'-effects of the enjoyment of lust. The simile of
the swallowed bait is an extension of the considerations on
'lust-after', in order to bring finally home the irrational
character of lust. While in quatrain I lust before consummation
was characterized by adjectives denoting violence and deception—in other words, wilful malice—quatrain II insists on
only one point: also before, but especially after, lust is irrespon-
sible; if its pursuit is irrational ($_6$*Past reason*),[47] no less irrational
is the revulsion after the event ($_7$*Past reason*), and therefore $_8$*mad*
in both these stages. The logical development of the quatrains
is now apparent: the first insists on lust 'now' and 'before', the
second on lust 'now' and 'after'—but while the adjectival
sequence seemed to imply a deliberate malice in the attempt to
secure sexual pleasure, the insistence on madness before and

[46] The already quoted essay by Richard Levin, 'Sonnet CXXIX as a "Dramatic"
Poem', contains an excellent analysis of the time-sequence of the poem, on which
Helen Vendler has based her very perceptive reconsideration of the sonnet,
polemizing with Jakobson's reading ('Jakobson, Richards and Shakespeare's
Sonnet CXXIX'). See also Ph. Martin, op. cit., pp. 55–61.

[47] Cf. *Lucrece*, line 243: 'My will is strong past reasons weak remooving', where,
of course, will = lust.

after 'lust in action' suggests that those who are the prey of sexual passions are no longer responsible for their behaviour. The attitude at this point is not so far from that of John Donne in his 'Farewell to Love', frequently quoted in connection with Sonnet 129[48] also in view of striking verbal parallelisms with quatrains II and III:

> But, from late faire
> His highnesse sitting in a golden Chaire,
> Is no lesse cared for after three dayes
> By children, then the thing which lovers so
> Blindly admire, and with such worship wooe;
> Being had, enjoying it decayes:
> And thence,
> What before pleas'd them all, takes but one sense,
> And that so lamely, as it leaves behinde
> A kinde of sorrowing dulnesse to the minde. (lines 11–20)

Also Donne defines the two moments, 'before' and 'after' the sexual enjoyment: 'Blindly' and 'woo' correspond respectively to 'Past reason' and 'hunted'[49] in line 6 of Sonnet 129; and there is a strong temptation to equate not only 'Being had' with 'Had' in line 10, but also 'before pleased' and 'behind . . . a . . . sorrowing dullness' with the statements in lines 11–12 of the sonnet. But, as Richard Levin points out,[50] Donne's treatment is 'essentially static (in that the speaker is not himself undergoing an experience in the poem, but is only developing a conclusion he had already reached)'; besides, while Donne concludes his 'Farewell' with a light-hearted and obviously unreliable resolution to shun women (with some regret: 'Ah cannot we / As well as Cocks and Lyons jocund be, / After such pleasures'!), crowned with a grimly obscene innuendo: 'If all faile, / 'Tis but applying worme-seed to the Taile', Shakespeare 'knows well' the impossibility of so easy an escape. He, therefore, though aware of both the pleasure and the 'sorrowing dullness' (bliss and woe) attending the enjoyment of love-lust, alters their sequence in quatrain III, which is particularly

[48] Sidney's sonnet on Desire (the last but one of *Certain Sonnets* appended to the 1598 *Arcadia*) is also associated by critics with Shakespeare's no. 129, but Sidney's attitude is one of mere abuse and rejection of lust in the name of virtue, 'Desiring nought but how to kill desire'.

[49] *Woo*, rhyming with *so* in Donne, seems to contain also the suggestion of *woe*, as in Sonnet 129, line 11.

[50] R. Levin, op. cit., p. 180.

dense with temporal pointers. While the first two quatrains stress in turn the 'before' and 'after' stages, the third manipulates with extraordinary ability the three moments, with no less than three references to each of them in separate lines: $_9In$ *pursuit*, $_{10}in$ *quest*, $_{12}Before$ mark the expectation of lust; $_9in$ *possession*, $_{10}having$, $_{11}in$ *proof* its enjoyment; $_{10}had$, $_{11}proved$, $_{12}behind$ its 'after'-taste. But there is a progressive attenuation of the negative views of lust before and after implied in the earlier parts of the sonnet. Line 9 sees it as 'made' or rendered utterly irrational by the tension of pursuit and enjoyment, and it is this irrational character that makes it impossible to 'have' it in any of its stages, except in excess: $_{10}extreme$ is repeated from line 4, implicitly recalling the first stage of lust, but emphasizing the least damning of the definitions contained there. It is subtly suggested that the ravages of lust are essentially confined to its preparatory stage, when it is still merely *Desire* —to use Sidney's definition. It is only as a consequence of excess in expectation, that, at the moment of fruition and afterwards (line 11: *in proof* and *proved*), it is both *bliss* and *woe*[51] together, excess of joy and excess of sorrow.

Having surveyed with a kind of rapid shuttle-movement the three moments of sexual passion in the first three lines of the quatrain (line 9 'before' → 'now' → line 10 'after' → 'now' → 'before' → line 11 'now' → 'after'), the last line returns to the more conventional antithesis, *before* versus *behind*. Once again, Levin's comment is illuminating (though I disagree with his contention that the sonnet represents the psychological reaction of a man 'to a recent sexual encounter'):

'a joy' is much less seriously qualified by 'a dream', a surprisingly mild negation which does not point to anything evil or even unpleasant in lust, but only to the transient nature of its satisfaction, and which leaves us with the impression (enforced by its crucial position as the last word before the couplet) that the entire disturbing experience is now fading out in the speaker's memory.[52]

[51] It is an established fact that the /oᵘ/ and the /u/ sounds were not sharply differentiated in Shakespeare's time, witness the puns on Rome/room in *Julius Caesar* and Donne's lines quoted above (see note 49). The omophony woe/woo implies, at least at subliminal level, the inclusion of the *wooing* stage ('before') also in this line devoted to the 'now' and 'after' of lust.

[52] R. Levin, op. cit., pp. 177 and 179. Cf. Ph. Martin's ingenious suggestion (op. cit., p. 61) for an alternative reading of line 12, based on the lack of punctuation in Quarto: '(lust is) facing a joy which lies behind a dream'.

In fact, the progressive toning-down of the connotative features had not been observed by earlier commentators, who saw the sonnet as a mere dogmatic condemnation of lust—K. F. Thompson, for instance, found that 'The word "dream" is difficult here', and translated it into 'nightmare',[53] while others referred to Tarquin's meditation on 'honour' versus 'lust' before he raped Lucrece (lines 211–12):

> What win I if I gaine the thing I seeke?
> A dreame, a breath, a froth of fleeting joy.

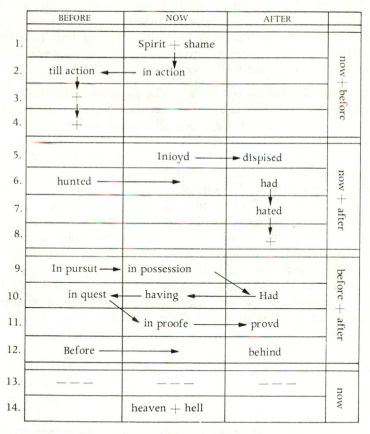

Fig. 11. Time-scheme of Sonnet 129

[53] K. F. Thompson, 'Shakespeare's Sonnet 129', *The Explicator*, vii (February, 1949), item 27; reprinted in Willen's and Reed's *Casebook*, pp. 273–4.

But also Tarquin, egging himself on to his foul enterprise, is describing the condition of satisfied lust in the mildest possible terms; 'behind a dream' is no more than Donne's statement that lust 'leaves behind / A kind of sorrowing dullness to the mind'.

'Before' and 'after' make us expect a 'now'; it is at this point that we rediscover also in the time-sequence the same break that we found in the sound-pattern and grammatical structure: after all the to-ing and fro-ing in time of the quatrains, line 13 affords no temporal indication, while line 14 suggests, through a parallelism of puns which I will examine in a moment, not a static but a dynamic condition of being, an abstract 'now', a present that keeps repeating itself like that of line 1 of the sonnet. Perhaps the diagram given in fig. 11 may best summarize the time-sequence in the sonnet.

2.1. The nibbler at the bait. The parallelism between the first and the last lines is based on nearly alliterative antinomic pairings (see § 1.8 above), but still more on the semantic polivalence of those which I have called the four imagined corners of the sonnet, its key words. The memorability of line 1 (one of the greatest in Shakespeare) is due not only to its density of sound but still more to its density of meaning: (a) 'Th'expence of Spirit in a waste of shame', at the level of purely verbal imagery may evoke the spilling and wasting (Lat. *spandere*) of precious liquid in a desert or wilderness (waste land—but note also the suggestion of expence = expanse, a desolate immensity). (b) But a more practical Elizabethan mind would recognize immediately the economic implications: *expense*, used only in two sonnets, nos. 30 and 94, had a very specific meaning: financial disposal of an estate easily turned to *waste* (Jakobson and Jones quote from *Lear*, II. i. 200: 'To have th'expense and waste of his revenues'),[54] so that lust in action would immediately appear as an unprofitable or downright mistaken and nearly criminal financial transaction. (c) 'Th'expence of Spirit', on the other hand, partook of another semantic area, very nearly scientific or medical. It was current knowledge or belief at the time that—to use the words of a learned book which Shakespeare knew, Timothy Bright's *A Treatise of Melancholie*

---

[54] Jakobson and Jones, op. cit., p. 15.

(1586)—'the excessive travaile of animal actions, or such as springe from the braine, *waiste and spende that spirite*' which is the intermediary between the body and the soul,[55] or rather 'is in the world the onely cheerer of all thinges, & dispenseth that life imparted of God to al other creatures'; the loss of reason, Bright adds, is due to the 'lavish *waste*, and predigall [sic] *expence of the spirite* in one passion, which dispensed with iudgement, would suffice the execution of many worthy actions besides'. 'Spirit', here, becomes more specifically the 'spirit generative', which was thought to originate and maintain physiological life.[56]

   This in turn leads to (d) a further way of reading the line as a sequence of *risqués double entendres*. As Fiedler[57] puts it: 'we are expected to know that *spirit* has the second meaning of *semen*, and *waste* is also to be read as *waist*.'[58] Or, more extensively, Jakobson and Jones:[59] '*Spirit*, in the vocabulary of Shakespeare's era, meant a life-giving, vital power manifested in mind and in semen as well; correspondingly, *shame* carried the meaning of chastity and genitalia as parts of shame';[60] therefore they paraphrase the line: 'The expenditure of vital power (mind and semen) in a wasting of shame (chastity and genitalia)'. The final outcome of these semantic ambiguities is that, while *Spirit* and *shame*, taken at their face value, appear antithetical (the spiritual principle versus physical unworthiness), at the level of innuendo they are one and the same thing:

---

[55] *A Treatise of Melancholie*, op. cit., pp. 250–1; the italics in this and the next quotation are mine. For Shakespeare's knowledge of Bright and the relation of spirit to body and soul see Interchapter, § 0 above, and especially note 1, and cf. J. Dover Wilson, *What Happens in Hamlet*, p. 319.

[56] Cf. P. Cruttwell, op. cit., p. 14, and Ph. Martin, op. cit., pp. 57–8. Bright uses the phrase 'expence of spirit' also earlier in his *Treatise* (p. 63), and the notion remained current in the seventeenth century: as W. R. Elton reminds us (*King Lear and the Gods*, p. 111), Francis Bacon maintained in *Sylva Sylvarum* (1627) that 'much use of Venus [=lust] doth dim the sight . . . The cause is *the expence of spirits*'. Donne was more precise on the results of the 'expense of spirit' in the practice of lust—in the poem quoted above ('Farewell to Love') he specifies: 'each such [sexual] Act, they say, / Diminisheth the length of life a day'.

[57] L. Fiedler, 'Some Contexts' etc., p. 64.

[58] Cf. *Hamlet*, II. ii. 231 ff.: '*Ham.*: Then you live about [Fortune's] waist, or in the middle of her favours?—*Guil.*: Faith, her privates we.—*Ham.*: In the secret parts of Fortune? O, most true; she is a strumpet.'

[59] Jakobson and Jones, op. cit., pp. 14–15.

[60] It would be better, perhaps, to refer directly to the Latin *pudor* (modesty, hence chastity), and *pudenda* (the unmentionable parts of the body).

the *thing*, in fact, 'which', in Donne's words, 'lovers so blindly admire'.

I believe that the *double entendre* is deliberate, because the covert allusions to the sexual organs are repeated with symmetrical precision and perfect tempo in the middle and at the end of the sonnet. What is the function of the 'expendable' sentence in the central lines of the poem (7–8), the only figure of simile? It introduces for the first time the human person— *the taker*—in what had risked to become only an abstract description of lust; but it is meant to recall as well the 'physical' presence of sex, the concrete 'thing' for the abstract lust; none of Shakespeare's contemporaries would have missed the real meaning of the one concrete noun in the passage, *bait*, a common metaphor used for instance by the author of Sonnet IV in *The Passionate Pilgrim* (a bawdy trifle on Venus and Adonis, sandwiched between two sonnets borrowed from *Love's Labour's Lost*):

> But whether unripe years did want conceit
> Or he did scorn to take the figured proffer,
> The tender nibbler would not *take* the *bait*
> But blushed and smiled at every gentle offer.

(lines 9–12)

The bait being what it undoubtedly is, it reflects an equivocal light on the 'tender nibbler', corresponding to the 'taker' of Sonnet 129—there is no need to call on Freud in order to learn about the phallic implications of the fish symbol.

The last line of the sonnet expresses the impossibility 'To shun the heaven that leads men to this hell'—so obvious a statement that Jakobson and Jones gave up at this point their 'tentative explanatory rewording' and reproduced the sentence as it stands in the original. The antithesis is emphasized by the alliteration and placing of *heaven* and *hell*, so that the two words are generally taken to refer respectively to the promised bliss of love and post-coital sorrow (enhanced by a sense of sin). This is not supported either by the temporal sequence we have already noticed, or by the general trend of the argument up to this point of the sonnet. The reference to the opening line of Sonnet 146, 'Poor soule the center of my sinfull earth' appears more promising, especially for those who consider the two poems closely connected as the concluding palinodes of the sonnet sequence: the two contrasted poles are the heaven of the soul—also idealized *love*—and the hell of the body, the sinful earth of *lust*.[61] This interpretation also seemed valid to those who were quick to discover in the word *hell* another obscene *double entendre*, the 'inferno' of line 12 of Sonnet 144 ('I gesse one angel [the lovely boy] in an others [the ill-coloured woman's] hel'). Fiedler, for instance, comments:[62] 'though [Sonnet 129] ends on the very pun we have noticed in 144, this time the equation of hell and the pudenda is intended to stir not the snigger but the shudder'. Perhaps this is too emotional an approach to the subject—there is no reason for snigger or shudder. What has been overlooked is the fact that, also in this case, the antithesis is only apparent on the rhetorical level; the two words *heaven* and *hell* actually carry the same (double) meaning. Heaven is a traditional metaphor, in conventional love-poetry, for the beloved, the poet's mistress not only in her idealized, but also in her physical aspect; heaven's bliss there-fore, the lover's crowning conquest, a consummation devoutly to be wished, is in fact the physical consummation of love. And in a sonnet so acutely conscious of paronomasiae based on minimal phonic variations ($_6$had/$_7$hated; $_8$mad/$_9$made—see § 1.7 above), it is not surprising to find an implicit pun on *heaven/haven*—a case in which the only phonic variant is in the length of the *e*-sound ($\varepsilon \rightarrow e^1$) and of which there is at least one other instance in Shakespeare.[63] The haven of the lover's bliss is hinted at with some restraint in *Taming of the Shrew*, v. i. 130–1:

> And happily I have arrived at last
> Unto the wished haven of my bliss;

but Carew's famous elaborate simile in 'The Rapture', of the sexual act as a ship entering port, is only a late reworking of an infinite series of repetitions of a euphemistic metaphor recurring with obsessive frequency in the Italian *novelle* of the fifteenth and sixteenth centuries; that Shakespeare was aware of its meaning is made clear in Sonnet 137 where, being conscious of the fact

---

[61] Cf. *Venus and Adonis*, lines 791–2: 'Call it not love, for love to heaven is fled, / Since sweating lust on earth usurpt his name.'

[62] Fiedler, 'Some Contexts' etc., p. 64.

[63] In the most rhetoric conscious of the Histories, *Richard II*, i. iii. 276: 'All places that the eye of *heaven* visits / Are to a wise man, ports and happy *havens*.'

that his lady *was* a whore, he speaks of being 'anchored in the baye where all men ride' (line 6).

Spirit and *shame*, the *bait* and the *taker*, *heaven* and *hell*, all the basic antinomies of the sonnet, its ideal boundaries and its antithetical centre (love versus lust, soul versus body), are—in their paronomasic values—all synonyms. Sonnet 129, on the surface an invective against lust, is in fact encompassed by the physical images of sex.

2.2. The maker and the taker.   Sonnet 129 is a dramatic meditation on the ethics of sex. I. A. Richards seems to be approaching this meaning in the Jamesian circumlocutions of the last paragraphs of his review of the Jakobson–Jones pamphlet.[64] He rightly warns us against the fallacy of 'mistaking a poem [. . .] for a preachment, a hortatory discourse', but feels compelled all the same to ask: 'What about the position which sonnet 129 is so intricately, so miraculously designed to define, to display and to sanction?' and again, 'Is not Shakespeare's view of lust now out of date? Does not a re-spelling of that old four-letter word with three letters instead, as *sex*, make all the difference in the world?' The replies are indirect and deliberately ambiguous, but I shall try—on the basis of his references and quotations—to give them a simpler form, or at least to say what I feel they ought to be, as one of the 'many readers, many minds' he mentions. Starting from the last question: there is no need for re-spelling, since Shakespeare's view of lust is actually an attempt to react both to the theological and moralistic condemnation *and* to the courtly idealization and sublimation of lust into love; for purposes of communication as well as aesthetics, he was bound to a system of linguistic signs which did not include sex in the modern acceptation; he did not break the system but devised new and revolutionary patterns and ways of organizing the signs, which would not only convey new meanings but ultimately renew the system itself. Shakespeare's subject in Sonnet 129 is actually sex—if we really need to use this word in order to emphasize the fact that his view is *not* out of date. The dramatic quality of the poem prevents it from being a mere statement: the inner tensions between old and new are fortunately unresolved, but the position that emerges (perhaps 'position' is the wrong word for such a dynamic, rather than static, attitude) is not different from that much more laboriously hinted at in Sonnet 20 (see Interchapter, above). Sex, or 'love's use', is one, and perhaps the most important, of the 'hues' in man's total being, his heaven and his hell—a heaven and a hell that cannot be told apart from each other (or both apart from man, since they are within him), like the enigmatic Phoenix and Turtle in Shakespeare's one truly metaphysical poem.[65] Richards rightly quotes from the *Phoenix and Turtle*, and (in order to find a more deliberately 'doctrinal' poetic expression of the same attitude) from John Donne, 'who, in Shakespeare's time, was the first man, they say, to use the word *sex* in its present dominant sense'. It is indeed, as Richards says, 'mutually illuminating to put a stanza of "The Exstasie" beside Sonnet 129:

> So must pure lovers' souls descend
>   T'affections and to faculties,
> That sense may reach and apprehend,
>   Else a great Prince in prison lies'.

What if the great Prince—in spite of all the surmises of the Donne scholars[66]—be, after all, the whole man, soul and spirit of sense, affections and faculties, all hues in his controlling? This may not be what Donne had in mind when writing his line, but what is not true of Donne may well be true of Shakespeare.

I have said that heaven and hell are both one, and both not outside but inside man, or rather part of him. Doctor Faustus could have told us as much with regard to hell;[67] but what about heaven and its traditional tenant? Also in this case Richards can suggest a reply, though in his usual devious way. He extracts it from the Jakobson–Jones's essay by putting to-

---

[65] On this see G. W. Knight, *The Mutual Flame*, an important book that frequently touches upon Shakespeare's feeling for the complex and contradictory unity of man's personality, but is distracted by too many side issues, so that, for instance, Sonnet 129—so important a poem from this point of view—is hardly mentioned at all.

[66] See the discussion in Appendix D of J. Donne, *The Elegies and the Songs and Sonnets*, ed. H. Gardner (Oxford, 1965), pp. 259–65. Dame Helen Gardner has no doubts that the 'Prince' is the soul in the temporary prison of the body.

[67] At least he should have learnt as much from Mephistophilis' words in *Dr. Faustus* (ed. J. D. Jump, 1962, sc. iii. 78): 'why, this is hell, nor am I out of it.'

gether in close sequence three quotations from different sections of their linguistic analysis of Sonnet 129:

(A) If the first centrifugal line [line 8 of the sonnet] introduces the hero, *the taker*, however, still not as an agent but as a victim, the final centrifugal line [14] brings the exposure of the malevolent culprit, *the heaven that leads men to this hell*, and thus discloses by what perjurer the joy was proposed and the lure laid. [p. 18].

(B) Both personal nouns of the poem (II *taker* and IV *men*) characterize human beings as passive goals of extrinsic non-human and inhuman actions. [p. 20]

(C) The final line seems to refer to the ultimate persona, the celestial condemner of mankind. [p. 27]

Richards limits his comment to two short sentences: 'These explications seem indeed to be reaching toward the "deep structure" of the poem. The interpreter seems to be placing Shakespeare at a viewpoint not too far removed from that of the author of *Milton's God*.'

I feel that to postulate for Shakespeare the Empsonian conception of a hostile God is not wholly warranted. Milton, at a time of open ideological warfare, when it was impossible not to take sides, had an overpowering background of Puritan theology; Shakespeare, more than half a century earlier, though certainly aware of the multiplicity of conflicting doctrines and new philosophies undermining the reassuring divinely established hierarchical order of the macrocosm, found himself in the eye of the ideological and theological storm without even fully realizing his position, except through his poet's gift of sensibility. In such circumstances his reaction would be not active opposition to the religious establishment, but covert radical doubt. His poetic strategy is shrewdly illustrated by William Elton in the concluding paragraph of his study of *King Lear and the Gods*:[68]

By depicting a superstitious pagan progressing toward doubt in *his* gods, Shakespeare secured for the play the approbation of the less speculative devout, who saw in its direction the victory of the True Faith [. . .]. Moreover, he obtained for it the interest of those more troubled and sophisticated auditors who were not to be stilled by pious assurances in the unsteady new world of the later

[68] R. W. Elton, op. cit., p. 338.

Renaissance. For the latter, *King Lear* carried its own *tua res agitur* significance.

Sonnet 129, a private poem, not a play for the public theatre, applies the same strategy with greater subtlety, because it has to satisfy not the indiscriminate audience's but the author's own mind. Jakobson and Jones, using to a purpose their linguistic scalpels, think they have reached the very heart of the matter when they expose the apparent antinomy between a passive human 'victim' (the taker of the bait, men led to hell) and a non-human agent—and, taking *heaven* at its face value, consider the Maker (who made the bait that makes the taker mad?) as 'celestial condemner' and 'malevolent culprit' at the same time. But: (a) is the reply to the question I have asked parenthetically really God? Or is it Lust?—(b) Is the heaven that leads men to *this* (not just *any*) hell really and only the heaven above? Or is it some other *thing*? I feel that Jakobson and Jones have given up their exploration too soon; it is quite acceptable as a stage of Shakespeare's mental progress, as a diagnosis of his dissatisfaction with current theological notions. But a deeper probe may reveal a further layer of meaning. The agents—heaven and the maker—the pudenda and lust—are both one, sex—and sex is human rather than non-human; in their turn men and the taker are not necessarily 'victims', but they are certainly *recipients* of sex's action. The human person and personality, the whole man, is by no means the 'passive goal of extrinsic non-human and inhuman actions'; on the contrary, he includes such actions, good or bad, creative or destructive as they may be. As in Sonnet 121, so also in Sonnet 129, Shakespeare's God is not Milton's God, but the man within (see ch. III § 3.4).

2.3. Deceptive palinode. To consider Sonnet 129 as a palinode, as Lever and Fiedler do, implies the acceptance of exactly that system of values—religious, ethical, and social—that the meditative poems call in question. A system of values upheld by such Court poets as Thomas Watson, whose 'passion' rejecting Love (that is *Lust*) is worth quoting in full in the English version (he provided also a longer text in Latin). It is no. XCVIII in his 'ΕΚΑΤΟΜΠΑΘΙΑ (1582), prefaced with the remark that 'The Author in this passion, telling what *Love*

is, easeth his heart, as it were, by rayling out right, where he
can worke no other manner of revenge':

> Harke wanton youthes, whome *Beawtie* maketh blinde,
> And learne of me, what kinde a thing is *Love*;
> *Love* is a *Brainesicke Boy*, and fierce by kinde;
> A *Willfull Thought*, which Reason can not move;
>   A *Flattring Sycophant*; a *Murd'ring Thiefe*;
>   A *Poysned choaking Bayte*; a *Tysing Griefe*;
> A *Tyrant* in his Lawes; in speach untrue;
> A *Blindfold Guide*; a *Feather* in the winde;
> A right *Chameleon* for change of hewe;
> A *Lamelimme Lust*; a *Tempest* of the minde;
>   A *Breach of Chastitie*; all vertues *Foe*;
>   A *private warre*; a *Toilsome webbe* of woe;
> A *Fearefull Iealosie*; a *Vaine Desire*;
> A *Labyrinth*; a *Pleasing Miserie*;
> A *Shipwracke* of mans life; a *Smoaklesse fire*;
> A *Sea* of teares; a *lasting Lunacie*;
>   A *Heavie servitude*; a *Dropsie Thurst*;
>   A *Hellish Gaile*, whose captives are accurst.[69]

Shakespeare is sure to have known Watson's collection of
eighteeners, a form that he himself experimented in, as some
of the poems in the *Passionate Pilgrim* seem to testify; and I
rather think that he remembered this particular passion when
listing the conventional accusations against Lust in the early
part of Sonnet 129. It is easy to point out also the parallel use
of 'bait', 'woe', 'hell' as the prison of the flesh, as the two poems
proceed.[70] But I feel that once again the correspondence is only
apparent: Shakespeare has chosen as a pattern on which to
model his sonnet what he knew to be an extremely thoughtless
repetition of a poetic convention, not in order to confirm it, but
to modify it from the inside and to expose its inconsistency. In
what is, in the 1609 Quarto, the very next sonnet to this,

[69] I am quoting from the text edited by G. C. Cecioni (Catania, 1964).

[70] It must be added that most of the same images are to be found also in Watson's
passion XVIII, notably 'A bayte for fooles' in line 5, and the whole of line 12, one
of the best in Watson's work: 'A private hell; a very world of woe', which Shakespeare may have remembered in his 'very woe'. But the 'passion', beginning with
a series of oxymora, is a conventional extended oxymoron itself, breaking up after
the second sestina, as Watson himself says: 'The second part is a sudden recantation
or excuse of the Authors evil words . . .' Besides, the image sequence does not
coincide with Shakespeare's.

no. 130, he has taken exactly the same liberty with another of Watson's passions: most critics agree that Sonnet 130, 'My Mistres eyes are nothing like the Sunne', is a deliberate parody of Watson's passion VII, the hyperbolical description of his mistress' beauty; Cruttwell[71] provides a line-by-line comparison showing Shakespeare's ironical reversal of the praises bestowed by Watson on each 'part' of his mistress. It is perhaps worth noticing that the two passions that Shakespeare has chosen for exposure, are the only two addressed to 'the general': as no. XCVIII begins 'Harke wanton youthes', so no. VII's first line is 'Harke you that list to heare what sainte I serve'.

If Watson's poem renouncing love is indeed a palinode, then Shakespeare's Sonnet 129 is not. Neither is Shakespeare, like Sidney, denouncing or renouncing 'Desire'; on the contrary, for him lust is murderous[72] and treacherous as long as it remains 'lust', that is to say unsatisfied desire. But in its satisfaction there is both bliss and woe, heaven and hell, spirit and shame, and that waste which is the inheritance of mortality, of human life. The poet's strategy in Sonnet 129 is very similar to that of Sonnet 94. There, the first line, 'Those that have power to hurt and will do none', seemed to repeat, and agree with, Sir Philip Sidney's chivalrous conception of the exercise of power: 'the more power he hath to hurt, the more admirable is his praise that he will not hurt' (see ch. II, § 2.1 above). In Sonnet 129 the initial hemistich, 'Th'expence of Spirit' would immediately suggest to a contemporary reader the current notion that 'the expence of spirit', through immoderate lechery, was the cause of rapid physical decay (see § 2.1 above). But in both cases the rest of the sonnet is a subtle confutation of the deceptively obvious premise: in 94 the mighty, far from being admirable, are revealed as the 'unmoved' movers, the subtle exploiters of their privileges; in 129 lust is not the body-and-soul-killing vice of the moralities or popular physiology, but, as sex, an essential element of the human personality. The strategy of devious implication based on progressive semantic variations is the same in both sonnets,

---

[71] P. Cruttwell, op. cit., pp. 18–19.

[72] It is significant that the only other two occurrences in the Sonnets of the adjective 'murderous' are both in the marriage group and refer to the refusal to generate, the rejection of the *use* of sex, which is called 'murdrous shame' in Sonnet 9 (line 14), and 'murderous hate' in Sonnet 10 (line 5).

but the tactical moves differ: in 94 a mirror-structure reflects the artificial social order of the octave in the metaphorical natural order of the sestet, while in 129 the forward rush, three times repeated in the phonic, grammatical, and logical patterns of the quatrains, ebbs back to a momentary rest in the couplet. What matters, in the end, is that both are perfectly achieved poems in which the complexity and subtlety of the moving thought and feeling are matched by the harmonious organization of all the contributing parts (sound, rhythm, syntactical and semantic values), with an over-all effect of forceful simplicity.

146

Poore soule the center of my sinfull earth,
My sinfull earth these rebbell powres that thee array,
Why dost thou pine within and suffer dearth
Painting thy outward walls so costlie gay?
Why so large cost hauing so short a lease,
Dost thou vpon thy fading mansion spend?
Shall wormes inheritors of this excesse,
Eate vp thy charge? is this thy bodies end?
Then soule liue thou vpon thy seruants losse,
And let that pine to aggrauat thy store;
Buy tearmes diuine in selling houres of drosse:
Within be fed, without be rich no more,
     So shalt thou feed on death, that feeds on men,
     And death once dead, ther's no more dying then.

CHAPTER V

POOR SOUL: SONNET 146
AND THE ETHICS OF RELIGION

0.1. The Soul as 'Thou'. No critic has missed the fact that Sonnet 146 is substantially 'different' from all the other Sonnets of Shakespeare. It has been associated at most with Sonnet 129,[1] as its partner in a formal palinodic close to Shakespeare's collection (see Interchapter and chapter IV, §§ 0.1 and 2.3 above). But more frequently it has been considered as the 'Holy Sonnet' or 'Divine Meditation' in a garland of love-poems. It is the 'Christian' or religious sonnet, as most critics agree to call it, starting with Hubler[2] (1952) who polemizes vigorously with the Bread Loaf School critics,[3] whom he finds too sophisticated; he maintains that 'the poem is Christian, and that Shakespeare presents Christianity without apology'. Cruttwell finds it 'explicitly and traditionally theological' and compares it with Donne's tenth Holy Sonnet.[4] Once this view has been adopted, the parallel with Donne seems inevitable, and is constantly repeated, at times with some caution,[5] but also to prove the inferiority of Shakespeare in respect of the Metaphysicals: Yvor Winters finds it 'somewhat commonplace when compared with the best of Donne's *Holy Sonnets*'.[6] The air of condescension is derived from Crowe Ransom, although he eschewed the term

---

[1] See P. Cruttwell, *The Shakespearean Moment*, p. 12; J. W. Lever, *Eliz. Love Sonnet*, pp. 180–1; L. Fiedler, 'Some Contexts' etc., pp. 89–90; N. Frye, 'How True a Twain', pp. 44–5; B. Stirling, 'Sonnets 127–154'; Northrop Frye is the only one of them who maintains that Sonnet 146, though linked by contrast with 129, is *not* a palinode.

[2] E. Hubler, *The Sense of Shakespeare's Sonnets*, pp. 59–63. Cf. Santayana's reservations, note 9 below.

[3] The reference is to the debate at the Bread Loaf School of English in 1942, between John Crowe Ransom, Reuben Brower, Daniel Aaron, Elizabeth Drew, and Donald A. Stauffer, who reported it under the title 'Critical Principles and a Sonnet', *The American Scholar*, xii. 1 (January 1943), pp. 52–62.

[4] P. Cruttwell, op. cit., p. 12.

[5] As, for instance, by Stephen Spender, for whom Sonnet 146 shows 'a mood curiously suggesting a religious sonnet by Donne' ('The Alike and the Other', p. 110).

[6] Y. Winters, 'Poetic Style' etc., p. 113.

'Christian' in favour of 'Platonic' ('it is the most Platonic or "spiritual" Sonnet in the entire sequence').[7] Fiedler, on the other hand, surprisingly rejects in this one case the Platonic interpretation: 'the poet in the end abandons the solution of the *Symposium*, the dream of Diotima, in favour of the Christian doctrine that there is no rebirth of beauty, except in God'.[8] I find this statement the only wrong note in Fiedler's admirably argued Platonic interpretation of the main body of the Sonnets: it is due perhaps to the difficulty of fitting 146 into the intellectual scheme he has devised, so that he has grown impatient with it. Leishman, who incidentally in his search for recurring themes and variations in the Sonnets does not even mention the atypical nos. 94, 121, and 129, tries to strike a balance between the two approaches:

If it were possible to use the word conventional in an unpejorative sense, I think it might be said that this is Shakespeare's nearest approach to an expression both of conventional Platonism and of conventional Christianity. It is unique among his sonnets, and is the only one having some real affinity with some of those sonnets full of *suspiria de profundis* written towards the close of his life by Michelangelo, the only sonnets, I think, except perhaps for some of Donne's *Holy Sonnets*, with which it is really comparable: true though it be that the sonnets both of Michelangelo and of Donne were full of clear and explicit expressions and professions of Christian doctrine which we do not find in this sonnet of Shakespeare's.[9]

The last paragraph with its apparent contradiction (Sonnet 146 has no explicit profession of that 'conventional Christianity' which is imputed to it at first) will be considered later in this chapter (see § 2.1 below). At the moment I wish to enlarge on the parallel with Michelangelo's Christian Platonism, which Leishman pursues in the next few pages of his book, in order to show the contrast rather than the identity of the positions of the two poets.[10] In fact Sonnet 146 may appear at first sight a

[7] J. C. Ransom, *The World's Body*, p. 298.

[8] L. Fiedler, 'Some Contexts', p. 90.

[9] J. B. Leishman, *Themes and Variations* etc., pp. 119–20. Compare the statement by George Santayana (*Interpretations* (1900), pp. 151–2) quoted by Rollins, *Variorum*, p. 375: 'The Sonnets are spiritual, but, with the doubtful exception of [146], they are not Christian'.

[10] I have tried to assess the affinities between Shakespeare's Sonnets and Michelangelo's in the introduction to my edition of *Shakespeare's Sonnets* (Bari, 3rd ed. 1971), pp. 32–3. But see on the subject G. W. Knight, *The Mutual Flame*, *passim*; he compares Sonnet 124 to Michelangelo's no. 39.

mere conceited repetition of Michelangelo's Sonnet 105, where
the Soul, the equal of God, passes beyond in the universal form
(trascende nella forma universale), while the body is only 'the
fair outside that pleases the eyes' ('l bel di fuor, ch'agli occhi
piace); where 'for the living, the dying part cannot appease
desire' (a chi vive, quel che more / Quetar non può disir) and
'lust is not love but unbridled will, soul-killing' (Voglia sfrenata
el senso è, non amore, / Che l'alma uccide). But the seeming
analogy is based on the assumption that Sonnet 146 is merely a
clever variation of the traditional, mediaeval 'Contrast of Soul
and Body'. Granted this starting-point, the experience of
Shakespeare's other dramatic meditations should warn us
against taking on trust the poet's acceptance of current ethical
commonplaces. Both Sonnets 94 and 129 started from similar
deceptively obvious current saws, but revealed a moral position
which was very nearly antithetical to the starting-point. So it is
rather surprising to find some very perceptive readers of the
Sonnets ready to take no. 146 at its face value, especially when
the whole poem insists, as we shall see, on a pattern of
reversal.

This pattern, which is both formal and conceptual, is explored
on the latter level by G. Wilson Knight,[11] as the paradox of loss
and gain mutually dependent on each other, not like the waves
of Sonnet 60 (see ch. IV § 1.8), but like the tides in 64, 'Increasing store with losse, and losse with store' (line 8). The paradox
is affirmed 'in terms of both (i) marriage-advice [by getting a
son, says Son. 11, 'As fast as thou shalt wane so fast thou
grow'st'] and (ii) literary-immortality [by writing verse, says
Sonnet 15, 'As he (= Time) takes from you, I ingraft you new']'.
In Sonnet 146 the paradox is 'firmly stated in religious terms [...].
It repeats, and interprets for us, our other thoughts on the universal principle of interaction and balance, loss and gain.
These [. . .] we have listed in relation to the temporal process,
as a natural phenomenon; in terms of the marriage, biological,
process; and in the literary-immortality thought-pattern.
Clearly we are to feel it as a universal principle of which all
these are aspects, and it is the principle that matters.' B. C.
Southam, in a controversial but very important essay, which I

---

[11] G. W. Knight, op. cit., pp. 92–3.

propose to discuss later,[12] takes issue with Knight's next paragraph, 'here, in our religious sonnet, the great thing is firmly said, because an adequate thought-mould, in terms of a religious tradition, is being used'. Southam's objection, that Shakespeare's 'subscription to Christian tenets' is far from proven, can be countered with the remark that Knight speaks of Shakespeare's 'use' of a religious thought-mould, not of his acceptance of the creed. In fact it could be maintained that also here, as in the Sonnets examined in the previous chapters, a traditional pattern of belief is used as a 'container' for new ethical considerations, or, if the metaphor seems more appropriate, as a set stage on which to perform a new and original dramatic agon.

A point of interest in Knight's remarks is represented by his tracing of the paradoxical exchange loss–gain back to the marriage sonnets. Those that have been interested in the formal organization or the imagery of Sonnet 146 have inevitably been reminded of the first group in the 1609 edition; Murray Krieger,[13] for instance, refers to the metaphorical structure of Sonnets 1 (on feeding) and 6 (the conquering worm), supported by other leading images in that group (economic processes, housing, clothing; see chapter I § 4 above). This link could be empirically confirmed by observing that this is the only other sonnet in the collection in which the proportional use of pronominal forms coincides with that in the marriage sonnets: there is no third person, only one first person (a possessive adjective in line 1), but at least ten *thou*s and *thy*s and possibly one *thee*. Which suggests that, though the second person is not really a 'person' but a personification, the speaker is taking up towards his Soul, the same attitude that we saw him assume (ch. 1 § 4) towards his friend and/or patron when trying to convince him to marry: paying homage and offering himself as the careful steward, promoting the material interests of his employer. The implication is a formal relationship, courtly and hierarchical, in which a sense of duty replaces all spontaneous feeling. There is no love for the Soul, only the conventional de-

[12] B. C. Southam, 'Shakespeare's Christian Sonnet? Number 146', *Shakespeare Quarterly*, xi (Winter 1961), p. 68.
[13] M. Krieger, *A Window to Criticism*, p. 128.

votion to a benevolent lord, in the interests of both master and servant.[14]

   What has emerged from a survey of some critical interpretations of Sonnet 146, is, so far, merely a general impression, in itself contradictory, of the purpose and purport of the poem. A closer approach to the meaning must necessarily be effected by way of the formal and semantic organization. But as soon as we take this road, we are confronted with a major crux which has bedevilled interpretation and effectively discouraged close verbal analysis.

0.2. Reversed concentric patterns and the emendation of line 2.   Here is the text from the 1609 Quarto, with the indication of the metrical breaks:

> Poore soule the center | of my sinfull earth,
> My sinfull earth | these rebbell powres | that thee array,
> Why dost thou pine within | and suffer dearth
> Painting thy outward walls | so costlie gay?
>
> Why so large cost | having so short a lease,
> Dost thou upon | thy fading mansion spend?
> Shall wormes inheritors | of this excesse,
> Eate up thy charge? | is this thy bodies end?
>
> Then soule live thou | upon thy servants losse,
> And let that pine | to aggravat thy store;
> Buy tearmes divine | in selling houres of drosse:
> Within be fed, | without be rich no more,
>
> So shalt thou feed on death, | that feeds on men,
> And death once dead, | ther's no more dying then.

Obviously line 2 will not do. It has one extra foot, and must therefore be emended. What editors find particularly suspicious is the uncommon repetition at the beginning of the line of the last three words of line 1.[15] Their instinctive reaction is to sup-

---

[14] Also Northrop Frye (op. cit., p. 49), remarks in passing that Sonnet 146 reproduces the exact imagery of the marriage sonnets—see quotations at the end of § 0.2 below.

[15] Uncommon in Shakespeare, though quite frequent in Daniel: e.g., in Sonnet XLIX of *Delia* the closing words of line 2, 'my chaste desiers', are repeated at the beginning of line 3, and 'celestial fiers' are both the closing words of line 4 and the opening ones of line 5. Schaar (*Sonnet Themes*, p. 105 n.) rightly remarks that '*anadiplosis* . . . does not occur in the *Sonnets*'. I rejected on this ground the possibility of a perfect though minimal anadiplosis in lines 8–9 of Sonnet 129

press them, as a printer's oversight; but then a foot is missing, and the two syllables must be supplied one way or another.[16] A minority of critics, on the other hand, have tried another way, avoiding the responsibility of interpolating something new into the text: they decided that the initial repetition is deliberate, and that the printer, misunderstanding the text, supplied two syllables of his own accord, and precisely the words *that thee*. Whichever way one chooses, the ultimate decision remains with the reading of the line one thinks most likely from the syntactical and semantic point of view as well as from the point of view of the prosody.

I. The first approach presents at least three major alternatives, always granting that *thee* refers to the Soul addressed in line 1:

(a) The two 'missing' syllables are an adjective (or past participle) plus a preposition, having to do with the Soul's enslavement to or deception by the *rebel powers*; in other words, the Soul is (I quote the most common emendations suggested) *fool'd by* (Malone), or *thrall to* (anonymous, Hubler, Leishman), or *foil'd by* (Palgrave, Redpath), or *press'd by* (Dowden), or *hemm'd with* (Furnivall), or *starv'd by* (Steevens), or *fenc'd by* (Sisson), or *trick'd by* (Lotham Davis), or *gull'd by* (Seymour-Smith) etc., the human passions, which are identified with the Body (*my sinful earth*). The contrast is limited in this way to Soul and Body, of which the *rebel powers* are the 'secular arm'.

(b) The 'missing' word is a present participle referring not to the Soul but to the Body, which supports the rebel powers: *feeding* (S. Evans) or *bearing* (Harrison) are the best-known emendations. In this case the earthly passions are considered as distinct from the Body, though fostered by and in league with it.

(c) The word is an imperative addressed to the Soul (Pooler suggests *Rebuke*, Tucker *Defeat* or *Cast forth*, Fiedler prints *Feed*

(see chapter 4, § 1.7 above); now I am ready to admit that I am contradicting myself in maintaining the presence of an extended anadiplosis in lines 1–2 of Sonnet 146. For his part, Schaar denies the possibility and suggests (op. cit., pp. 108–10) the reading 'imprison'd by' at the beginning of line 2, on the basis of a similarity with Sonnet XXVIII in Bartholomew Griffin's *Fidessa* (1596), but such an emendation is hard to accept on metrical grounds.

[16] In their edition of Shakespeare's Sonnets (pp. 336–8 and 358–9), Ingram and Redpath say that about four hundred different words or combinations of words used by Shakespeare would fit the pattern, and they list one hundred of them as the most likely.

not) to exhort it to reject human passions. As in the case of alternative Ia), the *rebel powers* are identified with *my sinful earth*, passions and body are one.

II. The second approach, which omits *that thee* and reads the line as 'My sinfull earth these rebbell powres array', was first suggested by Gerald Massey in 1866 and, exactly one century later, found the support of John Dover Wilson, whose argument in its favour is so neatly put that it must be reported at some length:

> It is clear that if 'that thee' be omitted we are left with a line both metrically satisfactory and pregnant in meaning, inasmuch as the word 'array' is now seen to carry the double sense of (i) 'defile' in reference to 'sinful earth' (see *O.E.D.* 'array' vb. 10), and (ii) 'clothe', referring to the 'costly gay' garments. 'Rebel powers' mean of course the fleshly lusts while 'these' may be rendered 'that everyone knows about'.... Finally, l. 2 is what Tucker calls a kind of 'parenthetical development' common in Sh. but, appearing to be incomplete to Thorpe or the printer, was supplied with 'that thee' to make sense.[17]

It will never be possible to decide which of the alternatives is correct. Metrically the solutions offered by (Ic) and (II) are perfect, the only difference being that in Ic the break falls after the third, and in II after the second foot (all the other lines of the sonnet have breaks falling in either of these positions); while (Ia) and (Ib) require spondaic or trochaic substitutions in the first foot—but line 5 has a spondee as its first, and a trochee as its third foot. Phonically the most attractive emenddation is the anonymous but widely accepted *thrall to* (Ia), fitting perfectly the prevailing *th/r* sound-pattern of the line (*th*ese *r*ebell ... *th*at *th*ee array); instead, adopting alternative II, the contiguity of the unvoiced and voiced *th* sounds in 'ear*th th*ese' may be unpleasing—though it is found again in line 13: dea*th th*at.

But the real issue is whether *these rebel powers* are to be taken as part of *my sinful earth*, or as a *tertium quid* linked with it but in fact external to it. The widespread inclination to adopt the Ia solution is largely conditioned by the interpreters' disinclina-

17 Dover Wilson's edition, p. 262.

tion to include a third party in the obvious contrast between
Soul and Body. Even Dover Wilson, who takes the opposite
view, hastens to assure the readers that line 2 is merely a 'parenthetical development', an expendable clause that need not
intrude in the main argument. The fact remains that the
alternative he has chosen (II) postulates a three-member concentric arrangement: the *Soul* as the centre, *my sinful earth*
(= the Body) enclosing it, and the *rebel powers* (= men's senses)
'arraying', that is to say clothing and enveloping in their turn,
the Body. It is true that in the rest of the sonnet the *rebel powers*
are lost sight of, but if we turn to the last but one line, exactly
symmetrical with line 2, we find the precise reversal of the
three-member concentrical arrangement: 'So shalt thou
[= Soul] feed on death, that feeds on men.' Here the *Soul* is the
outer circle, enclosing *death*, which throughout the poem has
been identified with the Body, the mortal part; and death in
turn engulfs *men* with their sensual passions.[18] (See fig. 12.)

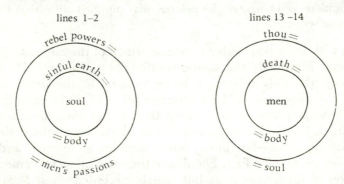

lines 1–2   lines 13 –14

Fig. 12. The pattern of lines 1–2 and 13–14 in Sonnet 146

[18] In connection with the graphic representation of lines 1–2 and 13–14 of
this sonnet, an interesting analogy is worth pointing out. In his admirable introduction to semiotics, *Il Segno* (Milano, 1973), Umberto Eco discusses C. S. Peirce's
paper on 'Existential Graphs', *Collected Papers* (Cambridge, Mass., 1931–5), iv,
347–573, where, following the models provided by earlier logicians, 'the nature
of the syllogism is illustrated by means of circles'. Eco (pp. 119–20) takes as an
example the proposition *All men are subject to passions—saints are men—saints are
subject to passions,* and represents it by way of concentric circles, like those in
our figures here, the centre being *Saints,* the next circle *Men,* and the outer one
Passions. A false syllogism, however, such as *No man is perfect—all saints are men—
no saint is perfect,* could not be represented in this way since, while the class *Men*

The acceptance of *rebel powers* as not just part of the Body, but as referring to the 'children of disobedience' mentioned in Ephesians 2:2, that is to say men in the toils of 'the lusts of our flesh', and therefore 'dead in trespasses and sins', confirms that pattern of reversal which rules the poem. A poem which, in Northrop Frye's words, tells the Soul, 'in the exact imagery of the opening [marriage] sonnets, not to devote all its attention to its 'fading mansion' which only 'worms' will inherit, but (in an astonishing reversal of eating metaphors) to feed on death until death disappears'.[19]

1.0. The Soul as vampyre: the morphologic structure.
The concentrical reversed semantic arrangements of the symmetrical lines 1–2 and 13–14 call attention to the whole structure of the poem. Its formal organization reflects that conceptual pattern clearly identified by Wilson Knight (see § 0.1 above): loss and gain mutually dependent on each other. It is an archetypal principle—*mors tua, vita mea*, the great cycle of all existence —which can be applied in a number of different fields; and this accounts for the abundance and variety of imagery in the sonnet. It is a principle that fascinated poets and artists of all countries and ages, and runs through the stories and novels of Henry James, who attempted, in *The Sacred Fount*, to apply it to human situations observed 'in vitro', in the aquarium-like atmosphere of the week-end guests in an English country house. James's critics have called it the vampyre-theme, since it represents human beings preying on each other, drawing their

does encompass the class *Saints*, the class *Perfection* does not include either, and must be represented by a separate independent circle. Reversing the process (instead of representing a syllogism by means of a graph, extracting from graphs the underlying syllogisms), it would be possible to suggest that the first and last two lines of Sonnet 146 harbour implicit syllogisms, viz., lines 1–2: *the body* (sinful earth) *is subject to passions* (rebel powers)—*the soul is enclosed in the body*— ergo *the soul is subject to human passions*; lines 13–14: *men are subject to death—the soul conquers death*—ergo *the soul conquers and rules men*. Shakespeare's art consists in transforming these commonplaces of devotional logic into a pregnant and revealing paradox through a linguistic manipulation centering on the question in line 8: *Is this thy body's end?* (see §§ 1.1 and following, below).

[19] N. Frye, op. cit., p. 49. See too the perceptive remarks of Elizabeth Drew on the circularity of the couplet (D. A. Stauffer, 'Critical Principles and a Sonnet', p. 58): 'the final couplet, then, with its circular movement, seems to convey on its deeper level the feeling that life is process, that being and becoming are one and inseparable. The individual life—not immortality, and not life in any one of its aspects—is in itself achievement and confirmation.'

physical or mental powers from others' losses.[20] This is exactly the relation postulated in Sonnet 146 between the Soul and the Body, the $_{3-12}$*within* and the $_4$*outward* or $_{12}$*without* of man: in the octave the Body grows rich by starving ($_3$*pine*) the Soul, in the sestet the Soul, made poor, is invited to become a vampyre in its turn, and to feed on the Body's $_9$*loss*, starving ($_{10}$*pine*) it to death. It is indeed vampyrism rather than cannibalism[21]—as some critics said—that Shakespeare is describing here.

The vampyre subject-matter conditions the formal structure in each detail. I have already mentioned the reversed parallelism of the opening and closing lines (1–2/13–14), and the obvious division of the sonnet into octave and sestet. The syntax of the sonnet emphasizes this division into two parts mirroring each other in reverse. Lines 1–2 are a formal address to the Soul— the dominating morphological feature in the vocative case. Lines 3–8 are a series of questions, the salient feature being the interrogative verbal forms. The first two questions fill exactly two lines each, the third one and a half, while the second hemistich of line 8 is an extra short question, breaking the rhythm established by the previous ones and acquiring therefore the same pre-eminence that, in Sonnet 121, was conferred on the first hemistich of line 9, 'No, I am that I am', by its being a break in the regular pattern of the poem. 'Is this thy bodies end' becomes the pivot on which the whole sonnet turns. In fact, as could be expected, Sonnet 146, as a contrast of Body and Soul (I am leaving out for the time being the third element at the two ends of it—the *rebels powers*, and *men*), is a sequence of antitheses: the attributes of Soul and Body are pitched against each other, so that the one is 'poor' and the other 'costly gay', the one is starved and the other richly painted, and so on. But, after the leading question has been asked, we shall see that, in the sestet, the attributes of the two contendants are reversed. Before passing on to the sestet, it must be observed that the octave

[20] See my essay 'Cups of Gold for the Sacred Fount', *The Critical Quarterly* (Winter 1965), pp. 301–16, and L. Edel, introduction to *The Sacred Fount* (New York, 1953), pp. xxvii–xxix. Georges Poulet, in *Les Métamorphoses du cercle* (Paris, 1961), p. 468, saw the structure of James's novel as based on a double spiral.

[21] The notion of cannibalism horrified E. Hubler (op. cit., p. 61), who found it in Ransom's words in the course of the Bread Loaf School debate: 'lines seven, eight, and thirteen are cannibalistic' (D. A. Stauffer, 'Critical Principles and a Sonnet', p. 61).

is apparently self-contained, framed by the key words, $_1Poor$ soul and $_8body's$ end: the two poles of its basic semantic system.

The frame of the sestet is even more perfect: it begins and ends with the same adverb, with different denotations—*then* at the beginning of line 9 is consecutive (= therefore) while *then* at the end of line 14 is temporal (= at that time). Like the octave, it contains in its first line the main axis word, $_9soul$, but, to complete the frame, the opposite pole, in the last line, is not the Body but $_{14}death$. In this way death is identified with the Body, a token of sad mortality. The mirror image of the octave is found also in the arrangement of the salient morphological features of the sestet. While the first part of the sonnet revealed a predominance of interrogative forms (lines 3–8), preceded by a vocative introductory address (lines 1–2), here we have a prevalence of imperative forms in quatrain III (lines 9–12), followed by the affirmative statements of the final couplet (lines 13–14). Once again, this section develops through antitheses, but those attributes that in the octave characterized the Soul, in the sestet characterize the Body, and vice versa: now the Soul is fed (line 12) while the Body is left to starve (line 10), the Soul is growing rich (line 10: *aggravat thy store*), while the Body is poor (line 12 *rich no more*); finally, and more significantly, the Soul lives (line 9) while the Body suffers loss (line 9) and, as we saw, is finally identified with death itself.

The reversed parallelism of octave and sestet is underlined by the presence of two pairs of antinomic constants—$_{1-9}soul$ versus $_8body/_{13-14}death$, and $_{3-12}within$ versus $_4outward/_{12}without$—and by the repetition of words which change sides in the two parts; I have already referred to $_{3-10}pine$ and $_1poor = _{12}rich\ no\ more$, but there is a more interesting case of hidden correspondence, based on a phonic pun. The word is $_5lease$, perfectly suited to the context of housing and economic imagery running through the quatrains of the sonnet: the lease is taken by the Soul on its 'fading mansion', the Body. A short lease is in itself a losing bargain, but this specific negative connotation (lease = loss), restricted for the modern reader to the field of meaning, was immediately apparent to Shakespeare's contemporaries thanks to the very sound of the word. *Lease* was pronounced not only like *leese* (an alternative form of *lose*) but also like *less*[22]—as testified by its rhyming with $_7$*excess*. This association *lease = loss*, referring to the Soul in line 5, is picked up by another rhyme-word in the sestet; but *loss* in line 9 refers, with the by now familiar inversion, to the Body instead of the Soul. It could also be argued, as an added symmetrical correspondence, that *no more* at the end of line 12 is another way of saying *less*; so that $_5$*lease* and $_{12}$*no more* provide a framing pattern for the two central quatrains.

The structure of the poem can, at this point, be summarized in Fig. 13.

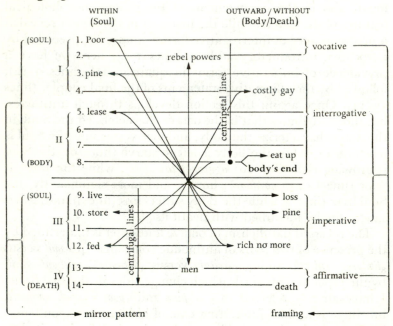

Fig. 13. Structural schema and pattern of reversal in Sonnet 146

1.1. The grasping landlord and the Body as mansion.
The pattern of reversal described above hinges and turns on the second hemistich of line 8: *is this thy bodies end?*, the odd one out, the extra question breaking the established rhythm of the octave. It is most appropriate that, as Krieger has very ably

---

[22] In Surrey's sonnet 'Alas, so all things now do hold their peace', *less* rhymes with *peace, cease*, and *increase*.

pointed out,[23] the question should be a pun, allowing for two different interpretations and replies, one reflecting on the rest of the octave, the other looking forward to the contents of the sestet. All the centripetal part of the poem leads up to this question; but the reply is given not to its original but to its alternative meaning, and thereby acts as the starting-point of the antithetical centrifugal section of the poem. The centrality of the question is emphasized by the fact that here we find the one and only non-metaphorical mention of the Body in the whole poem. Up to this point it had been alluded to as $_1$*my* sinful earth, $_4$*thy* outward walls, $_6$*thy* fading mansion, $_8$*thy* charge. The insistence on the possessive adjectives, and even more the shift after the first line from *my* (the speaker's) to *thy* (the Soul's) is significant: when thinking of the Body as his own, the poet had presented it as 'arrayed' (covered, defiled) by the rebellious senses, and housing in its turn a destitute Soul (Northrop Frye speaks of the allegorical castle of Alma in the moralities),[24] rendered practically powerless; but immediately afterwards, by adopting as a metaphorical system the contemporary practice in householding, the Body—the mansion—is no longer described as the speaker's own but as the residence of the Soul. The speaker has apparently placed himself at two removes from 'the' Body: (a) by disowning it; (b) by stating that it is tenanted by 'the' Soul (not *my* soul), which is itself not part of the speaker, but merely his interlocutor. The use of *thy* does not imply ownership by the Soul; on the contrary, the Soul has it merely on lease; like Eliot's Gerontion, we can conceive of the Soul as 'an old man in a decaying house'. We may well ask, who is the real owner, that does not contribute to the upkeep of his 'fading mansion', but lets the lessee, if he pleases, defray the 'large cost' of 'painting the outer walls'? The traditional Christian figure of the body as the temporary and temporal residence of the immortal soul, acquires a new relevance through the precise metaphorical terminology used at a time when most real estate was in the hands of a few aristocratic landlords, who would 'let so fair a house fall to decay',[25] or

[23] M. Krieger, *A Window to Criticism*, pp. 124-9.

[24] N. Frye, op. cit., p. 49.

[25] Sonnet 13, line 9—another marriage sonnet. The metaphor (here the house is both the estate and the future progeny) would have more point if the recipient of this group of sonnets were indeed a junior member of the landed aristocracy.

lease it out to ambitious social climbers ready to lavish fortunes for the sake of appearance on property not their own. 'Charge' in line 8, while at one level referring to the high cost of the up-keep of alien property, introduces a new topical metaphorical strand, connected with another practice of the decaying no-bility and aspiring gentry: their anxiety, so frequently satirized in poems, plays, and pamphlets from Donne and Marston to Middleton, to secure the wardship of rich orphans or mentally retarded heirs, in the hope of coming into possession or at least having the disposal of their estates.[26] After having pointed out the uselessness of wasting money on property belonging to other people, the poet warns the soul against this further mal-practice: the real heir to the 'charge' so artfully secured may well turn out to be not the guardian, but somebody else: the worms, death itself.

The question remains as to who is the real landlord, the aristocratic and miserly owner of the fading mansion. There are two possible replies, having ruled out death (the worms) since it has been identified with the heir, not yet in possession. One is the speaker himself, since he mentioned '*my* sinful earth'; but how could a temporary owner such as mortal man lease out anything to the immortal soul? He is but 'the pray of wormes, my body being dead,' (Sonnet 74, line 10), not the owner of the Body but one and the same thing with it. The second alterna-tive is more likely though more disturbing: it is the traditional universal owner, the supreme lord of creation—in the role of careless and avaricious landlord towards his poor but ambitious tenant, the Soul. I offer this as a further surmise toward the identification of that evasive concept, Shakespeare's God.

The leading question is very pertinent at this point: *Is this thy body's end?* Will the stately mansion which is the Body, decay utterly, shall it be inherited by the worms? Is death its end? Looking back at the octave, the reply is necessarily yes. If *end* is taken to mean as at first it must—terminus, finis—all that has been said up to now has gone to demonstrate that there is no other way out: the Body must die, it is death itself. The question is merely rhetorical. But the *end* becomes a turning-point, a new beginning, if the word is taken in its other basic acceptation, *end*

---

[26] The idiotic Ward in Middleton's *Women Beware Women* is an extreme example of this practice.

as 'purpose'.[27] Then the question is not the obvious rhetorical one, 'is death the way in which the body ends?', but 'is death the purpose for which the body exists?'—the interrogation is no longer rhetorical, it is a real problem that has to be faced, if not solved. The sestet is the poet's way of facing it.

1.2. The Body as servant and the Soul as Coriolanus.
Any attempt at replying to the leading question, seen in the new light, must start from a reassessment of the basic relationship between Soul and Body. This is done in the very first line of the sestet. The Body is not the decaying mansion that the Soul, like an enterprising gentleman with more ambition than substance, has leased from a great though mean Lord: neither is it the rich ward that the same gentlemanly Soul has secured in the misguided hope of improving his (the Soul's) own fortunes. In both cases, whether wasting an already meagre capital to 'improve' a perishable estate belonging to another, or, as the current expression was, 'begging for a fool', the Soul placed itself in a false position, practically becoming a prisoner, a suitor (indeed a beggar) of the Body, at the risk of following the latter's inescapable fate: death. In order to survive, the Soul must behave not like a dependant, but as a master, and a hard master at that: line 9 is peremptory: 'Then soul live thou upon thy servant's loss', a loss which is not merely economic and social but physical, is starvation to death. The Body's end is death indeed, but for another *end*, for the purpose of improving its master's train of life. The question about the purpose of the Body has found a reply: not *this*, the relationship described in the octave where the Body practically ruled the Soul, but that of serving, blindly and unquestioningly, that very Soul. Summing up, in the central question—Is this thy body's end—'this' is what has been stated in the first eight lines; the ambiguity is in the meaning of *end*: if it means 'ending' the reply is *yes*; if it means 'purpose', then the reply is emphatically *no*, not *this*. And the second reply conditions the centrifugal lines of the poem, starting fresh iconic trends based on what I have called before the vampyre theme.

Setting aside, for the time being, the moral implications of a

[27] M. Krieger (*A Window to Criticism*, p. 127) reaches the same conclusion, but his wording of the dilemma is conditioned by a different approach to Shakespeare's attitude.

type of imagery which, as the poem proceeds, becomes more
and more savage against the Body, degrading it from the role of
servant to that of slave and victim, and finally mere fodder, it is
proper to look at the iconic organization of the sonnet as a
whole, since it has a bearing on its formal structure. In his brilliant essay on the subject, Albert Gérard, after defining the
opposition *within* versus *outward* as the main axis of the poem,
identifies the two main iconic trends in the 'spending imagery'
dominating the first part and the 'feeding imagery' dominating
the second, each with subsidiary 'clusters of secondary images,
which form a coherent pattern'.[28] I have already explored one
of these not so 'secondary' clusters, and not just concerned with
'the metaphor of the body as a house', but developing it with
extraordinary consistency along the lines of contemporary real-
estate transactions. But the peculiar feature of this poem is that
these strands, though predominant in one part of the poem, do
not disappear in the next: they are present, though in a kind of
inverted position, applied to the opposite one of the two parties
in the debate. For instance, the spending—I would rather say
economic—imagery so prominent in the octave (even 'inheritors' in line 7 has to do with the transmission of property), reappears in lines 9 (*losse*), 10 (*aggravat thy store*), 11 (the whole
line is concerned with buying and selling), and 12 (*rich no more*);
the very word *tearmes* in line 11 sends us back to the contract for
the lease of the fading mansion (characteristically, the Soul is
told to renounce it, acquiring, instead of the short-term rights of
residence—*houres of drosse*—the eternity of *tearmes divine*); the
clothing metaphor touched upon in passing in lines 2 (*array*) and
4 (*costlie gay*)[29] is picked up unexpectedly in line 12.

This last reference has passed unnoticed since the reader, at
this point of the poem, is so engrossed with the increasing insistence on the startling and rather repulsive feeding imagery,
that he does not realize that the line '*Within be fed, without be rich
no more*' is the adaptation of a popular saw which had wide
currency from the middle of the sixteenth to at least the end of

[28] A. S. Gérard, 'Iconic Organization in Shakespeare's Sonnet 146', *English
Studies*, xlii (June 1961), pp. 157–9; included in Willen's and Reed's *Casebook*,
pp. 279–82.
[29] *Gay* is normally used of dress and attire, either directly or metaphorically,
as in the grim reference to the use of dead people's hair to make wigs, Sonnet 68,
line 8: 'beauties dead fleece made another gay'.

the seventeenth centuries. The proverb is 'the belly robs the back', or, in Cotgrave's version s.v. *Robbe*: 'Choyce food, and costlye fare, doe make the backe go bare'.[30] We have moved from the world of house-owners, aristocracy, and gentry, to the wisdom of the puritanical 'citizen', who, pressed by elementary economic needs, moralizes his forced choice between satisfying his justifiable hunger, or buying those dignified clothes (not necessarily 'costly gay') that will proclaim abroad his status, enabling him to climb another rung of the social ladder. The puritan justifies on the moral level his choice of the second alternative—in fact, earthly advancement—by condemning the fleshly pleasures of gluttony; but Shakespeare's advice to the Soul reverses the proverb: let the soul feed, renouncing its bodily garment. The implication is two-edged: (a) it unmasks the hypocritical piety of the original proverb: the dignity of dress is as earthly and materialistic a pursuit as the satisfaction of the belly; (b) the divine longings of the Soul are not different in quality from the earthly longings of the flesh.

If the reference to the outward dress that now must be 'rich no more', recalls the earlier clothing imagery, the rest of the line conforms in full with the dominant iconic strand in the second part of the poem—feeding–starving—present from lines 9–10 (*live* versus *pine*) and supreme in line 13. But also in this case the salient images of one section of the poem are anticipated in reverse in the other section: in line 3 the Soul is starved (*pine*), while in the closing lines of the octave, the earth-bred worms, inheritors of the Soul's excess of pampering of the Body in its charge, *eat* it *up*.

Side by side with these twisted and twisting iconic strands— economic, householding, clothing, and feeding/starvation— which change sides in mid-career, there is one metaphorical recurring motif that remains loyal to one side, and that the Body's; I am referring to the images of death that run through the sonnet from the very first line, where *sinful earth* implies mortality, followed up by the worms, and the Body's *end*. So too, the *loss* of the Body (line 9) is death, and the very name of death is at last mentioned and twice repeated in the final couplet: there is a crescendo that culminates in the replacement of the word *body* with *death*, making the identification of the two in-

[30] See Tilley, *Dictionary*, cit., item B228.

escapable. This treatment of the leading images contradicts Gérard's statement that, in this sonnet, 'the thought is simple and straightforward: there is no metaphysical ambiguity; even the metaphysical recognition of man's inner contradictions which characterizes Sonnet 129 is absent'.[31] I would rather say that the imagery of the poem moves constantly from the physical to the metaphysical and vice versa, and the very twisting patterns of reversal noticed in them bears witness to the poet's consciousness of the tensions and contradictions within man's frame. Apart from this point, Gérard's concluding sentences can be accepted in full, and provide a statement of the poem's structural solidity:

Sonnet 146 is a remarkable example of Renaissance organization both in structure and in imagery. With regard to subject matter and theme, it is constructed as a diptych, one panel dealing with things as they are, the other with things as they ought to be [. . .]. According to the principle of 'multiple unity', each part has its own clearly delineated individuality and rises to its own climax, but both parts are symmetrical and therefore integrated in the higher unity of the whole poem. Not only does each climax deal with death, but the imagic motifs (the outward inward contrast, the spending and feeding metaphors, the time and death motifs) recur with significant shifts and variations and skilful verbal echoes. There is even a smack of Renaissance préciosité in the pseudo-syllogistic conceit of the final couplet and in the unconvincing play on the word 'death' which, to one reader at least, unfortunately mar this otherwise finely woven poem.[32]

I feel that also the 'Renaissance préciosité' that perplexes, and in fact repels, the critic in the final couplet, has a reason. The iconic organization of this poem reproduces that of the marriage sonnets; even the 'worms inheritors' are the same which threaten the young man of Sonnet 6, who is invited to generate children since he is 'much too faire, To be deaths conquest and make wormes thine heire'; in Sonnet 13 the young man is told to provide in the same way against his coming 'end', so as to extend indefinitely the terms of the contract for the house of 'beauty which you hold in lease'; we have seen other similarities in the use of metaphors, and also the feeding–starva-

---

[31] Gérard, 'Iconic Organization' etc., p. 281.
[32] Ibid., pp. 281–2.

tion imagery is present in the very first sonnet, where 'thou'—
the self-centred youth—'Feed'st thy lights flame with selfe sub-
stantiall fewell, / Making a famine where aboundance lies', and
the poet exhorts him to:

> Pitty the world, or else this glutton be,
> To eate the worlds due, by the grave and thee.

Sonnet 146 echoes the sophisticated paradoxical style of the
marriage group—with the Soul replacing the young man—so
that it acquires the same formal ceremonial tone, that can easily
be taken for empty preciosity. But, this time, with a different
purpose; with obvious deliberation the parts are reversed:
while the youth was warned against being a glutton and feeding
upon himself, depriving in this way the world (earth and mankind) of its due, the Soul instead is *invited* to do the same thing,
to feed on that sinful earth which is death itself and which, like
the grave, feeds in its turn on men. The pattern of reversal holds
good not only within the sonnet itself, but within a wider context involving most of the hortatory sonnets.

The young man of the marriage sonnets is no Coriolanus to
the poet's Menenius; but Shakespeare is ready to take over that
part in Sonnet 146 with the Soul in the role of the Roman nobility, and to spin out his apologue on the necessary ruling
function of the belly-soul on the 'unruly members', the rebel
powers of the plebeian senses. Now, does the poet accept, in
Coriolanus or in Sonnet 146, Menenius' astute dialectics as absolute truth? Are the rulers (Coriolanus or the Soul) completely
blameless, and the rebels (Roman plebeians or merely 'men')
completely unjustified? The assumption of Menenius' role does
not imply a recognition of the character's moral integrity. The
question just asked cannot be answered decisively either way:
the greatness of a play like *Coriolanus* is in its capacity to reveal
the ambiguity of man's political and moral nature; the same
can surely be said of the paradoxical conceit at the close of a
poem like this—even if the compression required by the short-
ness of the sonnet-form as compared with a play makes for preciosity rather than nobility and amplitude of expression.

1.3. Reversing the sound-pattern. The pattern of reversal
in the poem is confirmed at the level of sounds. As in Sonnet
129 (see ch. IV § 1.1), the first and last lines are in sharp

phonic contrast. But while in that sonnet the pervasive presence of constant phonetic features lasted throughout the quatrains and the brusque sound-change took place in the couplet, in no. 146 there is a gradual but continuous alteration: the initial sounds are progressively overpowered by a new set, through a series of transitional stages. In the first line the dominant sounds are initial *s* and final *l* (*soule*, *center*, *sinful*), with unvoiced *r* as a subsidiary feature, lengthening the vowel sounds (Po*ore*, cent*er*, ea*r*th). The last line of the sonnet is characterized by the hammering repetition of the voiced dental *d* sound, helped out by both unvoiced and voiced *th* (An*d death* [. . .] *dead*, *the*r's [. . .] *d*ying *the*n). The intermediate lines exhibit mixed features: a general balance of sibilant and dental (t/d) consonant sounds, and a pervasive dominance of *th*, which is of course accounted for by the already noticed extraordinary number of pronominal forms in the second person singular.

It is impossible to determine the sound-pattern of line 2, since it depends on the type of emendation chosen (see § 0.2 above): the first alternative proposed would show already a predominance of *th* (*the*se, *that the*e, and a possible 'missing' word like *th*rall), while the second alternative, eliminating 'that thee' and reinstating 'My sinfull earth', would hardly depart from the pattern of line 1, adding to the unvoiced the voiced *r*, and insisting on the *s/l* sounds (*sinfull* ea*r*th the*se* *r*ebbe*ll* pow*res* a*rr*ay). The phonic link between lines 1 and 2 is reinforced by the repetition of one phoneme with the variation of the internal vowel sound: $_1$*Poore*/$_2$*powres*; a similar link holds together the next two lines: $_3$*pine*/$_4$*Pain*[ting], and the latter phonic association *p.n* is repeated in the first two lines of the sestet: $_9$u*pon*/$_{10}$*pine*. From line 3 the *s* sound is frequently associated with *t*—$_3$do*st*, $_4$co*st*lie, $_5$co*st*, $_6$Do*st*.

The two central lines of the poem, 8 and 9, those in which the semantic reversal takes place, are dominated by the intermediate sound between *t* and *s*: *th* (line 8 *th*y, *th*is, *th*y; line 9 *Th*en, *th*ou, *th*y). The sestet is, phonically, very closely knit through the repetition of phonemes and sounds throughout its lines: *th*ou in line 9 is found again in wi*th*ou*t* (line 12); the syllables before the breaks provide internal rhymes both in lines 10–11 ($_{10}$*pine*/$_{11}$*divine*) and 12–14 ($_{12}$*fed*/$_{14}$*dead*). The gradual taking-over of the dental sounds from *s/l* is realized

in two ways: (a) by sound-substitutions in words occupying the same positions in different lines—line 9 *liv*[e . . .] *losse*/line 11 *div*[ine . . .] *drosse*; (b) by reinforcing a *th* sound with a dental sound immediately preceding it twice in the same line: line 10, le*t tha*t/aggrava*t th*y. As the sestet proceeds, voiced 'prevail on unvoiced dentals: line 10 has four *t*, no *d*; line 11 two *d*, one *t*; line 12 one *d*, one *t*; line 13 three *d*, two *t*; line 14 four *d*, no *t*. The progress of the prevailing consonantal sounds could be summarized as follows:

$$1:s/l(r) \rightarrow 2:s/r(l) \rightarrow 3\text{--}6:st \rightarrow 8\text{--}9:th \rightarrow 10:t/th \rightarrow 11\text{--}13:t/d \rightarrow 14:d.$$

This scheme ought to be filled up with a number of details, but I shall only remark on the comparable change in the dominant vowel sounds between octave and sestet. Up to the middle of line 8 there is a prevalence of the long and short *a* sounds (ā, æ, ə); but the key word $_8end$ sets the tune for the sestet, where the short open ε sound is repeated in $_9$Then, $_{10}$let, $_{11}$selling, $_{12}$fed, and completely dominates the final couplet: line 13, death, men; line 14, death, dead, then.

In conclusion, phonically the sonnet reproduces the same formal organizational pattern that was evident on the morphologic, the semantic, and the iconic level. The first lines establish certain features, which are gradually infiltrated by 'foreign' elements; when the middle of the poem is reached, after a short precarious balance between old and new, the reversal of the parts takes place: in the second half of the poem the original features thin out while the new ones prevail, till, in the final couplet, the latter take over completely. In other words, passing through the bottle-neck of line 8, the proportions originally established are reversed. The over-all pattern could be graphically (or emblematically) represented by the figure of the hour-glass: the upper end being lines 1–2, with their apparent width and self-contained circularity of address to the Soul, whose centrality is firmly stated; the narrow central passage, the crossing of the ways, being the second half of line through which all the contents of the octave (questions, semantic values, images, and sounds) must be filtered and sift the nether end being the paradoxical and antinomic statem of lines 13–14, in which all those materials have rearrar

themselves in reverse, forming an antithetical mirror image of the top part of the poem.

1.4. The gyres, the gyres: the basic structure. The hourglass figure seems, at first sight, a fairly convincing, though rather sophisticated emblem of the structure of Sonnet 146—corresponding on the whole to the semantic schema given in § 1.0 above. All that has been said in this section has accepted the fact of the poem being constructed on the basic antinomy between Body and Soul. We could see the poem as moving from the medieval Christian conception of the soul as prisoner of the body, and as a 'detachable' part of man, to the Plotinian idea of the soul as 'all in all, and all in every part', so that 'it is more correct to say that body is in soul than that soul is in body'.[33] But the final couplet poses a problem, suggests a complexity that disturbs this elementary pattern. At first, the lines sound like a mere paraphrase of the Pauline vision of the final judgement, when 'the trumpet shall blow, and the dead shal be raysed up incorruptible, and we shall be changed' (1 Cor. 15:52); the feeding imagery is present in Paul's verses (ibid., 54–5) 'So when this corruptible hath put on incorruption, and this mortal hath put on immortalitie, then shall bee brought to pass the saying that is written, Death is swallowed up in victorie. O death where is thy sting? O grave where is thy victorie?' The first *Epistle to the Corinthians* maintains the doctrine of the resurrection of the body. Shakespeare, on the other hand, does not seem inclined to transcend the human level: the Body is inherited and eaten up by the worms, it ends for good, with no hope of resurrection—in fact the Body is death itself. In the marriage sonnets he had pointed out a different way to obtain victory over death: procreation would propagate the bodily form of the original model. Alternatively, poetry would give immortality, but not to a physical, rather to a mental image. In Sonnet 146 the victory is not that of man—the whole man, changed, re-formed, resurrected—over death, as in Paul, but that of the Soul after the destruction of the Body, which in turn has swallowed up man as he is. There will be 'no more dying' only for the Soul; but without death, there is also no

---

[33] See T. W. Baldwin, *Shakspere's Poems and Sonnets*, chapter VI, 'From Pistol to Plotinus', pp. 157–80.

man. Apparently Shakespeare cannot conceive of man as existing as a whole after physical death in a different dimension: he accepts the idea of a world of immortal souls—but the Soul is only one 'part', and without its Body and its senses cannot be called man, it loses its identity. In the temporal, earthly dimension the poor Soul may be the prisoner of the Body, which in turn is beset by man's rebellious senses; but when the imprisoned prince manages to control the rebellion, he becomes a bloodier tyrant than Time itself (see Sonnet 16), since he is not content to make the Body his slave, but imposes a death penalty on it which is the equivalent of a mass execution of the whole of mankind; in the extratemporal state there is no room for the rebels. It is a very high price to pay for the change of condition from 'poor soul' to 'pure soul', from this vile world to eternity. No wonder that the imagery of the couplet should be repulsive, a far cry from the triumphant close of Donne's tenth Holy Sonnet, so frequently compared with this: 'And death shall be no more; death, thou shalt die'.[34]

Lines 13–14 of Sonnet 146, then, do not merely mark the victory over death, the triumph of the incorruptible over the corruptible, of Soul over Body: there is a third party to be accounted for—individual humanity, with its sensual passions, its trespasses and sins. The 'men' of line 13 correspond to the 'rebel powers' of line 2: at both ends of the sonnet the characters involved in the dramatic confrontation are not two, but three. Therefore the simple figure of the hour-glass—suggested before as emblematic of the poem's structure—will not serve. (See fig. 14.)

The two ends or bases of the hour-glass include in point of fact three elements: a centre and two concentric circumferences. I must refer the reader to the diagrams in section 0.2 above, where I have already discussed this arrangement. The

[34] For a similar view of this false analogy, see B. C. Southam, op. cit., p. 71. Donne follows much more closely the Pauline doctrine: for him '*we* wake eternally' on Doomsday, while for Shakespeare only our souls, not our *selves*, do. A more disturbing suggestion was advanced to me in private conversation by Professor Witold Chwalewik, of the Polish Academy of Sciences: assuming Shakespeare was thinking in terms of Medieval (and Dantean) theological iconography, where hell is located in the centre of the earth, the first line of the sonnet would imply an identification of the human Soul with a personal Hell, 'the centre of my sinful earth'.

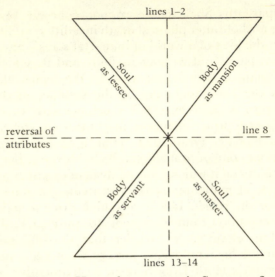

lines 1–2

Soul as lessee

Body as mansion

reversal of attributes — — — — — — — — — line 8

Body as servant

Soul as master

lines 13–14

Fig. 14. Hour-glass pattern in Sonnet 146

striking feature of the parallel patterns at the two extremes of the sonnet is that the sequence of their components is reversed: the soul, which is emphatically 'the centre' in line 1, becomes the outer circumference in line 13; inversely, the outer circumference in line 2 is represented by 'these rebel powers', that is to say men's passionate sensuous natures, while 'men' are the central point in the diagrammatical representation of line 13. The body occupies a middle position both at the beginning of the poem, as 'my sinful earth', and at the end, as 'death', with which it had been identified in lines 7–8. A reconsideration of the structure of the poem that takes into account its two extremes reveals that, if the Soul is the protagonist of the dramatic action taking place in the poem, the deuteragonist is not the Body—as in so much devotional literature—but Man and his rebellious senses. The Body in its turn is a constant, round which the two variables move; it is the character whose actions count only in relation to those of the other two. Basically passive, it is caught in their conflict, and is alternatively their testing ground and their instrument. The Body moves only from the spiritual death of sin (line 1), when it is the Soul's proud and fading mansion stormed by man's rebellious senses, to physical death (line 13), when it is the Soul's brutalized slave used to assassinate man himself.

In view of this the figure of the hour-glass must be radically modified. Both soul and man can be represented as points moving from one centre or apex at one end to a wide circumference at the other, describing therefore conical shapes, each with its apex in the centre of the other's circular base; we saw that in lines 1–2 the outer circle of man's 'rebel powers' has 'soul' as its centre, and in lines 13–14 the engulfing circle of 'thou', the soul, is drawn round a centre: 'men'. The resulting geometrical figure representing the basic structure of Sonnet 146 is that of two identical interpenetrating cones, opposed to each other.

No one familiar with the later work of Yeats can fail to recognize that this figure is but one of the diagrams out of his wild 'philosophical' treatise, A Vision;[35] a shape, according to his own account, suggested to him by the mysterious 'communicators' who inspired his wife's automatic writing. I may well be suspected, at this point, of juggling with esoteric notions, and trying to enrol the Bard in the ranks of the mysteriosophists —after all, this symbol, as a variation of Solomon's seal, was not unknown to the Rosicrucians, who were flourishing in Shakespeare's time and could boast of no less an adept than Francis Bacon. I have, of course, no such intention; Yeats's ultrasensorial experiences, his constant dabbling in the occult, were his own business, and they had a value (as he himself realized) only in so far as they provided him with miraculously apt images for his poetry. Witness, for instance, 'The Gyres', where, by invoking exactly this figure of the double cone, he produces a beautiful poem, quite apart from the symbolic meanings with which it is compacted. He adopted the gyres, or double cone, as the basis of his complicated cosmological 'system': the gyres symbolized the constantly antithetical movement in time and space of the life of the individual and of his inner nature, as well as the cyclic movement of human history. As I have tried to demonstrate elsewhere,[36] 'all, all those gyres and cubes and midnight things', that fill Yeats's pages, once

[35] 1st edition 1925, completely revised 1937.
[36] G. Melchiori, The Whole Mystery of Art: Pattern into Poetry in Yeats's Work (London, 1960), passim, and especially pp. 258–60.

they are divested of their esoteric paraphernalia, turn out to be—as Yeats himself recognized towards the end of his life—'stylistic arrangements of experience'—in fact, what we would call today semiotic patterns.

It is not unreasonable to think that Shakespeare, in a poem which is meant to express a basic mental conflict, involving antithetical attitudes towards ethical, religious, and human values, should have instinctively and unconsciously adopted an archetypal formal pattern: the two opposed and interpenetrating cones are the graphic representation of the impossible attempt at reconciling two urges, or drives, of opposite sign—specularly identical, each side wants to absorb and annihilate in itself the other. Indeed, in Sonnet 146 man rebels against the Soul (man's projection into eternity), and tries to smother it under an overrich raiment; the Soul in its turn wants to incorporate and nullify all mankind. But, under the influence

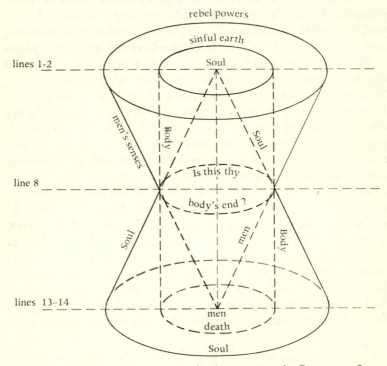

Fig. 15. The double cone as basic structure in Sonnet 146

of the traditional contrast of Body and Soul, the poet further complicated the pattern by inserting in the schema the Body itself, as part of man: there is an inner circle in the base of each cone, a constant presence throughout the poem, openly mentioned in the middle line, that is to say at the point of intersection of the two cones: is this thy body's end? The question with its ambivalent import, marks the reversal of the pattern. But the Body (sinful earth and death) remains the solid core of the sonnet, a cylindrical shape round which the two cones of Soul and man revolve.[37] I would suggest that the basic formal structure of Sonnet 146 is best represented in fig. 15; if nothing else, it should prove that Shakespeare is far from being a careless workman, even in a poem with a hopelessly garbled line, and where the deep structure was not adopted by deliberate choice, with full consciousness of its symbolic implications, but was instinctively suggested by the very complexity of the themes confronting him and conflicting with each other. It is in fact the visual, geometrical representation of the vampyre theme which we saw before (§ 1.0 above).

2.0. The rebel powers and they that have power (Sonnet 94).
Such exquisite geometrical circumvolutions would be utterly gratuitous if the formal structure were not matched by a meaning reflecting the same subtleties, the same contra-

---

[37] This seems to me a cruder and drier way of saying what Elizabeth Drew has expressed in very effective impressionistic terms, with the warning that it is 'something . . . impossible to defend or demonstrate logically': 'I do not believe that Shakespeare is making out a case for immortality, except as a formal device . . . Superficially I suppose we could call the doctrine of the poem Christian; it is conventional in its argument; it is almost sentimental in its doing away with the painful and the transient and the worthless, in its centering man's hope upon immortality and a system of future rewards and punishments. Yet in reading the poem I feel not a future but an immediate triumph over death. This is Shakespeare's "Sailing to Byzantium". And as with Yeats, his problem is to find some certain resting place for the human spirit, as the body betrays him. Both Yeats and Shakespeare resent "envious and calumniating time", and rebel against the inevitable fading of the body's mansion—this "tattered coat upon a stick". Although they bitterly proclaim that the body must know its place, the intensity of their rebellion only shows the intensity of their love. This feeling, for me, makes the last lines even more poignant than the opening, for Shakespeare's imaginative moving towards "terms divine", to him so tenuous, only increases the glory of the senses and of this world, which he has realized, here and elsewhere, so sharply. He is aware at once of the values of human flesh and human spirit.' (D. A. Stauffer, 'Critical Principles' etc., pp. 57–8).

dictions, the same adventurous feeling of re-exploring an im-
memorial ground beset by mystery. We have seen that, in spite
of the use of lexical and iconic codes connected with contemporary practices (domestic, real-estate transactions, feeding and
clothing, ethical and political issues),[38] the ground on which
the sonnet rests is traditional devotional literature, even Holy
Writ. The mystery is that of religious belief—but the approach
is that of lay morality. Sonnet 146 is a dramatic meditation
on the ethics of religion. Once again, the problem of Shakespeare's attitude to religious doctrine, in an age when established Christian theology was called in question from all sides,
must be faced. But before tackling it, there are one or two
more points to be cleared.

Sonnet 146 has a comparatively high number of words found
nowhere else in the Sonnets—hence the widely shared im-
pression that it is 'different' from the rest: e.g., $_1$*centre*, $_2$*rebel*,
$_2$*array*, $_3$*dearth*, $_7$*excess*, $_8$*charge*, $_{10}$*aggravate*. Most of these I have
already discussed, others are obvious; but *excess* is significant,
recalling the treatment of the excesses of the senses and of
sensibility in Sonnet 129 (see ch. IV. §§ 1.7 and 2.0), and the
excellence of Sonnet 94. There are other words, hardly found
elsewhere in the poems, that send us back to the latter sonnet:
$_2$*powers* in the plural is a nonce-word for the Sonnets (since there
was no compulsion to substitute here as in the plays the expression 'heavenly powers' for the forbidden name of God), but it
reminds us by contrast of the first line of Sonnet 94; these
powers are rebellious, confusedly arrayed like Jack Cade's fol-
lowers or the Roman plebeians in *Coriolanus* against 'them that
have' or rather 'Him that has power'. Neither in that sonnet
nor in the plays do the poet's sympathies go to the rebels, the
overthrowers of established order—but, again in each case,
there is no waste of sympathy either for the rulers. The vaguely
'political' implications of the first two lines of no. 146 become
more significant if we take into account the context of no. 94,
where 'They that have power' are 'unmoved' as stone:

[38] See Reuben Brower's remark in the Bread Loaf School debate: 'in the main
this complexity springs from the many fields of imagery which Shakespeare uses
in order to realize his argument—architecture, real estate, money, inheritances.
The metaphors derived from clothes and from eating give the sonnet a quality
of robustness and some humour throughout.' (D. A. Stauffer, op. cit., pp. 53–4).

> They rightly do inherrit heavens graces,
> And husband natures ritches from expence,
> They are the Lords and owners of their faces,
> Others, but stewards of their excellence:

I must refer back to chapter II for an exhaustive treatment of the poet's attitude to the mighty; the difference is that, in Sonnet 146, the rebellion is against the Almighty. The lines just quoted—an ironical assessment of the gifts of the great—are reflected in a peculiar way in Sonnet 146. In lines 3–6, the Soul, as yet 'poor' and innocent of the shrewd advice of quatrain III, does not behave like those that have power: instead of husbanding its meagre capital from 'expense', it wastes a 'large cost' on property not its own, courting bank-ruptcy; in fact, like the stewards of 94, it ministers to somebody else's 'excellence' or 'excess'. And here, in Sonnet 146, line 7, we come upon another nonce-word for the sonnets: *inheritors*—in the same way *inherit* in 94 does not occur elsewhere in the collection. The worms—i.e. death—inherit all worldly excess as the mighty inherit the ambiguous 'heaven's graces' (it is rather extraordinary that heaven should never be mentioned in the one 'holy' sonnet of Shakespeare) in addition to 'nature's riches'; in this case, the instinctive equation of 'they that have power' with the worms throws an additional ironical light on the great ones of this earth, but it also prepares us for the grim role of the Soul in the sestet of 146, where it becomes (or is invited to become) one of the Lords who are the death of their stewards in order to kill death itself. Also *stewards* in Sonnet 94 appears nowhere else in the Sonnets, while *servant* (in 146) is used in its usual courtly acceptation—the lover or client—in no. 57: but the two different words are obviously strictly related to each other: the situation in both 94 and 146 is the same—ruthless exploitation by the master of his dependants. With one difference: while the Lord in the earlier sonnet, like the one in Shakespeare's reading of the parable of the talents, will do no hurt and be content to exploit the administrative skill of his steward (making him do the 'dirty work'), the 'servant' of the Soul is treated like the succubus of a vampyre, drained of his very life-blood. The difference, though, is quanti-tative rather than qualitative: the moral oppression of the one is the equivalent of the physical suppression of the other—and in neither case is there a hint at Sidney's natural aristocratic 'fairness' of behaviour to one's inferiors:

> On servants' shame oft Maister's blame doth sit.
> (*Astrophil and Stella*, Sonnet 107, line 12)

Shakespeare, moving in lower circles of society, was accustomed to a much cruder view of the master–servant relationship than the one Sir Philip Sidney could afford to entertain—a view based on direct experience of everyday practice.

It may be observed at this point that in both instances it is the poet himself that seems to encourage the Lord to adopt this tyrannical—or vampyristic—attitude towards his servants. I would reply by calling attention to two points: (a) as in Sonnet 94 the stand taken by the speaker is sardonic, it seems to be even more bitterly so in 146, as witnessed by the type of imagery used; (b) the speaker is not to be identified with the poet Shakespeare: he is a narrator, at most a producer, or a character, as much as, say, Menenius—and we must doubt very much that Shakespeare the man, or his ethical ego, would make Menenius' apologue his own statement of an absolute truth.

The two sonnets, 94 and 146, are mutually illuminating. What emerges is a singular equation of political with religious points of view, revealed also in conceptual and verbal parallelisms. When placed in the light of a 'natural' ethical code—not aristocratic, or puritanical, or manicheistic, or even mercantile—the outcome of this equation is disconcerting, especially if we had assumed Shakespeare's acceptance of traditional religious views. For one thing, the Soul fills a series of roles that tend to mark it out, more and more, in theatrical terms, as the villain—but without the villain's inescapable retribution. In order to clear up this point it is perhaps better to have a second look at those texts that the interpreters who consider Sonnet 146 as the expression of the poet's Christian orthodoxy have pointed out as the bases of its inspiration.

2.1. Corinthians and Colossians: Shakespeare versus Paul. I find that I have already dealt at some length (see § 1.4 above) with 1 Cor. 15, commonly accepted as the starting-point of the Christian meditation in Sonnet 146, and as the source of some of its imagery. We saw that the apparent similarities did not extend to the doctrine of the resurrection of the body of man, which is fundamental in Paul—the Soul postulated by Shakespeare debars the Body and men as such from any hope of new life after death. What is missing in the sonnet is the specifically *Christian* idea of redemption, the belief that (1 Cor. 15:21–2): 'For since by man came death, by man came also the resurrection of the dead. For as in Adam all die, even so in Christ shall all be made alive.' The same peculiar omission is apparent when we look at the context of the earlier passage from 1 Corinthians which is also frequently placed side by side with Sonnet 146: 'But I beat down my bodye, and bring it into subjection' (9:27). In the sonnet, the speaker exhorts the Soul not only to enslave, but to starve the Body, while in 1 Corinthians it is the preacher himself—as a whole man, soul and body, spirit and senses—who fills at the same time the roles of both master and servant: 'For though I be free from all men, yet have I made my selfe servant unto all men, that I may winne the more.' (9:19) Instead there is no possibility of gain for the servant (the Body) in the sonnet—only, and emphatically, *loss*: it is left to *pine* in order to *aggravate* the Soul's *store*. B. C. Southam has rightly stressed the 'pejorative force' of the verb 'to aggravate' in Shakespeare's usage in the plays (it is a nonce-word in the Sonnets): not 'to increase', or 'strengthen, add weight to', but 'to make more serious, to make worse'; and the critic reads the whole line as a piece of savage irony against the Soul: '*Store* does not refer to the waiting joys of heaven but to the punishments in hell (or conscience) which are being prepared for a master who has acted in such an un-Christianlike way towards his servant.'[39] I have no quarrel with the ironical purport not only of this line, but of the whole sestet; my only objection to this interpretation is grounded on the fact that it presupposes a Christian point of view in Shakespeare himself—you cannot accuse somebody else of being un-Christian unless you yourself are Christian. This is in contrast with the attitude emerging from the poet's 'reduction' of the Pauline doctrine—an attitude which carefully eschewed the specifically Christian elements in it, the very idea of redemption. (The position is quite different in *The Winter's Tale* and in the other romances—but they belong to a later period, and ideas *do* change with the years).

[39] B. C. Southam, op. cit., p. 70.

Other texts of the Apostle are relevant to Sonnet 146, especially if taken in connection with the 'political' Sonnet 94, taking a disenchanted view of the hierarchical order of society. One of them, Ephesians 2, I have mentioned before (§ 0.2 above) in commenting upon the 'rebel powers' who beset both body and soul and who can be identified with the 'children of disobedience'. The context is interesting:

And you hath he [Christ] quickened, who were dead in trespasses and sinnes, Wherein in time past yee walked according to the course of this world, and after the prince that ruleth in the air, even the spirit that now worketh in the children of disobedience: Among whome we also had our conversation in time past in the lusts of our flesh, in fulfilling the will of the flesh, and of the minde (2:1–3).

Here again the stress is on the regeneration of man the sinner—the rebels are Satan's party, but even those who belonged for a time to that party can 'wake up eternally' after the death which is life on this sinful earth. The children of disobedience are mentioned in a similar context in chapter 3 of Colossians, where mortification is advised: 'Mortifie therefore your members which are upon the earth: fornication, uncleanness, the inordinate affection, evill concupiscence, and covetousnesse, which is idolatrie: For which things' sake the wrath of God commeth to the children of disobedience. Wherein ye also walked once, when ye lived in them' (3:5–7). But now, 'Set your affections on things which are above, not on things which are on the earth. For yee are dead, and your life is hid with Christ in God' (3:2–3). The chapter ends by listing the duties of those who wish to receive 'the rewarde of the inheritance' of the Lord Christ (3:24)—among them, the servants: 'Servants, be obedient unto them that are your masters according to the flesh in all things, not with eie-service, as men pleasers; but in singlenes of heart, fearing God' (3:22).

Passages like these seem to contain most of the doctrinal materials that went into Sonnet 146: the sinful earth, the rebel powers, mortality and mortification (in its etymological sense, 'making dead'), death and life, the inheritance, the master and the servant. But these materials have changed their doctrinal features by the admixture, not only on the iconic but also on the conceptual level, of the brutal facts of experienced reality, economic, legal, political, and social relations and transactions. Even the highest promise of biblical doctrine, the eternal reward for the suppression of bodily lusts, 'is conceived', as B. C. Southam puts it, commenting on line 11, 'as a spiritual bargain concluded on grossly commercial terms, where the antithesis of *tearmes divine* and *houres of drosse* impress the inequality of the deal'.[40] Having excluded the mediation of Christ, God made into Man, Man and God in one, Shakespeare must see Soul and Body as merely antagonistic to each other, with Man as the sufferer; feeling that by the loss of his body he will no longer be *man*, he has to rebel, to take the Body's side; that is why man replaces the Body as the main opponent of the Soul, and views the supreme Lord of creation as the grasping Landlord, the patron who on the one hand exploits the Soul, and on the other protects and abets its unscrupulous practices against the Body. It is exactly the same view that Shakespeare had taken in Sonnet 94 of the behaviour of 'They that have power'.

Leishman's remark, reported at the beginning of this chapter (§ 0.1 above), that, while 'the sonnets both of Michelangelo and of Donne are full of clear and explicit expressions and professions of Christian doctrine', we do not find the doctrine at all in Shakespeare's Sonnet 146, is quite correct. Donne's poems, for all their apparent obscurities and contradictions and involutions, are quite consistent with the religious-doctrinal background of his time. For the reader familiar with that background (and the Pauline doctrine is particularly prominent in his later work) Donne's metaphysical perplexities are much plainer than the three or four sonnets in which Shakespeare faces metaphysical problems. Donne, though placing Man always right in the middle of the picture, expresses a hard-won orthodox Christian view of his relation to God, helped out by theological doctrines; Shakepeare's religion, by comparison, is not theological—it is, I would say, anthropological, or rather anthropocentrical. Hence the difficulty of this sonnet, and the misunderstandings of most critics. I feel that, once again, B. C. Southam puts the matter rightly:

There are in the Sonnet a number of Biblical echoes which superficially run the poem along a conventional course, and the values

40 B. C. Southam, op. cit., pp. 70–1.

of the poem seem to be those of the prosperous Elizabethan world.
But it is Shakespeare the humanist speaking, pleading for the life
of the body as against the rigorous asceticism which glorifies the
life of the spirit at the expense of the vitality and richness of sensuous
experience. Neither spiritual nor bodily life can be fulfilled at the
other's cost, for the whole man, body and spirit indivisible, will
suffer thereby. We can see how very much higher is the charity
which motivates this sonnet than the type of Christianity which
moves on the surface of the poem, and at which the irony is
directed.[41]

2.2. Poor man, the centre. The very structural pattern itself of the sonnet bears witness to this attitude of Shakespeare's:
the poem starts from the traditional view of the centrality of
the Soul, enclosed in the prison of the Body, only to expose its
fallacy by a series of transitions which leave us in the end with
poor unaccommodated and sinful man as the centre of a hostile
and murderous universe, where the only certainty—the certainty of death—is provided by the Body. As Lear says of
Edgar (III. iv. 105–12):

> Is man no more than this? Consider him well [. . .] Thou art
> the thing it selfe; unaccomodated man, is no more but such
> a poore, bare footed Animall as thou art. Off, off you Lendings.

This is much the same question as in Sonnet 146: Is this thy
body's end? The end, the purpose of the Body is indeed *this*:
to be the only constant, and therefore *true*, thing in an arbitrary
universe dominated at all levels, physical, and metaphysical,
by greed and hypocrisy, the deception of 'appearance'.

I have said Man—but Shakespeare uses the plural. His concern is not with an abstraction, a personification, but with
concrete living people, I, thou, you, they, the others, the infinite
number of individual men, the living and the dead, with their
feelings, their actions—good or bad—their passions, their sins.
An infinite horde of rebel powers—desperate adventurers, one
and all—perpetually doomed to defeat by the orderly and well-
trained celestial host of the great Lord of creation. The poet
knows how unworthy the rebels are, and tries to judge them
objectively, to withdraw his sympathy—but the fact remains
that they are the one thing he really knows for certain and
cares for, since he is one of them.

[41] B. C. Southam, op. cit., p. 71.

And here we discover the one feature in common to all four dramatic meditations: whatever their starting-point—the exercise of power or social worth, the ravages of lust, or the misery and triumph of the Soul—the real concern that emerges in the final couplet is always the same—the 'wearisome condition of humanity'.[42] This is less apparent in Sonnet 94, though the sudden change from the singular of quatrain III to the plural of the couplet is in itself significant: the single 'sommers flowre' is turned into the whole garden of the State and the world itself, where 'sweetest things turne sowrest by their deedes'; besides the whole sonnet is concerned with men as political animals, as members of a peculiarly ordered community, of which the poet explores the ambiguous inner relationships. In the other three sonnets (and practically nowhere else in the collection)[43] *men* punctually appear in the closing lines:

121 Unlesse this generall evill they maintaine,
     All men are bad and in their badnesse raigne.

129 All this the world well knowes yet none knowes well,
     To shun the heaven that leads *men* to this hell.

146 So shalt thou feed on death, that feeds on *men*.

Lines, in each case, which show an extraordinary ambivalent attitude, where a seemingly negative judgement is counterbalanced by a deep sense of charity and solidarity. It is the same ambiguous attitude that we find in Shakespeare's approach to his great tragic heroes—Hamlet, Lear, Macbeth. And not to them only—could not the same be said of his villains, his fools, his lovers, even the English kings of the Histories?

This study of the Sonnets—or rather of some of them—may have at least one use: to show that Shakespeare, also in his lyrical poetry, is *the* great dramatist. Either by establishing a dramatic relationship between an I and a You; or, when

---

[42] The next few lines from Fulke Greville's famous chorus in *Mustapha* (piratically published in 1608) are relevant: 'Born under one Law, to another bound: / Vainly begot, and yet forbidden vanity; / Created sick, commanded to be sound: / ... Is it the mark or Majesty of Power / To make offences that it may forgive?', where 'Power' formally refers to Nature, but such a Nature that reminds us of its Creator.

[43] The only other two sonnets in which *men* is found in the final couplet are nos. 18 and 81; in both cases the word refers to the future generations that will testify to the qualities of the friend immortalized in the poet's lines.

deliberately facing the world of It, of meditation and reflection on seemingly abstract issues, by always returning to the main concern of his plays, the nature and condition of individual man. The metaphysical issues are not evaded: they are made to coincide with the human dimension. The masterly, infinitely varied, treatment of the strict poetical structure of the sonnet-form, does not allow for overflows: nothing is left outside. The world of infinite space and its Lord must inhabit the narrow room of the sonnet; which is the domain of poor man, the only real, true, knowable being in creation, with his endless variety and contradictoriness. Man is the God of this world—he is also the poet, who says I AM THAT I AM.

APPENDIX

Statistical Tables

TABLE I

Words most frequently used in five sequences and number of occurrences per sonnet

Author	Total: all sequences		Sidney (1591) Astrophil and Stella		Daniel (1592) Delia		Drayton (1594) Ideas Mirrour		Spenser (1595) Amoretti		Shakespeare's Sonnets (1609)	
Sonnets in each seq.	452		108		50		51		89		154	
	No. of occurrences	Occurrences per sonnet	No. of occurrences	Occurrences per sonnet	No. of occurrences	Occurrences per sonnet	No. of occurrences	Occurrences per sonnet	No. of occurrences	Occurrences per sonnet	No. of occurrences	Occurrences per sonnet
1. The	1,441	3·18	228	2·11	262	5·24	198	3·88	311	3·49	442	2·87
2. And	1,397	3·09	247	2·28	224	4·48	161	3·15	275	3·09	490	3·18
3. My	1,356	3·00	298	2·75	233	4·66	254	4·98	179	2·01	392	2·54
4. To	1,251	2·76	276	2·55	174	3·48	114	2·23	270	3·03	417	2·70
5. Of	1,162	2·57	291	2·69	143	2·86	142	2·77	216	2·42	370	2·40
6. I	970	2·14	257	2·37	139	2·78	75	1·47	155	1·74	344	2·23
7. In	940	2·07	246	2·27	95	1·90	112	2·19	164	1·84	323	2·09
8. That	906	2·00	249	2·30	126	2·52	51	1·00	208	2·33	322	2·09
9. With	682	1·50	169	1·56	74	1·48	100	1·98	159	1·78	180	1·16
10. *Love*	556	1·23	131	1·21	67	1·34	67	1·31	68	**0·76**	223	1·44
11. Her	539	1·19	102	**0·94**	169	3·38	86	1·68	231	2·59	51	**0·33**
12. Thy	526	1·16	93	**0·86**	77	1·54	79	1·54	15	**0·16**	272	1·76
13. But	504	1·11	150	1·38	41	**0·82**	22	**0·43**	128	1·43	163	1·05
14. A	487	1·07	117	1·08	66	1·32	67	1·31	68	**0·76**	169	1·09
15. Me	471	1·04	141	1·30	56	1·12	24	**0·47**	83	**0·93**	168	1·09
Thou											235	1·53
Is									103	1·15	182	1·18
Which									105	1·17		
So					56	1·12			93	1·04		
For											172	1·11
Not											166	1·07
Thee											161	1·04

N.B. This table extrapolates from the lists of verbal frequencies provided by Donow those words which, in the five sequences taken as a whole, occur on an average at least once per sonnet. When, in a single sequence, any one word falls below such average, the figure is given in **bold type**. I have added at the bottom of the table those words which exceed the once-per-sonnet minimum only in one or two sequences, while remaining below it in all the rest.

TABLE II

Personal pronominal forms in five sonnet sequences

	In all five sequences		Sidney		Daniel		Drayton		Spenser		Shakespeare	
Number of words in the sequences	53,115		12,791		6,920		5,768		10,000		17,676	
Number of pronominal forms	7,010		1,579		946		755		1,225		2,505	
% of pron. forms per total no. of words	13·2		12·34		13·67		13·09		12·25		14·17	
Number of Sonnets	452 Sonnets		108 Sonnets		50 Sonnets		51 Sonnets		89 Sonnets		154 Sonnets	
Pron. forms	Total number	%	Total number	%	Total number	%	Total number	%	Total number	%	Total number	%
First person												
(a) Singular	2,972	42·4	740	46·8	456	48·1	374	49·5	428	34·9	974	38·9
(b) Plural	96	1·4	23	1·5	10	1·1	13	1·7	14	1·1	36	1·4
TOTAL No. FOR FIRST PERSON	3,073	43·8	763	48·3	466	49·2	487	51·2	442	36·0	1,015	40·3
Second person Sing. and plural	1,794	25·6	323	20·5	184	19·5	156	20·7	198	16·2	933	37·2
Third person Singular:												
(a) masculine	529	7·5	168	10·6	21	2·2	57	7·5	91	7·4	192	7·7
(b) feminine	890	12·7	165	10·5	214	22·6	114	15·1	312	25·5	85	3·4
(c) neuter	293	4·2	59	3·7	23	2·5	5	0·7	79	6·5	127	5·1
Plural	436	6·2	101	6·4	38	4·8	36	4·8	103	8·4	158	6·3
TOTAL THIRD PERSON	2,148	30·6	493	31·2	296	31·3	212	28·1	585	47·8	562	22·5
General total all three persons	7,010	100·0	1,579	100·0	946	100·0	755	100·0	1,225	100·0	2,505	100·0

N.B. The gender distinction only occurs in the third person singular. In the second person also the number distinction is made impossible by the frequent use of the plural form for the singular. Pronominal forms tabulated: First person—singular: *I, me, myself, my, mine*;—plural: *we, us, our* (*selves*), *ours*. Second person: *thou, thee, thy* (*self*), *thine, you, ye, your* (*self*) or (*-selves*), *yours*. Third person—singular, masculine: *he, him, himself, his*; feminine: *she, her, herself, hers*; neuter: *it, 't, its*—plural: *they, them, themselves, their, theirs*.

TABLE III

Frequencies of connotative words

	All five sequences		Sidney		Daniel		Drayton		Spenser		Shake-speare	
	Total no. occurrences	Occurrences per sonnet	Total no. occurrences	Occurrences per sonnet	Total no. occurrences	Occurrences per sonnet	Total no. occurrences	Occurrences per sonnet	Total no. occurrences	Occurrences per sonnet	Total no. occurrences	Occurrences per sonnet
1. Love	556	1·23	131	1·21	67	1·34	67	1·31	68	0·76	223	1·44
2. Eye[s]	307	0·67	68	0·63	47	0·94	52	1·02	45	0·50	95	0·61
3. Heart	253	0·56	66	0·61	47	0·94	32	0·62	45	0·50	63	0·40
4. Fair	220	0·48	40	0·37	34	0·68	34	0·66	61	0·68	51	0·33
5. Sweet	215	0·47	58	0·53	19	0·38	27	0·53	39	0·43	72	0·46
6. Self	209	0·46	52	0·48	17	0·34	4	**0·07**	46	0·51	90	0·58
7. Beauty	190	0·42	40	0·37	20	0·40	30	0·58	16	**0·18**	84	0·54
8. See	178	0·39	47	0·43	21	0·42	27	0·53	22	0·24	61	0·39
9. Time	127	0·28	7	**0·06**	16	0·32	12	0·23	13	**0·14**	79	0·51
10. True/Truth	127	0·28	32	0·29	10	0·20	6	**0·11**	11	**0·12**	68	0·44
11. World	116	0·25	8	**0·07**	21	0·42	31	0·60	23	0·25	33	0·21

N.B. The words listed (including their inflected forms) are those which, over the whole body of 452 sonnets considered, occur at the rate of at least 0·25 per sonnet, i.e., once in every four sonnets. Lower rates for any of them in any single sequence are shown in **bold type.**

APPENDIX

TABLE IV

'I' and 'Thou' in Shakespeare's Sonnets

Pronominal forms	In all 154 sonnets		In Sonnets 1–17 (marriage group)	
	Total occurrences	Occurrences per sonnet	Total occurrences	Occurrences per sonnet
I—I'll	351		16	
me	168		2	
my—mine	455		13	
TOTAL 1ST PERSON SING.	974 (51·1 per cent)	6·35	31 (16·3 per cent)	1·82
thou	235		47	
thee	161		18	
thy—thine	316		52	
you—ye	116		17	
your—yours	105		25	
TOTAL 2ND PERSON	933 (48·9 per cent)	6·05	159 (83·7 per cent)	9·35
General total	1,907 (100 per cent)		190 (100 per cent)	

GENERAL INDEX

The letter 'n' after the page number indicates mention in a note. Italics indicate quotation from or extended treatment of the author or work mentioned.

INDEX OF SHAKESPEARE'S WORKS

Italics indicate quotations from or extended treatment of the work mentioned.